KARL MANNHEIM AND THE CONTEMPORARY SOCIOLOGY OF KNOWLEDGE

Karl Mannheim and the Contemporary Sociology of Knowledge

Brian Longhurst
Research Fellow
Department of Social Policy and Social Work
University of Edinburgh

St. Martin's Press
New York

First published in the United States of America in 1989

Printed in Hong Kong

ISBN 0–312–02017–1

Library of Congress Cataloging-in-Publication Data

Longhurst, Brian, 1956–
Karl Mannheim and the contemporary sociology of
knowledge.

Bibliography: p.
Includes index.
1. Mannheim, Karl, 1893–1947—Contributions in
sociology of knowledge.   2. Knowledge, Sociology
of—History—20th century.   I. Title.
BD175.L66   1989   306′.42′0924   88–4627
ISBN 0–312–02017–1

To Bernadette

Contents

List of Figures

Acknowledgements

Many people have helped with the preparation of this book. Nick Abercrombie must be singled out for special thanks. Others who have helped greatly are Steve Ackroyd, Valerie Chuter, Maeve Conolly, Jane Mark-Lawson, Scott Lash, Mike Savage, Michalina Vaughan, Alan Warde and Annie Witz. My biggest debts are to Bernadette Oxley and James Longhurst.

Introduction

In this book I seek to elaborate Karl Mannheim's work to aid contemporary analysis in the sociology of knowledge. This form of sociology is undergoing a stimulating revival at the moment, after a substantial period of relative inactivity. As will become clear as my analysis proceeds, I see the sociology of knowledge as a broad discipline which incorporates many subtypes of study.

I use the 'sociology of knowledge' to refer to all forms of analysis of belief, knowledge, discourse, culture and texts within society. However, I realise that there are distinctions within the approach in the way that there are particular specialisms within any discipline. It is my contention therefore that the contemporary sociology of knowledge includes and draws upon the work of theorists like Foucault, Bourdieu and Elias[1] as well as the varied approaches to the study of scientific knowledge.[2] In addition, it includes the study of texts, as developed in literary studies,[3] cultural studies and cultural theory.[4]

In varied ways, from different perspectives and with distinctive aims, these specialisms are all concerned with the relationship between knowledge or belief and society, but disappointingly they have tended to remain relatively separated. This is regrettable as insights from one approach can often help to overcome difficulties in another. However, confluences are increasingly occurring as, for example, in the development of analysis of scientific texts or scientific practices as texts.[5] Such occurrences are very welcome and hopefully they will flourish as those working within one specialism become more aware of the value of others.

Part of the aim of this book is to provide a framework to facilitate such confluences of interest. This does not mean that the difference between these approaches can be ironed out or ignored; they are real and, indeed, fruitful; however, I do suggest that an overall perspective can advance theoretical and empirical work in the sociology of knowledge. My contention is that Karl Mannheim's work provides the outline of such a framework. In this respect, then, this is not just a book about Mannheim, though by necessity it is that.

Over the past decade the revival of interest in the sociology of knowledge has been reflected in the reconsideration of Mannheim's work. Several important studies[6] have appeared, which have considerably influenced the interpretation detailed in the book. However, I feel that all of these books, some more than others, have failed to show why Mannheim is relevant to the contemporary sociology of knowledge. They neglect to provide a sufficient justification for the attention paid to this 'classic'. In this book I interpret Mannheim, with the purpose of showing the relevance of his general approach to current work. This interpretation can stand alone and the differences of my views from those associated with others will become clear as the analysis unfolds. In this respect I hope that this book will be used by those seeking a concise introduction to Mannheim's sociology of knowledge. However, I would be unhappy if this was all that was drawn from it. Consequently, the second part of the book shows how the structure of Mannheim's work can be used along with other approaches to formulate an overall framework for the sociology of knowledge.

The first part of the book, therefore, is concerned with the interpretation of Mannheim. In chapter 1 I outline the movement of his work as a whole, setting this in the context of his residence in Hungary, Germany and England. Whilst it is clear that it is necessary to divide Mannheim's work into several phases to aid the interpretation, it should not be thought that such phases are totally distinct and completely internally coherent[7]; they are *relatively* clear and distinct, but as many recent analysts have recognised, Mannheim's work should be seen as a whole. Themes which he developed in his native Hungary recurred in his sociology of knowledge and English writings. Most of Mannheim's work is interesting and much of it has a great deal to say to contemporary sociology; however, I suggest that his detailed sociology of knowledge articulated in Germany has particular relevance.

In chapter 2 I analyse the different aspects of this sociology of knowledge, maintaining that it is structured by Mannheim's stress on the inherently competitive struggle between social groups. Knowledge is a resource and weapon in this competitive struggle. The discussion in this chapter provides a base for the development of Mannheimian themes in the second part of the book.

In chapter 3 I begin by considering the main criticisms which have been made of Mannheim's work. I argue that whilst some of the points made expose flaws they do not invalidate Mannheim's approach. I examine in detail the alleged deficiencies of Mannheim's sociology in the areas of relativism and intellectuals. I maintain that Mannheim's accounts are much more detailed and coherent than many of his critics suggest and that these areas do not pose particular problems for the sociology of knowledge, though they should be explored in future research. In the final part of this chapter I provide a constructive critique of Mannheim, drawing out those themes to be explored further in chapter 4.

In chapter 4 I take Mannheim's work as the starting point for the contemporary sociology of knowledge. I argue that Mannheim's stress on competitive struggle needs to be recast into struggle contextualised by the structural properties of contemporary societies, and I examine these structures. In addition, I maintain that Mannheim's distinction (which is not always consistently expressed) between the specific and general—the surface and underlying—categories of knowledge is very useful in the analysis of contemporary belief. I recategorise Mannheim's distinctions whilst retaining their essential focus. Finally, in this chapter, I develop Mannheim's analysis of interests and commitments, arguing that the concept of interest is essential to the contemporary sociology of knowledge. I examine some of the debates which have taken place around this concept and show how use can be made of various recent accounts. The aim of this chapter is to produce a framework which can be elucidated further in the course of future empirical and theoretical work.

Some pointers to how this blueprint can be used are provided in the conclusion, where I begin an analysis of conservative thought. This is a form that Mannheim was particularly interested in and I take many cues from his analysis—which I discuss in detail in chapter 2.

This book, then, has several aims: it interprets Mannheim, shows how his work is relevant to the contemporary sociology of knowledge and provides the beginnings of an enhanced Mannheimian framework. Its main point is to show the importance and contemporary relevance of Mannheim's sociology of knowledge.

Part I
Karl Mannheim's Sociology of Knowledge

Part I
Karl Mannheim's Sociology
of Knowledge

1 Text and Context

One of the main contentions of this book is that Mannheim's most important contribution to sociological understanding is the detailed sociology of knowledge which he developed in Germany in the mid- to late 1920s. However, this perspective can only be properly understood in the context of the unfolding of his thought as a whole which, in turn, can only be fully comprehended against the background of political and intellectual trends of the period. Consequently, this chapter is devoted to a description of Mannheim's thought as it developed over his residence in Hungary, Germany and England. In the course of this survey certain key themes in Mannheim's work will emerge.

Main concern	Residence	Dates	Main themes
1. Idealist philosophy	Hungary/ Germany	up to early 1920s	General philosophical questions, especially ethics, epistemology and cultural change
2. Hermeneutics	Germany	c. 1920–23	The synchronic interpretation of meaning within a culture
3. Historicism	Germany	1924	The diachronic interpretation of meaning
4. Detailed sociology of knowledge	Germany	1924–29	Analysis of correspondence between society and knowledge, incorporating insights from previous periods but developing the sociological aspects
5. Sociology of knowledge and politics	Germany	1929–33	The nature, ethics and effects of social theory, and general sociology of knowledge
6. General analysis of society, planning and reconstruction	England	1933–47	The planning of the new society, developing views on the crisis in values, the need for democracy and educating the citizen

FIGURE 1.1 *Phases in Mannheim's Work*

3

The main phases in Mannheim's work can be summarised as in Figure 1.1[1]:

HUNGARY: PHILOSOPHY AND CULTURE

Karl Mannheim was born into a Jewish, bourgeois family in Budapest in Hungary in 1893. He showed intellectual flair at an early age and by the beginning of the First World War had studied at the University of Budapest and abroad. Mannheim's thought was formed in an atmosphere of concern with general philosophical questions, especially in the areas of ethics and epistemology, which were bound up with the issue of cultural change. He became involved in the debates about the nature, methods and leadership of a proposed 'cultural revolution', which preoccupied him all through the First World War. Mannheim was in contact with the two main poles of the Hungarian debate on cultural and intellectual change. He had attended the meetings of the Social Scientific Society, an important forum for the discussion of positivist social analysis and its introduction into Hungarian intellectual life. However, more prominent at this stage of Mannheim's life was his association with a small group of intellectuals led by Georg Lukács.[2]

Mannheim's early concern with culture is brought out in his youthful letters to Lukács. For example, he states that:

> We have to see through our own humanity that bond which ties us, and have to seek through this understanding the form which determines the way in which one man may approach another. Thus I wish to approach you through the possibilities ensured by culture.[3]

The Lukács' group rejected any 'positivist' or 'mechanistic' understanding of society and was dissatisfied with the existing political arrangements and intellectual atmosphere in Hungary. The way forward was seen to be through the spiritual renewal entailed in a revolution in culture.[4] The members' views were rooted in a dissatisfaction with the existing political and intellectual arrangements in Hungary; however, they rejected a materialist Marxist critique of this society. Hungary was to be changed by spiritual renewal[5] led by those who had reached a significant level of cultural awareness. Mannheim set out many of the themes that were central to the group in his introductory lecture of 1917, entitled 'Soul and Culture'.[6]

Ideas that were initially articulated in this period of Mannheim's life remain strong through all his writings. The centrality of ethical renewal is paramount in much of his later work, where it is often joined with a plea for human direction by those in possession of the correct values.[7] These themes are of a more political/ethical nature, and while they are of fundamental importance in the understanding of Mannheim's thought, they do not exhaust its content. In general terms, Mannheim's work at this stage fitted into a traditional philosophical mould, and his concerns were with the analysis of particular philosophers and 'cultural' figures.[8]

As the political situation developed, with the successive social crises towards the conclusion of the First World War, many of the Hungarian intellectuals forsook their previous 'idealist' stances and came to support Marxist analyses of the problems of their society.[9] Mannheim did not follow Lukács into the Hungarian Communist Party in 1918 and even at this early stage in his life he was reserved about Marxism and the role of the revolutionary party. However, this did not prevent him from becoming involved in the establishment of the Hungarian Soviet Republic in 1919, when he taught philosophy at the University of Budapest.

This Soviet Republic lasted only a short while before it was deposed by the reactionary forces of Admiral Miklas Horthy, who then held power until 1944. Mannheim's connection with the University was sufficient reason for him to leave the country and go to Germany.[10]

GERMANY: FROM PHILOSOPHY TO HERMENEUTICS

After an initial stay in Freiburg, Mannheim settled in Heidelberg, where he had studied before the First World War. He married the psychologist Julia Lang in 1921, and the period in Heidelberg was, on the whole, a happy one for both of them. However, this was tempered by Mannheim's occasional 'homesickness' and by the fact that his path through academic circles in Germany was not always as smooth as he might have desired. His attempt to become a licensed lecturer at Heidelberg was marked by conflicts among the faculty and university administration over the issue of whether Mannheim should be required to obtain German citizenship before a lectureship could be awarded. This opposition was eventually overcome in 1926.[11] It is obvious that Mannheim still felt attached to his native country and was unsettled at times in Germany. However, at other points he was appreciative of the possibilities of intellectual exchange opened up by Weimar society, though after the rise of the Nazis Mannheim pointed to the way in which the structure of Weimar had opened a route to dictatorship.[12]

During the early part of his residence in Germany, Mannheim published his doctoral dissertation on the 'Structural Analysis of Epistemology', which represents the culmination of, as well as the beginning of the transition from, Mannheim's early idealist phase.[13] After this, Mannheim became increasingly concerned with hermeneutic issues of the interpretation of meanings within culture, showing the increasing effects of the German environment upon him.[14]

In 'Structural Analysis of Epistemology' Mannheim elucidates his theory of the structure of epistemology. The relations between the knower, the known and the to be known, which make up epistemology are, for Mannheim, based upon the more specialised disciplines of psychology, logic and ontology.[15] This discussion is not as interesting for present purposes as some of the other issues raised in a more peripheral fashion.

Three themes which resonate through Mannheim's subsequent work are raised through his discussion of epistemology. Firstly, the nature of interpretation; secondly, the differences between art, the cultural and the natural sciences; and, thirdly, the traps involved in the historical relativisation of thought.

First, Mannheim argues that philosophy has moved away from attempting to understand complex phenomena in terms of the analysis of simple constituents and towards beginning with the complex general picture and understanding simple, specific manifestations in terms of their place in the whole.[16] This is an early introduction of the hermeneutic problem of the relationship between the whole and the parts, which Mannheim returns to later in his work.

Second, at several points in this paper, Mannheim compares art, natural science and philosophy with respect to truth claims.[17] He contends that science is always striving towards the elimination of competing theories in the drive to reach the one certain truth. Art is the opposite in two senses: firstly, one art work never disproves another and secondly, art works can coexist as different views of the world. Philosophy falls in-between these two extremes in that while attempting to reconcile competing approaches, or eliminate the false claims of one approach, it still recognises that there are perennial philosophical problems, which recur in the course of history.[18] It is important to recognise that Mannheim introduces this comparison at several places in his sociology of knowledge. In these cases sociological/cultural analysis is contrasted with both natural science and the history of art production.[19]

Third, Mannheim recognises that cultural products result from historical processes, and is aware that this introduces the danger of relativism as, if meaning is thought to be relative to a historical period, it may become unavailable to a contemporary analyst. He notes, therefore, that

> The historical interpretation of a meaningful whole is a possible and necessary task, but all too often the mistake is made of trying to explain the meaning itself with reference to the temporal features of the works in question—with reference to empirical, real factors. If we seek to validate or invalidate meanings by means of such factors, we shall inescapably fall into relativism. The temporal as such only contains the conditions for the realisation of meanings, but not the meanings themselves; they can only be represented by means of a structural analysis.[20]

In the rest of this essay Mannheim effectively brackets off the historical element in the development of meaning. This is a procedure that is repeated in his more hermeneutic writings. The best representation of the concerns of this later period of Mannheim's work can be found in 'On the Interpretation of *Weltanschauung*', which expresses Mannheim's desire to interpret the nature of the *Weltanschauung* (world-view) that structures the culture of a society.[21] More specifically, Mannheim asks how the 'spirit of an age' can be known, and seeks to understand the nature of the relationship between this spirit and its manifestations in particular cultural products or actions.

This reintroduces the issue of the relationship between the whole and the parts, discussed previously in his work on epistemology. The relationships involved here can be clarified by taking the example of the interpretation of a novel, for example, George Eliot's *The Mill on the Floss*.[22] This novel can be used to provide information about the nature of the place of, and constraints upon, Victorian women, as revealed in the character and development of Maggie Tulliver: the reader is educated about Victorian society by reading the book. However, at the same time the novel is a product of the times, and is interpreted against the *known* background of the Victorian period. The novel is understood against a given context, and what is learned about Victorian society is *assumed*, and used to provide meaning. In this sense the meanings that a book provides change as the knowledge and interpretation of the period change due to struggles in the present. Thus, *The Mill on the Floss* may be interpreted as presenting a sympathetic picture of the struggles for independence of a Victorian woman, but this interpretation is partly the product of the struggles of feminism and feminist literary criticism in the present.[23] This process of interpretation of context through text and text through context, or the whole through parts and parts through the whole, is often called the 'hermeneutic circle'; however, as the analysis deepens and becomes more marked over a period of time, the circle is best thought of as a continuing spiral (or helix) of interpretation.[24] This can be represented diagrammatically as follows:

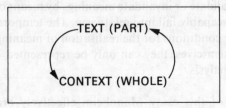

FIGURE 1.2 *The Hermeneutic Circle*

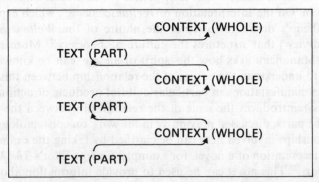

FIGURE 1.3 *The Hermeneutic Spiral or Helix*

In his work on hermeneutics Mannheim sees the cultural products (text-part) as documents of the *Weltanschauung* (context-whole) of a period. The *Weltanschauung* is understood through the analysis of the product, and the meaning of the product through the interpretation of the *Weltanschauung*. Mannheim's approach at this stage of his work is fundamentally static: he freezes a picture of a culture at one time and attempts to show the relationships and meanings operating at that point. The next significant development in Mannheim's thought stems from his increasing awareness of the dynamic movement of society.[25]

Mannheim's developing appreciation of the historical dimension to culture is illustrated by the difference between two long essays published as *Structures of Thinking*.[26] In these analyses Mannheim is concerned with clearing away the obstacles in the path of the production of the sociology of culture and a cultural sociology. This theme is especially prevalent in 'The distinctive character of cultural sociological knowledge'. Despite Mannheim's increasing awareness of sociology, this essay has marked similarities to 'On the Interpretation of *Weltanschauung*', utilising the category of *Weltanschauung* in the analysis of the social nature of culture.[27]

In the later essay, 'A sociological theory of culture and its knowability (conjunctive and communicative thinking',) Mannheim begins to approach these issues in a rather different way, stressing the importance of history as a cultural science as well as the dynamic development of the social. He combines this with an emphasis on the historical standpoint of the subject who is seeking an interpretation and understanding of history. This process of development is carried on in the next phase of Mannheim's work.

GERMANY: FROM HISTORICISM TO THE DETAILED SOCIOLOGY OF KNOWLEDGE

In the five years from 1924 to 1929 Mannheim produced his most important work, moving from the synchronic interpretation of cultural phenomena to a fully developed sociology of knowledge. Mannheim's movement out of the hermeneutic phase was particularly affected by the works of Ernst Troeltsch and Lukács, and is represented by the essay on 'Historicism'.[28] Mannheim's previous friendship with Lukács was obviously of some importance here, but the positions that Lukács was now advancing were significantly different from those of his earlier Hungarian period. In *History and Class Consciousness* (1923) Lukács produces a Hegelianised-Marxist view of the formation of the world-view of the proletariat and its development in the process of history, arguing that only the proletariat can gain a complete view of the nature of society.[29] Mannheim felt that it was necessary for the analyst of culture to confront these positions, writing that

> Today it is impossible to take part in politics, even to understand a person—at least if we don't want to forego present-day interpretive techniques—without treating all these realities which we have to deal with as having evolved and as developing dynamically.[30]

In 'Historicism' Mannheim, as in his hermeneutic period, still seeks an understanding of the nature of the cultural totality; however, he now stresses that this is a product of a continuing historical development.[31] In accord with his earlier positions, historicism, as the advocacy of the continuing historical evolution and realisation of meaning, is seen as a particular *Weltanschauung*,[32] to be analysed utilising the category of documentary meaning developed in 'On the Interpretation of *Weltanschauung*'. However, the analysis is marked by the beginnings of the transition to a more developed sociological understanding of the nature of the whole. 'Historicism' is a vehicle for this development, which can be illustrated by a consideration of the change involved in the meaning of *Weltanschauung*. In Mannheim's hermeneutic work, the '*Weltanschauung*' is a macro-entity underlying (or incorporating) the whole of the culture. By contrast, in the developing sociological orientation, Mannheim increasingly stresses the way in which *Weltanschauungen* become expressed by particular social groups.[33] As Lukács developed the idea of class world views, so Mannheim saw perspectives as corresponding to the 'location' of the individual.[34]

While, in these respects, it is important to note the role of Lukács' *History and Class Consciousness* in the development of Mannheim's work, it is a mistake to seek out simple parallels between Mannheim and Lukács.[35] The fact that Lukács' work was to move Mannheim in a particular direction does not mean that he adopted Lukács' perspective or simply adapted it beyond its Marxist origins. At this juncture some important differences should be noted.

First, Lukács adopts a Marxist view seeing society as consisting of classes existing in struggle, which is ultimately determined by the movement of the dominant mode of production: a perspective that Mannheim never adopted.[36] Second, while it is correct to argue that 'in Lukács, the idea of "mission" is associated with the proletariat', it is incorrect to correspondingly simply say that 'in Mannheim it becomes associated with the intellectual elite'.[37] The place of the intellectuals in Mannheim's thought is different structurally from that of the proletariat in Lukács' theory. Lukács tends to see the role of the proletariat as determined within a general philosophy of history. For Mannheim the intellectuals can (and perhaps should) reconcile competing truth claims, but there is not the same weight of historical necessity behind this. Intellectuals are also quite likely to sell their pens to the highest bidders.[38] It is important to realise that Mannheim's development of the sociology of knowledge was not a 'bourgeoisification' of Lukács. Lukács' work is one impetus for the development of the sociology of knowledge, but this is a distinctive position.[39]

'Historicism' marks the transition in Mannheim's work from the hermeneutic phase illustrated by 'On the Interpretation of *Weltanschauung*' to the beginning of his development of a detailed sociology of knowledge. This sociology of knowledge is itself subject to a process of development. Mannheim sets out the ground for study in 'The Problem of a Sociology of Knowledge'[40] and 'The Ideological and the Sociological Interpretation of Intellectual Phenomena'.[41] This is theoretically and substantively developed in 'The Problem of Generations'[42] and 'Conservative Thought',[43] before reaching a new synthesis in 'Competition as a Cultural Phenomenon'[44] and *Ideology and Utopia*.

In addition to taking account of the historical dimension of culture, Mannheim felt, after 'Historicism', that he had to take greater account of the sociological aspect. The work of German sociologists such as Scheler and Alfred and Max Weber was obviously important here.[45] In 'The Problem of a Sociology of Knowledge' Mannheim continues to reject Marxist positions, mainly because he thinks that there can be no direct and straightforward correspondence between knowledge and classes as

> Differentiation in the world of the mind is much too great to permit the identification of each current, each standpoint with a given class.[46]

Mannheim rejects the Marxist idea that each class has a set of structurally determined interests as being one-sided, replacing it with the more general idea that certain groups are 'committed' to particular ideas, as he states,

> indirect 'committedness' to certain mental forms is the most comprehensive category in the field of the social conditioning of ideas.[47]

'The Problem of the Sociology of Knowledge' represents the first real articulation of a developed sociological position in Mannheim's work. Analysing the competing *Weltanschauungen*, Mannheim seeks to detail the different social groups 'that champion each', and once these have been specified, to consider the 'social strata' to which they 'correspond'. Accordingly, Mannheim argues that

> we can understand the transformation of the various ideologies only on the basis of the changes in the social composition of the intellectual stratum corresponding to them.[48]

This position illustrates the development in Mannheim's concept of *Weltanschauung*, which now refers more to forms of thought which are articulated by intellectuals representing different social strata. It should be stressed that the intelligentsia is seen as articulating and systematising the ideas that correspond to social groups.

The more sociological position that Mannheim had begun to develop at this point was reinforced by the paper that he published in 1926 on the 'Ideological and the Sociological Interpretation of Intellectual Phenomena'. Here, Mannheim distinguishes 'intrinsic' analysis, where an idea is discussed without being placed in any context, from 'extrinsic' interpretation, where a form of thought is considered from 'without', placed in a context, and seen as 'functionally' related to other ideas or 'material' factors.[49] Sociological analysis is a specific type of material, extrinsic interpretation in which ideas are functionalised in relation to the 'economic-social' sphere. The work of Marx is *one* source of this idea of 'extrinsic' interpretation; however, Marx is still presented as being one-sided and as lacking a full conception of the complexity of the relationship between ideas and social structure.[50]

The papers on 'The Problem of a Sociology of Knowledge' and 'The Ideological and the Sociological Interpretation of Intellectual Phenomena' introduced the initial background theoretical framework of Mannheim's detailed sociology of knowledge. This is then deepened through the discussions of 19th-century German conservative thought and generations.

In his attempt to formulate a coherent model of the nature of German conservatism, Mannheim always describes its opposition to ideas such as abstraction, a progressive view of history, and, in general, the 'rationalism' associated with the rising bourgeoisie. After delimiting the nature of conservative thought, Mannheim turns to the issue of its expression by particular social groups. This is analysed through a consideration of the intellectual spokespersons of conservatism, those 'mercenary pamphleteers' who sold their pens to the declining ruling nobility.[51] Conservative thought thus arose from those social groups which opposed capitalism, and it is this which gives the oppositional quality to the ideas of conservative intellectuals.

Mannheim's work on conservatism defines a body of ideas which is related to the social structure through a consideration of the thought of those intellectuals who articulated conservatism for groups marginalised by the rising bourgeoisie. At this stage of his work Mannheim had not theorised the nature, and relationships between these groups: areas which are considered in his next important work.

In this essay on 'The Problem of Generations' Mannheim concentrates on the analysis of a particular group to which knowledge is to be related. He is dissatisfied with what he sees as the limitations of an analysis restricted to the narrow sense of class, wishing to broaden this with the concept of social location, one of the most important of which, as well as class, is generation.

Through his analysis of this social location, Mannheim widened the range of social groupings that were to be seen as possessing relevance for their correspondence to particular forms of knowledge. However, this begs the fundamental questions of how these groups are to be related together, and whether there is a principle for the structuring of the relationships between them? Mannheim answers these questions in his important essay on 'Competition as a Cultural Phenomenon', where he argues that inter-group relations are inherently competitive. For Mannheim 'competition must be regarded as a feature not merely of economic life, but of social life as a whole'.[52] Here Mannheim also maintains that thought is used as an instrument of collective struggle. He argues that competition enters into every aspect of culture: 'The point I want to make is that processes of change in the deepest strata of world interpretation, modifications of the categorical apparatus itself, can to a large extent be explained in terms of competition'.[53]

By this stage in his intellectual career Mannheim had developed the main themes of his sociology of knowledge. He argued that society was divided into social groups, which produce particular potential social locations for the individual actor, and relate to particular knowledges. The explanation for the adoption of a form of thought by a group, and of the nature of the relationship between groups, is to be found in the area of competition, which places groups in antagonistic relations to one another.

The high point in Mannheim's development of a detailed sociology of knowledge came in 1929, with the publication of the first German edition of his most famous work, *Ideology and Utopia*. The original German edition of this work consists of parts II–IV of the subsequent English edition, published in 1936, which added Mannheim's article on 'The Sociology of Knowledge' and a special introduction written for the English reader.[54] It should be stressed, therefore, that *Ideology and Utopia* is not a unified book, and that the book itself can often be confused with the particular essay on 'Ideology and Utopia' which it contains.[55]

The distinctions Mannheim draws within the category of ideology, and between Ideology and Utopia, are of great importance. For Mannheim systems of belief are formed in the competitive struggle between social groups over power or domination. Ideology refers to the system of belief of dominant groups which 'are so interest bound to a situation that they are simply no longer able to see certain facts which would undermine their sense of domination'.[56] Ideologies typically take the form of beliefs whose contents could not actually be realised.

Utopian thinking, on the other hand, is not antiquated, but is, rather, oriented to the future, seeking to transform the present reality. If ideological thought is characteristic of dominant groups, utopian ideas are appropriate to rising groups. The utopian of the ascendent bourgeoisie, in the context of the feudal order, for example, was the idea of freedom, 'in the sense of bursting asunder the bonds of the static, guild and caste order, in the sense of freedom of thought and opinion and the unhampered development of the personality'.[57] Mannheim concentrates most of his attention on the concept of Utopia, tracing the history of the 'Utopian mentality' from its first form, the organic chiliasm of the Anabaptists, to its more recent manifestations in socialism and communism.

Mannheim's concepts of ideology and utopia could be used in the analysis of forms of thought in contemporary Britain. For example, it might be argued that the 'monetarist' economic policies, adopted by the Conservative government, are 'ideological', representing the interests of threatened ruling groups whereas the 'protectionist' economic aims of some sections of the Labour Party are utopian, in attempting to break out of the confines of a world economic system, and pave the way towards a new economic order.

In Mannheim's detailed sociology of knowledge action is a fundamental part of human life and typically occurs as collective action
undertaken by social groups or classes in pursuit of some common
purpose. Such collective action necessarily involves struggle and
competition between groups pursuing their own goals. As far as
Mannheim is concerned the most important focus of inter-group
struggle is power: groups compete for domination over one another.

Thought is to be explained by its use as an instrument in competition. Belief is correlated with social location and different groups will
therefore have different systems of ideas according to their different
situations. Thus, 'Different interpretations of the world for the most
part correspond to the particular positions the various groups occupy
in their struggle for power.'[58] These were ideas that were to be hotly
contested after the publication of *Ideology and Utopia*.

GERMANY/ENGLAND: FROM THE SOCIOLOGY OF KNOWLEDGE TO SOCIAL RECONSTRUCTION

The success of *Ideology and Utopia* aided Mannheim's advancement
in the German academic world and in 1929 he became Professor of
Sociology at the University of Frankfurt. Here Mannheim worked in
close proximity to the members of the Institute for Social Research,
more commonly known as the Frankfurt School. Adorno, Horkheimer and Marcuse all published analyses of Mannheim's work, but
Adorno's critique most clearly expresses some of the fundamental
differences between the Frankfurt School's critique of ideology and
Mannheim's sociology of knowledge.[59]

For Adorno the sociology of knowledge is blind to the structural
contradictions of capitalist society, and consequently is a sceptical
rather than 'critical' discipline, which 'calls everything into question
and criticises nothing'.[60] The sociology of knowledge is also seen to
lack the subtlety of a Marxist critique, as it 'translates dialectical
concepts into classificatory ones'.[61] Politically the sociology of knowledge leads to 'reformism' and mistakes the structural location of the
intellectual stratum; 'The very intelligentsia that pretends to float
freely is fundamentally rooted in the very being that must be changed
and which it merely pretends to criticise.'[62]

Despite their intellectual attacks on Mannheim members of the
School moved in partly similar circles. For example, Adorno and
Mannheim are both mentioned in Hannah Tillich's memoir.[63] The

common experience of emigration may have contributed to the feelings of 'loyalty' that Adorno expressed towards Mannheim in 1934. However, before this Mannheim's relationship with the Frankfurt School 'seems to have been a cool one'.[64]

Ideology and Utopia represents the high point of Mannheim's development of a detailed sociology of knowledge and after this he increasingly concerned himself with more general problems of sociology and society, though these had, of course, always been present in the sociology of knowledge. Consequently Mannheim stresses the duality in the nature of the relationship between society and knowledge. Knowledge corresponds to social positions and people's behaviour is moulded by society.[65] However, on the other hand, the understanding of social processes, produced by the sociology of knowledge, that determine 'mental and moral life',[66] can be used to change that society and the individual's place in it. Mannheim wishes to study the 'hidden' structural processes,

> to gain an insight into the pattern of their interplay, and thus become able, at the bidding of an autonomous will, to master them and put them at the service of an educational work in personality formation which one can pursue consciously in full freedom and responsibility.[67]

Mannheim believed that education has a large role to play in the development of a new consciousness and,

> The elucidation of the typical influences at work in the everyday life of an industrial society will make it easier to develop in the individual the necessary skills, and also to cultivate in him, in a planned fashion, the attitudes likely to enable him to withstand damaging influences.[68]

Mannheim, obviously partly in response to the increasing political conflict in Weimar Germany, centred his work around these issues and this period represents a bridge between his detailed development of the sociology of knowledge and his lengthy work on social reconstruction after his move to England.

This successful period in Mannheim's life was brought to a close by the advent to power of the Nazis at the beginning of 1933, forcing him to leave Frankfurt and Germany. Once more Mannheim became refugee and exile, but at this juncture it was as much his Jewish background as his political views that led to his emigration.[69]

Mannheim took up a post as lecturer in sociology at the London School of Economics (LSE) in 1933.[70] Whilst there is a definite change in the *style* of Mannheim's work after his emigration to England, it is still rooted in the same concerns, and has fundamental themes in common with those which he had developed up to that point. This, of course, is not to argue that the new intellectual atmosphere did not have its effects on Mannheim's work and his developing awareness of the work of Anglo-Saxon scholars is visible.[71] In a broad sense, however, Mannheim was still concerned with the issues of cultural and political crisis, as well as the need to produce a better-educated, more 'responsible', population. The cultural atmosphere that Mannheim was to draw on in Britain of the 1930s and 1940s was to be conducive to the development of these themes, and led him into the more substantive consideration of possible ways forward.[72]

The first major work that Mannheim published after his emigration was *Man and Society in an Age of Reconstruction*,[73] the original German-language version being produced in Holland in 1935, with the enlarged English edition following in 1940. In this book Mannheim adopts a broad-based, 'mass society' thesis, and whilst the exact details and parameters of this are assumed rather than worked out in detail, themes characteristic of the approach are prominent.[74] First, he operates with an elite-mass dichotomy, though this is also combined with other concepts of social division.[75] Second, Mannheim is fearful of the effects that propaganda may have, though he does envisage its continued use in the planned society of the future.[76] Third, he is afraid of the danger of 'mass-crowd' behaviour.[77] Fourth, combining the 'aristocratic' and 'democratic' variant of mass society theory, he comments on the penetration of the exclusivity of the elite by mass elements, and on the dictatorship of the elite over the mass.[78] Finally, Mannheim utilises a theory of totalitarianism, this being tied up with implicit analyses of the rise of Fascism, which he had, of course, just experienced at first hand in Germany.[79] This mass society vision informs much of the specific content of this book. However, Mannheim's analysis is also determined by his interpretation of the force and nature of historical and political development. This is one of the main reasons for his abandonment of the specific problems of his detailed sociology of knowledge. His move to England, whilst having distinct effects on his work, is not at this stage as significant as the fact that he fled from a Fascist regime involved in the totalisation and centralisation of power.

In *Man and Society*, Mannheim characterises the 19th century as dominated by the liberal order, and argues that this society, founded on the unregulated trade cycle, unextended democracy, free competition and ideas of competitive individualism, had developed from feudal society. This liberal order was now in a state of flux due to the growth of a mass of separated individuals and economic concentration. The result of this process could either be totalitarian dictatorship, or planned democracy founded in the still living remnants of liberal *laissez-faire* capitalism.[80]

Mannheim argues for planned democracy, but devotes much of *Man and Society* to a sociological analysis of the fluidity of contemporary society. His theses on the inevitability of planning and the need for the sociologist to be involved in this are central themes of this phase of his work. The sociological involvement in the plan is to come from above, with the sociologist in the role of 'expert'. Mannheim's analysis of the division of the elite from the mass is carried through, in that he envisages the existence of elites in the future, planned society, one example here being the sociological elite. This elite, rather than 'dominating' society, is to act in an advisory capacity, producing analyses of society based on a scientific sociology, but within the parameters of social practice and possibility.[81] This theme parallels Mannheim's belief in the necessity of the 'spiritual renewal from above' advocated in his early years in Hungary, as well as the role that he envisaged for the sociology of knowledge in his later German years.[82]

In *Man and Society* Mannheim moved on from the detailed sociology of knowledge. However, the basic tenets of a sociology of knowledge are accepted as given, being one of the bases of the study and are expressed in forms such as knowledge being related to action, parts of consciousness to groups, and forms of investigation to 'ages'. Given this base, the lack of attention that Mannheim pays to the difficulties and sophisticated discussion of his earlier writing is arresting.

Mannheim's later work develops logically from that preceding it. His general views of the nature of society and its problems were developed quite early and his later approaches must be seen as refinements and developments of these. Thus, the sociology of knowledge rests on positions that were developed in the early period, and which are further explored in his work on social reconstruction.

The products of Mannheim's English period are by no means an uncommon mode of sociological intervention in the classical style.

The subjects of the books are broad ones, and Mannheim seeks to detail the structure and development of the age of reconstruction. He attempts to delimit the nature of people and their society in contemporary and previous periods of history, considering such issues as the relative effects of instincts as opposed to social conditioning. His main concern, however, is with developing a general theory of the nature of social organisation as a whole, which can be used as a guide in the process of reconstruction.

These themes are developed as Mannheim's work progresses. The essays published as *Diagnosis of Our Time* in 1943 reflect Mannheim's increasingly explicit concern with the role of values in social and political life.[83] He argues that democracy can only operate with a set of participatory values, which are to be fostered through a new morality. The titles of the essays illustrate Mannheim's interests at this point in his career. He is concerned with the analysis of contemporary society and the nature of its crisis, which is manifested in phenomena such as the conflict of values and the alienation of young people. Part of the solution to these conflicts is to come through the educational process, which itself must be democratically based to avoid the danger of indoctrination. A new morality is to be provided through the adoption of an integrative Christian spirituality.

Diagnosis of Our Time is less explicit in its adoption of a mass society view, but this is still manifested in Mannheim's concern with phenomena such as 'mass psychoses'. Mannheim also continues to be very concerned about the nature of the inevitable transition from *laissez-faire* to planned society. He argues that the embryonic planned society can develop along democratic or dictatorial routes. In this context he produces the thesis of the 'Third Way'. The 'First Way' of social organisation and development is *laissez-faire*, an historical option no longer open in the present situation. The 'Second Way' is that of dictatorship as expressed in the totalitarian societies of Nazi Germany and the Soviet Union. The 'Third Way' is that of democratic planning as argued for by Mannheim. These positions are linked with Mannheim's view of conflict in Western societies. He argues that the Second World War has changed what was previously a conflict between capitalism and communism to one between democracy and dictatorship.[84] This, of course, was a perspective that was to gain much ground in the sociological and political analyses of the 1940s and 1950s, as well as being expressed in literary forms.[85] The need for democratic planning is therefore brought about by the nature of historical development itself.

This process of democratic planning could only be properly understood and controlled once the 'crisis in valuations' of existing society
was resolved. In showing that modern society is suffering from this
malady, Mannheim, in a familiar sociological fashion, produces a
typology of historically existing societies and their corresponding
value systems.[86] He argues that in 'Primitive Society' there was a
'consensus' based on the similarity and closeness of the interacting
people. In pre-capitalist, feudal societies there was again a consensus
in values, but this was differently based in the acceptance of a
religious value system. This was broken down by the rise of liberal
laissez-faire, characterised by a plurality in the field of values.
Initially, this helped this form of organisation to dominance, but
eventually led to increasing social conflict and crisis. *Laissez-faire* is to
be followed by either authoritarian dictatorship or consensual planning. In a consensually planned society there will be no irreconcilable
difference in values, an acceptance of the democratic 'rules of the
game', and even the planning of areas of non-consensus, to enable
release of the tensions that might build up in the otherwise agreed
harmony. In elucidating these themes, Mannheim draws upon a
general sociology of knowledge, arguing that the state of values
corresponds to the general organisation of society.

Mannheim argues that Christian spirituality should be at the centre
of the consensus in values in the democratic, planned society.[87] His
participation with British religious and cultural thinkers, including
T. S. Eliot, in the discussion group known as the 'Moot' reflects the
importance that Mannheim accorded to this area, as well as the
difficulties that he had in addressing a sociological audience.[88] Mannheim's involvement with this group parallels that in the Hungarian
Lukács circle, as both groups were concerned with finding a resolu-
tion to the perceived crisis in culture. The proposed solutions, while
differing in specific content, do have a significant similarity in the need
to assert a new set of values, which at the moment is seen as only
existing in certain elite groups.

The concern with the propagation of a new morality is reflected in
Mannheim's increasing stress on the importance of education, and in
1946 he took up the Chair in the Institute of Education at the
University of London. The themes that Mannheim was addressing at
this stage of his career are explicated in *An Introduction to the
Sociology of Education*,[89] edited by W. A. C. Stewart and published in
1962, long after Mannheim's death in 1947.

Freedom, Power and Democratic Planning, edited by Hans Gerth and Ernest K. Bramstedt and published in 1951, reveals the increasing complexity and detail of Mannheim's views on the state of society and the possibility of planning.[90] This book shares many themes in common with Mannheim's other general works on the state of contemporary society, such as the need for planning, the disintegration of *laissez-faire* society, and the dictatorial and democratic alternatives to this. There is a subtle difference here, however, as Mannheim believes that the breakdown of *laissez-faire* and its values was caused more by its decay than its inherent nature. For example, he places more weight on the pathological nature of monopolisation, which he discusses in the following fashion:

> As long as society was regulated by a natural interplay between small self-contained units, mutual controls could work. One individual could control the other, or one group the other, or the group the individual. Just as in economic life where huge combines with their monopolies replace fierce competition between small enterprises, so in other spheres complex social units arise that are too arbitrary to reorganize themselves, and must be governed from a centre.[91]

For Mannheim a democratically planned society is necessary for the preservation of 'civilisation'. While this is historically determined, it still needs active human intervention to bring it about. The prime responsibility for this action lies with the upper reaches of society rather than with the mass behaviour of the organised working class. Again, as in many other of Mannheim's works, the educated are to lead the masses.

The analysis in *Freedom, Power and Democratic Planning* then splits into a consideration of the new institutions, structures, methods, and corresponding values, which are necessary in the new, planned society. Mannheim is again concerned to prevent the collapse into an atomised, valueless society, by the formulation of a coherent, educated value system. Accordingly, certain aspects of the nature of the future planned society are made clearer—for example, 'competition' will remain.[92] In addition, there will be 'controls', a 'mixed economic system' and a ruling class.[93] The press and radio will be democratically controlled, as these have massive potential influence in a mass society.[94] Public accountability is seen as being at the heart of democracy,[95] and the operation of the BBC is, to a large degree, paradigmatic of the type of neutrality that Mannheim wishes to see.[96] In the discussion of these issues *Freedom, Power and Democratic Planning* is an advance on the other general works.

The general sociological position which underpins these detailed works on planning and social reconstruction can be found in *Systematic Sociology*.[97] Published in 1957 and edited by J. R. Eros and W. A. C. Stewart, this is based on lectures given at the LSE in the 1930s. Here, Mannheim reasserts a central theme when he argues that 'Competition, like struggle, is a universal category of life—in biology we speak about a struggle for life—and it is a general category of social life'.[98]

While books such as *Freedom, Power and Democratic Planning* and *Systematic Sociology* are significant works, revealing Mannheim's positions on various issues, it is important to remember that they were edited and published after his death. This means that it is sometimes difficult for the general reader to decide upon the degree of editorial contribution to the final text, which in the case of *Freedom, Power and Democratic Planning* seems to have been very considerable. The question of the degree of editorial input is also relevant to the evaluation of the collection published as *Essays on the Sociology of Culture*,[99] which consists of essays written by Mannheim in the later part of his stay in Germany. These essays address the issue of the nature of the sociology of the mind, the 'problem of the intelligentsia' and 'the democratisation of culture'. The degree of editorial influence on Mannheim's most important essays from the 1920s, collected in *Essays on the Sociology of Knowledge*, published in 1952, and *Essays on Sociology and Social Psychology*, from 1953, would also be a worthwhile topic for further investigation.[100]

MANNHEIM'S SOCIOLOGY

Mannheim's short life from 1893–1947 was packed with experience of important political and intellectual developments. He twice had to leave a country because of his political affiliations and consequently was pushed into the role of refugee and exile.[101] His moves from Hungary to Germany and from Germany to Britain were not easy, though in moving from Hungary to Germany he went to a country where he had studied before and which shared a Central European culture in many respects. Mannheim's move to England was more difficult, involving an adaptation to a very different social structure, culture and intellectual tradition. However, this picture should not be overdrawn as, in England, Mannheim did find an intellectual atmosphere that paralleled and further stimulated themes which had always been present in his work. Mannheim's stress on planning in his later works, for example, is not just a response to his new environment, but is a logical development from the positions that he had set out and begun to develop in both his Hungarian and German phases.

The response to Mannheim's work in England was not always encouraging for him, however.[102] In 1945, he was subject to an attack by Montgomery Belgion,[103] who, in his attempt to free England from 'German' intellectual influence, managed to more or less misrepresent all of Mannheim's positions on significant issues, especially on the difference between the natural and cultural sciences, a point which Mannheim brings out in his reply.[104] In a general sense, while Mannheim is often thought to be one of the classical thinkers in sociology, there has actually been relatively little development of substantive themes and issues that his work raises. It is to the identification, and critical development, of these themes, that this book is mainly devoted.

In his work Mannheim drew on the intellectual traditions of Hungary, Germany and England. His general and political views remained structured by his earliest experiences and contacts in Hungary. He was always convinced of the need for social change toward a more democratic, ordered society, which was to be guided by those in possession of the requisite level of culture. Mannheim's period in England inflected this in particular new directions, but his general position remained the same. In the more narrowly defined intellectual sense, Mannheim began with a period of concern over idealist philosophical questions, as raised by classical philosophers and novelists such as Dostoyevsky, moved through brief hermeneutic and historical phases, before increasingly concerning himself with the development of a detailed sociology of knowledge incorporating new insights as well as some themes from the earlier work. The development of this sociology of knowledge reached its peak in *Ideology and Utopia*, where Mannheim set out his most explicit scheme in the sociology of knowledge. After this he broadened his work, attempting to provide a characterisation of the social structure and values of contemporary advanced Western society as a whole, as well as discussing the role of sociology and the sociologist in the fostering of a new value system. These were issues that Mannheim worked and refined, developing them in his more specific discussions of political sociology and education, until his death.

Most of Mannheim's best and most interesting work was written (or at least published) in the essay form. His reasons for doing this stem, at least partly, from his belief in the trail-blazing nature of sociological knowledge. Mannheim thought that many of his statements were only provisional and wanted to produce half-formed ideas which others could either take up and refine or discuss and reject. In these respects Mannheim did not attempt to produce a completely closed and unified general theory or system. This means that whilst his essays are often very stimulating and thought-provoking, they do tend to suffer from a certain truncation of argument. However, it is Mannheim's role in prompting thought about particular general ideas in the sociology of knowledge that is most important and the nature of this sociology of knowledge will be discussed in detail in the following chapter.

2 Mannheim's Sociology of Knowledge

In this chapter Mannheim's sociology of knowledge is analysed more closely. I concentrate on his work from 'The Problem of a Sociology of Knowledge' to *Ideology and Utopia*. However, as Mannheim's thought is, in the broad sense, a development of core themes, the presentation of the sociology of knowledge also involves drawing on some of his other writings when these clarify his more specific ideas. In any sociology of knowledge there are, as Merton has stressed, three crucial areas which are relatively separated. These are the social, knowledge and the relationship which is held to exist between these two.[1] In this chapter this relationship will be placed under the rubric of determination, and will be considered after the discussions of the meanings which Mannheim accords to the social and knowledge.[2]

THE SOCIAL

In any discussion of the nature of the social or society there are two broad questions which need to be considered. These are, firstly, what are the constituent elements of the social and, secondly, how are these elements related? One answer to the first question might be that society consists of classes which, in answer to the second question, exist in relations of struggle and conflict because of the exploitative relations which exist at the heart of their relationship.[3] The examination of these questions structures the following analysis of Mannheim's view of the social in his sociology of knowledge.

In this sociology of knowledge proper Mannheim refers to a plurality of groups to which knowledge can be related and which make up the structure of the social. The most important of these are class and generation. The examination of how Mannheim builds up the concept of generation provides a clear indication of how he looks at the nature of society, and of his category of social location in particular, which is central to his sociology of knowledge.

Generations

For Mannheim, generations are of fundamental contemporary importance.[4] He notes that

> The problem of generations is important enough to merit serious consideration. It is one of the indispensable guides to an understanding of social and intellectual movements. Its practical importance becomes clear as soon as one tries to obtain a more exact understanding of the accelerated pace of social change characteristic of our time.[5]

He begins his essay on generations, however, by criticising some of the existing literature on this concept. He divides this into two main types, the 'positivist' and the 'romantic-historical'. These are French and German phenomena, respectively. Mannheim accepts neither of these approaches but uses them as an orienting device for his own work.[6]

At the root of this lies Mannheim's idea of 'location'. In the case of generation, what underlies this as a social location is the 'biological rhythm in human existence'. However, this does not mean that the biological determines the social,[7] a point that he makes many times throughout the essay, for example:

> Now one might assume that the sociological phenomenon of location can be explained by, and deduced from, these basic biological factors. But this would be the mistake of all naturalistic theories which try to deduce sociological phenomena directly from natural facts or lose sight of the social phenomenon altogether in a mass of primarily anthropological data.[8]

The category of generation location is based on factors such as birth, death and ageing and importantly *implies* a *potential* for a particular experience and way of looking at the world. Generation location is only a base, however, and 'falls short of encompassing the generation phenomenon in its full actuality'.[9] Mannheim therefore moves a step closer to the 'real' with the idea of 'generation as actuality', which exists 'only where a concrete bond is created between members of a generation by their being exposed to the social and intellectual symptoms of a process of dynamic destabilisation'.[10] This is part and parcel of general increasing dynamism in society.[11]

Mannheim draws out this distinction between generation location and generation as actuality through the difference between the town youth and peasants, a somewhat confusing comparison given that he is comparing a regional category with an 'economic' one. However, his meaning is relatively clear, when he states that:

> the young peasants we mentioned above only share the same generation location, without, however, being members of the same generation as an actuality, with the youth of the town. They are similarly located, insofar as they are potentially capable of being sucked into the vortex of social change, and, in fact, this is what happened in the wars against Napoleon, which stirred up all German classes.[12]

In addition to 'generation as actuality' Mannheim develops the category of 'generation unit', through an analysis of political ideas and history. He notes that

> Both the romantic-conservative and the liberal-rationalist youth belonged to the same actual generation, romantic-conservative and liberal-rationalism were merely two polar forms of the intellectual and social responses experienced by all in common. Romantic-conservative youth, and the liberal-rationalist group, belong to the actual generation but form separate 'generation units' within it. The general unit represents a much more concrete bond than the actual generation as such.[13]

Mannheim produces therefore a threefold categorisation of generation: generation location, generation as 'actuality' and 'generation unit'. The most important concept here is that of generation location, which is a specific case of the more general concept of social location. As Mannheim says,

> The fact of belonging to the same class, and that of belonging to the same generation or age group, have this in common, that both endow the individuals sharing in them with a common location in the social and historical process, and thereby limit them to a specific range of potential experience, predisposing them for a certain characteristic mode of thought and experience and a characteristic type of historically relevant action.[14]

Thought is, then, a collective experience, and individuals are members of a social group to the extent that they share a common social location. This emergence is a contingent matter and cannot be settled *a priori*. The social structure places individuals into social locations which, in turn, generate common experiences and thinking. Of these locations, generation and class are accorded the most importance. However, compared with the theoretical analysis of generation the concept of class is underdeveloped.

Class

The lack of theoretical development of the concept of class in Mannheim's work has aided many commentators in their assimilation of Mannheim's concept of class to that of Marx. The falsity of this becomes clear once the place of class in Mannheim's work as a whole is understood.[15] When Mannheim talks of class he tends to use this to refer to the area of political activity rather than economic determination. For example, he very rarely mentions the economic aspects of society of even specific areas such as the production process or the workplace. This gives a particular gloss to his accounts of the rise of capitalism, which is signified by the *political* and *intellectual* ascendancy of the bourgeoisie. In this respect rationalism is considered to be the intellectual expression of the bourgeoisie. Class may be thought to be the most important social location, but it does not exist prior to other social locations and if it is more important it is mainly because of its political effects.

In summary, then, Mannheim divides the social into a plurality of social locations. These imply a particular potential for experience and action. By extension of his analysis of generation, it can be seen that at the more substantive levels of analysis there will exist actual groups (following the concept of generation as actuality) and the subdivisions of these groups into units (following the idea of generation unit). Whilst Mannheim argues that the emergence of social locations and consequently other groups is a historically contingent phenomenon, the relationship between these groups is structured by a particular phenomenon—the competitive nature of human social life.

The principle of the structuring of the social: Competition

The most straightforward exposition of Mannheim's idea of competition can be found in his essay on 'Competition as a Cultural

Phenomenon'.[16] Mannheim begins this conference paper[17] by following the position advocated by the previous speaker, von Wiese. He states that

> I shall simply submit without discussion the correctness of his main contention that competition must be regarded as a feature not merely of economic life, but of social life as a whole, and I propose to outline its role as a determinant in intellectual life, where its importance has so far been least recognized.[18]

Mannheim stresses that he is not producing an economically determinist account of the social or of thought.[19] Competition has been mistakenly thought of as an economic phenomenon as it was first manifested in this sphere. However, group competition is fundamentally a political phenomenon. Social groups and the thought they produce are structured by the competition for *power*. As Mannheim notes,

> every historical, ideological, sociological piece of knowledge (even should it prove to be absolute truth itself), is clearly rooted in and carried by the desire for power and recognition of particular social groups who want to make their interpretation of the world the universal one.[20]

In general he argues that

> Different interpretations of the world for the most part correspond to the particular functions the various groups occupy in their struggle for power.[21]

Mannheim argues that there are four 'pure types' of competition which produce particular types of knowledge.[22] The first two involve the stabilisation and containment of competition. These are 'on the basis of a consensus of opinion, of spontaneous co-operation between individuals and groups' and 'on the basis of the monopoly-position of one particular group'.[23] The other pure types depict more 'unresolved' competition. The third rests 'on the basis of competition between many groups, each determined to impose on others their particular interpretation of the world.'[24] This is termed 'atomistic competition'.[25] The final type is 'on the basis of a concentration round one point of view of a number of formerly atomistic competing groups, as a result of which competition as a whole is gradually concentrated around a few poles which become more and more dominant'.[26]

Despite initially presenting these categories as ahistorical 'pure types', Mannheim argues that they represent stages of history. The change from the first to the later types is symptomatic of the increasing dynamism of society, with the second 'pure type' being 'shattered by the tensions prevailing in an increasingly dynamic society'.[27] The increasing social conflict characteristic of the third period has potentially dangerous consequences as

> Everything seemed to go to pieces, as though the world in which one lived was not the same. In place of the old order, we now have the multi-polar conception of the world which tries to do justice to the same set of newly emerging facts from a number of different points of view.[28]

The similarity between this view and the one that Mannheim develops in his later, more general, work is striking. Thus it is important to see that the fourth 'pure type' describes an 'ordering' of competition:

> As a reaction to the increasing fragmentation brought about by atomistic competition, a fourth type of competition developed, which is the dominant type in our era—a process of concentration of the competing groups and types of orientation.[29]

In 'Competition as a Cultural Phenomenon' Mannheim assumes that competition is at the base of human associative life. This is not a theory of human nature, a theme which, although present in parts of Mannheim's work, is never central.[30] This base determines the production and structuring of ideas. As Mannheim says

> The point I want to make is that processes of change in the deepest strata of world interpretation, modification of the categorical apparatus itself, can to a large extent be explained in terms of competition.[31]

The effects of competition: the example of the rise of the Nazis

Mannheim stresses competition at various other stages in his work, and one interesting example is contained in *Systematic Sociology*, where he discusses the effects that competition has on the selection of dominant groups and thought patterns.[32] This general position is used to examined the rise to power of the Nazi Party in Weimar Germany. Mannheim contends that

> Not all Germans changed their minds between 1930 and 1933, but in the very same society different methods of social selection, brought about by competition and struggle, drew out different types of people.[33]

These people were able effectively to propagandise their views, provoking 'social imitation' which 'helped to spread this new type of behaviour and this mental pattern'.

This discussion rests on two important assumptions. First, that the media of communication have direct propagandistic effects which affect the socio-psychological processes at work in the diffusion of ideas. Second, that society has become divided into 'bare individuals' who are open to manipulation by elites, which themselves change due to the processes of competition and selection. Both of these are fundamental and characteristic assumptions of 'mass society' theory.

Mannheim's argument here can be represented in diagrammatic form as appears in Figure 2.1.

Whilst in his earlier work Mannheim did not adopt such a strong 'mass society' thesis, the essential structure of argument remains the same: groups exist in relations of antagonism and competition due to the effects of the competitive process at the heart of human social existence. In their attempts to 'win' the competition, groups adopt and foster particular forms of thought which serve these goals. The Nazi groups coming out of a particular phase of competition produced racist and Nationalist ideas which became widespread and ultimately aided their gaining of power.

The competitive nature of social life means that it is always prone to twin dangers. On the one hand there is the risk that society will fall

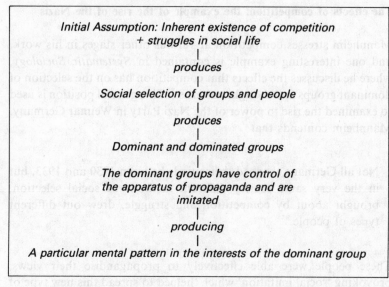

FIGURE 2.1   *The Effects of Competition in a Mass Society*

apart into a totally unstructured and chaotic state; and on the other,
that one group may be able to seize power and exercise it in a
dictatorial fashion. Mannheim, in his attempt to combat both of these
results, argues that the proper organisation of competition will only
be found in a particular mode of ordering, both in the intellectual and
political senses.

This introduces Mannheim's concern with issues of order, as the
groups which are engaged in a competitive struggle for power have to
be ordered to prevent continuing and increasing political conflict.
This concern is also manifested in the ideational realm, where he
argues for the particular synthesising and ordering role of sociology.
Sociology integrates the results from the particular social sciences.
This is linked to Mannheim's view that all knowledge is partial: a
theme that will be considered below. Mannheim therefore seeks to
impose both political and intellectual order on the disarray produced
by the inherently competitive nature of social life.

These positions were implicit even in Mannheim's very early work
and the theory of cultural revolution was as much a way of imposing
order on society as of changing it in a revolutionary fashion. The

significant split in the Hungarian group between those who did or did not follow Lukács into the Communist Party can, to a large extent, be seen as revolving around this issue of the nature of ordered social change. These themes are carried through to Mannheim's later general work on planning, where the stress is placed on the need to educate people to the level of appreciation of ordered social democracy through the regeneration of an appropriate value system.

The dominant view of the social: a summary

The coherence of Mannheim's thought on the social can now be seen. He argues that the essence of competition lies at the heart of human associative life. The antagonism between different social groupings produces political conflict. During this struggle over political power and domination, groups draw upon and create forms of knowledge, which they attempt to use to advance and defend their positions in society's hierarchy.

The structure of this argument remains constant throughout Mannheim's work even though the *contents* of it change as the focus of his work and the nature of the political/cultural/intellectual situation changes. This has the effect of filtering the core themes of Mannheim's work into particular substantive and detailed writings. In the period when Mannheim worked in detail on his sociology of knowledge he argued that the growth of anarchic political relations and the subsequent development of dictatorship can be traced back to the inherently competitive nature of social life.

In the Hungarian period the competitive essence of society is seen by Mannheim to be producing cultural crisis. In the English period the same essence produces the massification and individuation of society and the consequent dangers, which can only be resolved through the cultivation of an ordered democracy. In all of these cases the situation produced by competition requires the creation of a new form of order, and the intellectual stratum has a large role to play in this. In the Hungarian situation the ordering was to take place through the process of cultural revolution, and in the German context through the sociology of knowledge, which would provide a basis for the reconciliation of the claims of different groups. In the English period order was to be provided by the democratic plan and the respiritualisation of society through the new value system.

Some subsidiary themes

In Mannheim's main development of the sociology of knowledge his stress is on social groups and social locations based in the competitive nature of society. However, it is important to notice that at other points in his work Mannheim tends to neglect the level of social groups. As has been noted, in his later work, from *Man and Society* onwards, Mannheim becomes progressively less concerned with issues of class domination and group competition and much more absorbed with the problem of the integration of the individual *into* the group and consequently into society. This reflects the growing impact of mass society theory on Mannheim's work, but also an account of what might be the dangers of intense group conflict, as, for Mannheim, the competition of groups over fundamental issues may ultimately undermine beliefs and shared values. This separation of the individual member of society from his/her immediate social groupings produces a crisis in 'valuations' and consequently a need for new theoretical and value systems. Thus, there is a development in a particular direction here, rather than the simple substitution of a sociological theory of the individual and society for one of Marxian class conflict.

The focus on 'society' as opposed to the social groups which make it up also comes through in Mannheim's sociology of knowledge. Mannheim sometimes relates knowledge to the form of competition that is seen as characterising a particular society at a particular time.[34] This 'broad' view of the social is also revealed in the work of Mannheim's hermeneutic phase, where society is not made up of social groups, but of actors orienting themselves to the underlying *Weltanschauung*.[35] The significance of these different views of the social will become clear once the nature of the whole analysis that Mannheim adopts for the relating of knowledge to the social structure is considered.

In addition to considering the relation of the individual to society and group competition, Mannheim often divides the social into dominant and dominated, or ruling and ruled.[36] In his earlier sociology of knowledge this is often couched in Marxist terminology, whilst in his later sociology of planning and general sociology he makes greater use of concepts such as mass and elite. The fundamental dichotomisation is the same.

To recapitulate, the main view that Mannheim adopts on the nature of society sees it as a fundamentally competitive sphere, made up of different social groups. The best example of the relations involved here is the manner in which different social classes are in competition for political power and dominance over other classes.

KNOWLEDGE

The second important aspect of any sociology of knowledge is the nature of knowledge itself. Again, there are two fundamental issues which should be considered. First, it is important to determine what is meant by knowledge, to decide whether the sociology of knowledge studies ideologies, discourses, commonsense or ideas, for example. It is important to analyse what a thinker is denoting with these concepts. Second, there is the question of how one variant of knowledge is to be separated from another within the proposed categories. For example, it is important to know how to separate conservative from bourgeois or socialist thought. In this section I will primarily address the first question, leaving consideration of the second to the conclusion of this chapter where I discuss Mannheim's substantive study of conservatism as an example of his sociology of knowledge.

At different points in his work Mannheim adopts different categories of knowledge. There are constant themes in these discussions, however, and the positions he advanced in his early, hermeneutic essay 'On the Interpretation of *Weltanschauung*' were to remain influential.

The construction and interpretation of meaning

In 'On the Interpretation of *Weltanschauung*' Mannheim produces protocols for the study of cultural objects. These phenomena are organised into 'styles'. He argues that

> Just as the 'physical object' of science is totally different from the object of immediate everyday experience and is constituted, one might say, by the method of physics, so, for example, 'style' (to take an example from aesthetics) also is a novel kind of object, brought

into being by the methodological analysis of stylistic historical studies.[37]

The parallels between this type of general study and the specific examination of artistic products are explicit. The theme of the need for the sociologist of knowledge to adopt methods that have been successful in the specific studies of art history is a very strong one in Mannheim's work.[38] In this essay, however, the concept of a cultural product is used in the much wider general sense to refer to any product of human interaction. Culture is here given an anthropological, rather than aesthetic, meaning.[39]

Apart from the level of the cultural product, the more general level studied in this essay, that of *Weltanschauung* (world-view) can also be seen as a form of knowledge. In this essay Mannheim relates specific products or acts to the general cultural outlook of a whole age or society. The central issue then becomes one of how this is to be carried out. Mannheim wishes to produce both a knowledge, and a theory, of the total outlook, but the problem is that this totality can only be studied indirectly. The only way of reaching an understanding of the *Weltanschauung* is through the analysis of the meanings of the cultural products, mediating between the analyst and the *Weltanschauung* itself.

Mannheim argues that any cultural product consists of three layers of meaning: 'objective meaning', 'expressive meaning' and 'documentary or evidential meaning'.[40] Mannheim uses the hypothetical example of a friend of his giving alms to a beggar to bring out the differences between these levels of meaning. The objective meaning of an act or product inheres in that act itself. To refer to Mannheim's example, in this case the objective meaning of the situation is 'assistance' and 'the distinguishing mark of such a meaning is that it can be fully grasped without knowing anything about the "intentional acts" of the individual "author" of the product or manifestation'.[41]

The second level, expressive meaning, involves the consideration of what an actor intended or wishes to express by any particular act.[42] To return to the example, Mannheim argues 'that when my friend caused an event to happen the objective meaning of which was "assistance" his intention was not merely to help, but also to convey a feeling of sympathy to me or to the beggar'.[43] The expressive meaning of the act may be interpreted to be 'sympathy'.

The third level of meaning, documentary meaning, is the most important for Mannheim in this essay. This performs the function of linking the cultural product to the *Weltanschauung*, as the act is a *document* of the wider perspective. As Mannheim argues:

> Whenever a cultural product is grasped not only as expressive but also as documentary meaning, it again points beyond itself to something different—with the qualification, however, that this 'something different' is no longer an intentional content actually entertained by my friend, but his 'essential character' as evidenced by his action.[44]

In general,

> Nothing will be interpreted in terms of consciously intended meaning, or in terms of objective performance; rather, every behavioural datum will serve to illustrate my synoptical appraisal of his personality as a whole; and this appraisal need not be limited to his moral character—it may take his global orientation as a whole into its purview.[45]

In Mannheim's example the documentary meaning of the act may be hypocrisy.

It is possible to utilise Mannheim's categories in the analysis of other cases. Take, for example, Roland Barthes' discussion of 'a young negro in a French uniform' who is 'saluting, with his eyes uplifted, probably fixed on a fold of the tricolour', as shown on the cover of *Paris Match*.[46] It could be argued that the objective meaning here is that the soldier is saluting the flag of the country whose army is being served. In addition, the objective meaning might also entail ideas about military life and discipline. At the level of the expressive meaning of the act, the soldier may be expressing loyalty to the country being served. On the level of documentary meaning, when considering the act as a whole, it can be viewed as a document of the ideological incorporation of Black Africans into the French army. Of course, this is only an interpretation of the act depicted, the interpretations of the photograph and the act of taking it would be different.

Mannheim's essay on the interpretation of world-views utilises the study of art as an example of the sort of method to be followed in wider cultural analysis. It illustrates, in general, Mannheim's early

	Mannheim's Example	Barthes Example
Act	Friend giving alms to a begger	Black soldier saluting
Objective meaning	alms	saluting
Expressive meaning	sympathy	loyalty
Documentary meaning	hypocrisy	ideological incorporation

FIGURE 2.2   *Summary of two Examples of Interpretation of Meanings.*

procedures for the relating of a set of ideas to a wider context. Fundamentally, Mannheim is performing a particular type of what he was later to call 'extrinsic interpretation'.[47] He will later make the point that 'extrinsic' interpretation of ideas is not necessarily sociological, and what he is doing here is to relate one cultural meaning to the context of meaning which is outside it but which also incorporates it (that is, the *Weltanschauung*). However, it is possible to see the particular development of Mannheim's thought in this area. While he never argues for an 'intrinsic' interpretation of ideas, where ideas are not to be related to any context, what is to count as a proper 'extrinsic' interpretation changes as his work develops.

Mannheim is also concerned about the issue of cultural fragmentation and hopes that the methods he elucidates in 'On the Interpretation of *Weltanschauung*' will go some way towards alleviating this problem. He notes that

For one thing, our search for a synthesis will then be in a position to encompass every single cultural field. The plastic arts, music, costumes, moves and customs, rituals, the tempo of living, expressive gestures and demeanour—all these no less than the theoretical communication will become a decipherable language, adumbrating the underlying unitary whole of *Weltanschauung*.[48]

In this essay, then, Mannheim relates cultural products to the whole world-view of a society through the interpretation of meaning. The world-view *underlies* or *encapsulates* the acts being interpreted and refers to a whole age or society. At this point Mannheim does not relate the cultural product or the world-view to social groups. The issues that structure the analysis are derived from the concerns of idealist philosophy and hermeneutics. These are issues which will remain important but become more subordinated to sociological questions as Mannheim's work develops toward the sociology of knowledge. In these senses, at this stage, Mannheim thinks of knowledge in terms of widespread world-views and the relations between these are not explored in a detailed sociological way.

Ideology

The category of knowledge which lies at the base of Mannheim's sociology of knowledge is ideology. His attempts to refine the use of this concept contain some of the most fascinating insights in his work. In his earlier sociology of knowledge (before *Ideology and Utopia*) Mannheim is generally wary of the category of ideology and uses it very sparingly. For example, in his essay on 'The Ideological and the Sociological Interpretation of Intellectual Phenomena', he comments on the pejorative meaning of ideology, even though he retains the concept.[49]

In this essay Mannheim discusses the distinctions between interpreting an idea as an 'idea' or as an 'ideology'. The operation of considering forms of knowledge as 'ideas', that is, from *within*, is called 'ideological' analysis by Mannheim. On the other hand, the study of forms of knowledge as ideologies, that is, from 'without' (as functionally related to something else) is termed 'extrinsic' analysis. Mannheim contends that

> The same idea (in the sense of any intellectual-psychological content whatever toward which there is a conscious orientation) appears as 'idea' as long as one attempts to grasp and interpret it 'from within' but as 'ideology' when one considers it from points of view that lie outside of it, particularly from 'social existence'. In this sense, every idea (whether intrinsically true or false) may be considered both 'from within' and from 'existence'.[50]

He makes the point even clearer in the following passage:

> The difference between idea and ideology, then (in the sense of the present study), is not merely one of point of view but is the result of

a fundamentally different attitude towards the same intellectual phenomenon, of a fundamentally different way of looking at it.[51]

The double reference of ideology in this essay, as describing an ideological process of interpretation and as a category of knowledge, when considered extrinsically, is rather confusing on first reading, but it does illustrate the dual meaning of ideology that has grown up in the sociology of knowledge. On the one hand ideology can be taken to mean a set of coherent ideas and, on the other, may refer pejoratively to a set of ideas or process of thought.[52] These different meanings run through Mannheim's use of the term.

Mannheim's fullest development of the concept of ideology comes later in his sociology of knowledge. In *Ideology and Utopia* it is developed in parallel with 'utopia'. At this point in Mannheim's work these concepts have particular meanings; fundamentally they are seen as instruments for use in political action. An ideology is a tool used by ruling groups to maintain their power, and a utopia is a weapon for ruled groups to utilise in their attempt to gain power. None of these groups seeks to produce true knowledge about the world and consequently, for Mannheim, ideologies and utopias do not contain a correct understanding of the whole situation. The inevitable partiality of these forms of thought means that any person in pursuit of true knowledge has to approach them critically to find out what insights they express and then synthesise, in an attempt to grasp the whole picture. An ordered, complete, understanding of the world can only be obtained through these processes of particularisation and synthesis.

Mannheim's account of the nature of ideology in his essay on 'Ideology and Utopia' is one of the most well-known parts of his work. His first step is to distinguish the particular from the total form. In the area of the particular form of ideology, only part of what an opponent in a dialogue is saying is doubted due to his/her social position. In the total form, the whole conceptual framework of the opponent is thrown into doubt, as it is seen as reflecting his/her social position. This distinction is not, however, simply between psychological and sociological aspects—an overneat distinction which has partly resulted from the 'individualistic' example Mannheim utilises here.[53] This type of illustration is common in Mannheim's expositions, but it can lead to confusion. To a large extent the difference between the particular and the total is one of the degree to which the conceptual apparatus is dependent upon social functions, rather than being centred in the nature of the processes at work, or any intent on the part of the actor. Mannheim is talking about a sociology of knowledge rather than a psychology,[54] his own confused comments on the nature of interests not withstanding.

The distinction between the particular and the total concepts of ideology is historical as well as categorical and Mannheim devotes a good part of his essay on 'Ideology and Utopia' to this aspect. The total concept of ideology develops from the particular, as time goes on. The rise of the bourgeoisie has an important place in this. Mannheim argues that

At first, in the course of this ever-deepening disintegration naive distrust becomes transformed into a systematic particular notion of ideology, which, however, remains on the psychological plane. But, as the process continues, it extends to the noological-epistemological sphere. The rising bourgeoisie which brought with it a new set of values was not content with merely being assigned a circumscribed place in the old feudal order.[55]

To reach the stage where the sociology of knowledge is possible, however, the total conception of ideology must be divided into special and general variants. The special formulation of the total concept is where 'one does not call his own position into question but regards it as absolute, while interpreting his opponents' ideas as a mere function of the social positions they occupy'.[56] 'In contrast to this special formulation, the general form of the total conception of ideology is being used by the analyst when he has the courage to subject not just the adversary's point of view but all points of view, including his own, to the ideological analysis.'[57]

This has political resonances as 'it becomes the task of the sociological history of thought to analyse without regard for party biases all the factors in the actually existing social situation which may influence thought'.[58] Mannheim castigates Marxists, arguing that they relate the ideas of opponents to social positions while refusing to examine their own views in this manner. Mannheim rejects such an approach, contending that all political thought is dependent upon social position/location. There are no exceptions, and in this respect, Marxism itself is no more correct than other forms of social thought.

In addition to making these distinctions, Mannheim discusses the issue of the nature of truth, distinguishing between the 'evaluative' and the 'non-evaluative' types of the general form of the total concept of ideology. In the non-evaluative sphere truth is of no importance. The investigator can simply, and empirically, relate knowledge to social position. In the evaluative realm analysis goes beyond this to consider the relative truth claims of the different knowledge forms. However, as Mannheim recognises, this introduces the problem of the nature of truth; if all knowledge is socially related, is truth also social? Mannheim argues that there is no ahistorical truth, and that 'The modern investigator can answer, if he is accused of evading the problem of what is truth, that the indirect approach to truth through social history will in the end be more fruitful than a direct logical attack'.[59]

The distinction that Mannheim draws here is, however, not as clear as might be hoped. The problem is that direct evaluative assumptions are entailed in the non-evaluative realm. Mannheim says that 'we have, then, as the theme of this non-evaluative study of ideology, the relationship of all partial knowledge and its component elements to the larger body of meaning, and ultimately to the structure of historical reality'.[60] The problem here is that there is no justification offered for the assumption that particular knowledges are partial. It tends to be assumed that knowledge is like this by nature: to say that knowledge is socially determined is to say that it is partial. As Mannheim says, 'only when we are thoroughly aware of the limited scope of every point of view are we on the road to the sought-for comprehension of the whole'.[61] Mannheim likewise assumes that ideology involves distortion.[62]

Mannheim produces then a detailed set of distinctions within the concept of ideology. He separates the particular from the total, the special from the general form of the total and the evaluative from the non-evaluative. These distinctions can be represented diagrammatically, as below:

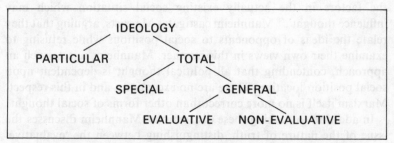

FIGURE 2.3   *Distinctions in Mannheim's Concept of Ideology*

Despite these distinctions, however, Mannheim also uses the concept of ideology to refer in a general sense to 'a system of ideas'. This can lead to confusion in *Ideology and Utopia*, where utopias are at times referred to as ideologies.

It is also clear that even at this late stage of the development of his sociology of knowledge Mannheim is not consistent about the forms of knowledge that the sociology of knowledge is to consider, though he mainly concentrates on the area of relatively formalised sets of political beliefs or ideas. This is also an issue in the interpretation of Mannheim's later, more general, works, where forms of knowledge are considered as 'values' or as 'mind' for example.[63] These are then related to the general nature of society, the structure of the distinctions here having themes in common with the discussion of worldviews in 'On the Interpretation of *Weltanschauung*'.

Despite his continuing use of the concept of ideology in both the detailed sense, and in the form of a system of ideas (or world-view) which is correlated with a particular social location, Mannheim is always worried about the pejorative connotations that were attached to it. At various points in his work he develops concepts which incorporate and replace the category of ideology, and these will now be discussed.

Other categories of knowledge

In various places Mannheim uses the concept of perspective to describe forms of knowledge, pointing to the perspectives that are developed in the course of the unfolding of history. Mannheim relates the occurrence of perspectives to 'epochs' of history.[64] In turn, the perspectives can only be understood 'perspectively' by the analyst, as the standpoint of the sociologist 'is itself a product of history'.[65]

This term and its use is carried through into *Ideology and Utopia*, where in 'The Sociology of Knowledge' Mannheim writes that

> In the realm of the sociology of knowledge, we shall then, as far as possible, avoid the use of the term 'ideology' because of its moral connotations, and shall instead speak of the 'perspective' of a thinker. By this term we mean the subject's mode of conceiving things as determined by his historical and social setting.[66]

Another important concept which Mannheim uses as the object of analysis for the sociology of knowledge is that of 'style of thought'.

This is specifically introduced in the essay on 'Conservative Thought', where its uses are noted:

> At the heart of this method is the concept of a style of thought. The history of thought from this point of view is not mere history of ideas, but an analysis of different styles of thought as they grow and develop, fuse and disappear; and the key to the understanding of changes in ideas is to be found in the changing social background, mainly in the fate of social groups or classes which are the 'carriers' of these styles of thought.[67]

Mannheim derives this concept from the study of styles in the history of art,[68] repeating a similar orientation to that found in his earlier work on the interpretation of world-views. The concept is to be used in an analytic as well as a descriptive sense:

> it is our contention that human thought also develops in 'styles', and that there are different schools of thought distinguishable by the different ways in which they use different thought patterns and categories. Thus it should be just as possible to 'place' an anonymous piece of writing as an anonymous work of art, if we only took the trouble to reconstruct the different styles of a given epoch and their variations from individual to individual.[69]

Like the category of perspective, 'style of thought' is retained by Mannheim in his later theoretical development of the sociology of knowledge. In his article on the 'Sociology of Knowledge' Mannheim produces the following summary of his position, which shows how he attempts to integrate some of the different aspects which have been discussed in this section. He maintains that

> There are two levels on which the task of imputation may proceed. The first (*Sinngemasse Zurechnung*) deals with general problems of interpretation. It reconstructs integral styles of thought and perspectives, tracing single expressions and records of thought which appear to be related back to a central *Weltanschauung* which they express.[70]

The first level built up ideal types. The next stage of interpretation is sociological:

When the structures and the tendencies of two styles of thought have been worked out, we are faced with the task of their sociological imputation. As sociologists we do not attempt to explain the forms and variations in conservative thought, for example, solely by reference to the conservative *Weltanschauung*. On the contrary, we seek to derive them firstly from the composition of the groups and strata which express themselves in that mode of thought.[71]

It should be clear from this discussion, that the categories of knowledge (and the relationships between them) that Mannheim develops are not as consistent as might be desired. Generally, however, it is important to note that he does normally make a distinction between a specific category and the wider form of which it is a part. For example, the specific ideas of bouregois ideology are based in a wider style of bourgeois thought.[72] What makes this rather confusing, however, is the way in which categories at times cross from the wider to the specific mode, or even mediate between them. This is especially the case with the concept of a 'style of thought'.[73] This distinction between the general and the specific will become clearer in the analysis of 'Conservative Thought' (see below).

Non-socially determined forms of thought: Natural Science and Traditionalism

While Mannheim is not as consistent in his analysis of natural science as might be wished, he is generally loath to subject it to analysis by the sociology of knowledge.[74] He presents many arguments about the development and history of science, where he stresses its 'immanentist' character: its procedures and methods develop according to an internal logic of their own. Most of the examples that Mannheim gives have come from mathematics and he is very fond of stating that $2 \times 2 = 4$ is a universally understood relation.[75] He also notes that

> The peculiar phenomenon of change of meaning does not occur in these fields. The Pythagorean theorem meant just the same for the Greeks as it does for us. A technical invention, as technical invention, e.g. an axe, does not change its meaning in the process of time.[76]

Mannheim adds a footnote to this which tends to confuse rather than clarify his position:

Technology can, however, be enveloped in magic. In such cases, of course, the magical interpretation which accompanies the technical invention as such belongs to the psychic-cultural inventory of the epoch in question, but later stages may lay bare the purely technical elements of the invention—and improve upon it in 'progressive' fashion.[77]

How the purely technical aspect is to be separated from others is perhaps not as clear as Mannheim seems to think.

Much of the recent work in the sociology of knowledge has been concerned with the study of scientific knowledge and has been critical of positions such as that adopted by Mannheim. However, there is no real reason why Mannheim's general arguments could not be used in the analysis and understanding of science even if he does not do it himself.[78]

A second example of the autonomisation of a form of knowledge is revealed in Mannheim's discussion of traditionalism in his essay on 'Conservative Thought'. Here he argues that 'Traditionalism signifies a tendency to cling to vegetative patterns, to old ways of life which we may well consider as fairly ubiquitous and universal.'[79] Mannheim gives the following explanation of this type of thought (and hence of action consequent upon it):

The word 'traditionalist' describes what, to a greater or lesser degree, is a formal psychological characteristic of every individual's mind.[80]

A tendency to 'traditionalism' is, then, an inherent part of any human being's psychological make-up. Mannheim, in effect, produces a philosophical anthropology: human beings are naturally traditional. This is rather an unusual position to find in his work. Generally if he makes similar assumptions, they are about the nature of human associative life, for example, that it is inherently competitive, rather than about human nature itself.

To recapitulate on the arguments in this section on knowledge, I have demonstrated that Mannheim adopts different positions on the names to be given to the forms of knowledge that the sociology of knowledge studies. His earlier, hermeneutic positions involved the attempt to interpret the nature of a *Weltanschauung* as revealed by particular documentary products. In his sociology of knowledge proper he moves to the analysis of the 'world-views' that are attached to particular social locations and often uses ideology to denote this form of knowledge. In his later sociology of knowledge he produces a set of categorisations which develop the concepts of ideology and utopia. However, because of his worries about the pejorative meanings attached to the concept of ideology, he developed other terms at different points in his sociology of knowledge, the most important of these being 'perspective' and 'style of thought'. He continues to use both of these in his later sociology of knowledge, drawing distinctions between specific and wider forms of knowledge. It is this separation of levels which is the most important part of his analysis, no matter how the levels are labelled.

Finally, it was demonstrated that Mannheim did not subject all forms of knowledge to social analysis and that he importantly exempted both natural science and traditionalism. The detailing of these categories provides an answer to the issue of the nature of the knowledge to be studied by the sociology of knowledge posed at the beginning of this section. Mannheim also provides some pointers to how one form of knowledge may be separated from another. I discuss this further in considering Mannheim's analysis of conservative thought.

DETERMINATION

The nature of the relationship between the social and knowledge is a critical part of the sociology of knowledge. There are two interrelated issues here. First, the general character of the relationship must be considered, and second, relatedly, the examination of *how* and *why* the particular relationships identified by the sociology of knowledge exist, must be pursued. Mannheim's work raises and addresses many of the most important problems in this realm.

Mannheim produces what initially seem to be a plurality of different characterisations of the nature of the general relationship between knowledge and social structure, leading Merton to think that this 'leads to vagueness and obscurity'.[81] However, whilst Mannheim's positions are not as clear as one might like here, there is a logic in their development and use.

Correspondence

At various points in his work, Mannheim makes use of a theory of correspondence to describe the relationship between knowledge and social structure. For example, he argues in 'Historicism' that

> If the autonomizing, sectionalizing mode of thought may be regarded as corresponding to a social structure which allowed a maximum dissolution of the social bonds and which produced an economy consisting of liberalistically independent, atom-like units, then the present trend toward synthesis, toward the investigation of totalities may be regarded as the emergence, at the level of reflection of a force which is pushing social reality into more collectivistic channels.[82]

This broad perspective is reiterated in Mannheim's later sociology of knowledge, where, for example, he contends that 'corresponding to the dual meanings of the term ideology which are designated here as the particular and total conceptions respectively, are two distinct currents of historical development'.[83]

Mannheim develops more specific aspects of the relation of correspondence at different points in his work. In 'The Problem of a Sociology of Knowledge' he introduces the concept of 'constellation', saying that

> the term 'constellation' may designate the specific combination of certain factors at a given moment, and this will call for observation when we have reason to assume that the simultaneous presence of various factors is responsible for the shape assumed by that one factor in which we are interested.[84]

The sociology of knowledge itself is a form of thought which is produced in a specific constellation of factors. These are 'the self-relativization of thought and knowledge', 'the appearance of a new form of relativization introduced by the "unmasking" turn of mind', 'the emergence of a new system of reference, that of the social sphere, in respect of which thought could be conceived to be relative', and finally, 'the aspiration to make this relativization total, relating not one thought or idea, but a whole system of ideas, to an underlying social reality'.[85]

This is a more complex version of the general correspondence theory. Instead of drawing a simple parallel between the separated spheres of the social and knowledge, Mannheim introduces a number of different aspects which form the background to the sociology of knowledge. These are both 'real' and 'ideal'. There is a distinct parallel here between this theory and the uses of function and functional system in other forms of sociology, and Mannheim does in fact use the concept of function at points in his work.

His general use of function parallels that of 'correspondence'. In 'The Ideological and Sociological Interpretation of Intellectual Phenomena', for example, Mannheim maintains that 'we do not stop at the suspension of intrinsic interpretation but, at the same time, relate the intellectual content to something we posit outside it, as the function of which it then appears'.[86] The different factors in a constellation are functionally and correspondingly related. In addition to this general position, however, Mannheim also develops his theory of correspondence in a more specific direction.

Group struggle, competition and correspondence

In his essay on 'Ideology and Utopia' Mannheim argues that 'It is extremely probable that everyday experience with political affairs first made man aware of and critical toward the ideological element in his thinking'.[87] In common with the analysis in 'Historicism', Mannheim stresses that the process of change in thought is the result of the process of the development of history. Significantly, however, he adds a greater specification of detail here, and stresses the political dimensions of these developments.

These elements are first introduced in detail in 'The Problem of a Sociology of Knowledge', as part of Mannheim's development of a more sociological view. He notes that there are 'various "world postulates", systems of *Weltanschauung*, combating each other'. These are 'championed' by different social groups and only when these 'intellectual strata' are specified, can we ask which 'social strata' correspond to them. This leads to the conclusion that 'we can understand the transformation of the various ideologies only on the basis of changes in the social composition of the intellectual stratum corresponding to them'.[88]

In effect, Mannheim produces two general theories of the nature of the relation between knowledge and social structure using the category of correspondence. Generally, he argues that developments in thought can be correlated to, or seen to correspond with, developments in society and history. More specifically, he contends that ideologies or styles of thought relate to particular social groups. It is the second of these theories which has more contemporary relevance and interest. However, it does pose some further issues. Notably, those of why particular forms of thought are related to particular groups, and how this relation operates? One classical strategy for coping with this issue is to argue that groups adopt or create forms of thought in accordance with interests. However, Mannheim is not disposed to this solution. He characterises interests in the following fashion in his essay on 'Ideology and Utopia':

> the particular conception of ideology operates primarily with a psychology of interests, while the total conception uses a more formal functional analysis, without any reference to motivations, confining itself to an objective description of the structural differences in minds operating in different social settings. The former assumes that this or that interest is the cause of a given lie or deception. The latter presupposes simply that there is a correspondence between a given social situation and a given perspective, point of view, or apperception mass. In this case, while an analysis of constellations of interests may often be necessary, it is not to establish causal connections but to characterize the total situation. Thus interest psychology tends to be displaced by an analysis of the correspondence between the situation to be known and the forms of knowledge.[89]

In this passage Mannheim is separating the particular from the total forms of ideology and restricting the concept of interest to the arena of the former. However, at other points in his sociology of knowledge, Mannheim does produce a theoretical scheme utilising a concept which parallels interest. This is based in his theory of competition. Mannheim argues:

> Competition controls not merely economic activity through the mechanism of the market, not merely the cause of political and social events, but furnishes also the motor impulse behind diverse interpretations of the world which, when their social background is uncovered, reveal themselves as the intellectual expression of conflicting groups struggling for power'.[90]

As has already been seen, Mannheim thinks that competition is inherent in social life. Groups made up of socially located individuals exist in relationships of political struggle, attempting to secure or retain dominance. These groups produce or use thought in such struggles. In a Marxist sociology of knowledge it would be argued that classes in conflict, having been placed in this relation due to their relationships to the means of production, produce or utilise knowledge in the attempt to further their interests. For Mannheim, Marxism one-sidedly stresses economics in the development of history. At times he thinks that this conception of Marxism has some validity, but ultimately, in his view, it should be purged of its one-sidedness, and its 'polemical', 'political' character stripped away.

Mannheim therefore doubts the value of interest, as a general mechanism for characterising the relationship between knowledge and the social structure. In 'The Problem of a Sociology of Knowledge' he 'replaces' this with the concept of 'committedness', arguing that 'direct "committedness" to certain mental forms is the most comprehensive category in the field of the social conditioning of ideas'.[91]

Mannheim criticises Marxism for being propagandistic, and maintains that 'Marxism consists in directly associating even the most esoteric and spiritual products of the mind with the economic and power interests of a certain class'.[92] Interests are only a specific direct case of commitment, and the difference between them is illustrated by the different forms of knowledge that are subject to these different relations:

> it may be that we profess a certain economic theory or certain political ideas because they are in keeping with our interests. But surely no immediate interests are involved in our choice of a certain artistic style or style of thought; and yet these entities also do not float in thin air but come to be developed by certain groups as a result of socio-historical factors. In the case of ideas held because of direct interest, we may speak of 'interestedness'; to designate the more indirect relation between the subject and those other ideas, we may use the parallel expression 'committedness'.[93]

There are, then, processes of competition between groups, at work in both the general social and the more specific economic/political levels. In the latter, the relationship between groups and knowledge is more clearly based in interest formed by competition and it is possible cautiously to use the concept of interest. However, in the wider case forms of thought are produced because of commitments. This is the wider category of which interest is a sub set. Groups are committed to particular forms of knowledge because of the role that they play in competition. Despite this detailed theory, however, Mannheim is still worried about the general meaning of determination in his later sociology of knowledge.

'Existential determination', dynamism and ordering

In his essay on 'The Sociology of Knowledge' Mannheim character-ises the sociology of knowledge 'as a theory of the social or existential determination of actual thinking'.[94] However, he realises that 'deter-mination' may possess a particular type of 'positivistic' connotation for an English-speaking audience and thus introduces the following explanation:

> Here we do not mean by 'determination' a mechanical cause-effect sequence: we leave the meaning of 'determination' open, and only empirical investigation will show us how strict is the correlation between life-situation and thought-process, or what scope exists for variations in the correlation. [The German expression '*Seinsverbun-denes Wissens*' conveys a meaning which leaves the exact nature of the determinism open.][95]

It is this passage which especially opens Mannheim to Merton's charges of vagueness. However, it is important to realise the context within which Mannheim developed this theory.[96] There are reasons why he adopted such a position which cannot be reduced to a simple oversight, though, of course, these do not in themselves refute the charge of vagueness.

One aspect of the situation which produces this general, later position on determination is Mannheim's dislike of the Marxist sense of causation. This is a point which has already been mentioned in the specific sense in relation to the concept of interest. However, in the general sense Mannheim thinks that Marxism is like many other approaches in its partiality or one-sidedness. Part of the reason for Mannheim's rejection of 'mechanical' theories of causality stems from his desire to produce what he saw as a non-dogmatic, complete picture of social life, which would be able to analyse the complex linkages between different aspects of the social structure and thought.

The political developments in Germany in the 1920s and 1930s in which Marxism played a part also had their effects on Mannheim's views. One way of overcoming the intellectual and political turmoil was to synthesise competing sets of ideas, but it was also important not to have a closed mind on contemporary developments. 'Closure' in the area of determination would be a prime example of the kinds of intellectual and political dogmatism which Mannheim saw himself as fighting against.

In addition to his views of Marxism and developments in German social and political life it is important to remember Mannheim's stress on the development of history and the subsequent dynamic nature of both society and knowledge. Mannheim was deeply concerned with social change and historicity at various points in his work.[97]

From the more specifically historicist phase of his writing Mannheim retains the idea that society is becoming increasingly dynamic. A sense of history and of dynamic development are important aspects of his thought. However, order needs to be formed out of this rapid change. Mannheim wishes to place a grid of classification and typology over society.

These themes have their effects on the concept of determination since, because of the nature of the historical process, the nature of the relation between social structure and knowledge is altering in an accelerated fashion. To a large degree Mannheim accepts the inevitability of this. However, he desires a new form of order to counteract the dangers inherent in massification. The concepts that he develops in the field of determination attempt to take these issues and problems into account. These aspects form one set of sources for Mannheim's openness on the nature of determination in a general sense. The other main set derives from his use of the theory of interpretation derived from hermeneutic writers.[98]

The interpretive links between knowledge and social structure

The positions which Mannheim elucidated in 'On the Interpretation of *Weltanschauung*' had effects on his later work. It will be remembered that in this essay Mannheim argued that knowledge of the *Weltanschauung* of an age can only be obtained through the indirect route of the analysis of documentary meanings. Diagrammatically this can be represented as follows:

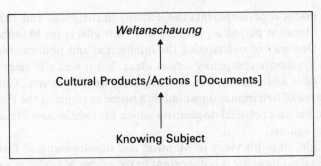

FIGURE 2.4   *The Process of Interpretation of Weltanschauung in Mannheim's
Hermeneutic Work*

However, it should also be remembered that the *Weltanschauung*
incorporates both the cultural product and the knowing subject. We
live in terms of world-views and our cultural products and actions
constitute them. This leads into some of the important technical issues
in hermeneutic social science, notably around the problem of the
relationships between the whole and the parts—the *Weltanschauung*
and the cultural product, as it is thought that there is a paradox here.[99]
As Mannheim himself expressed it:

> we understand the whole from the part, and the part from the
> whole. We derive the 'spirit of the epoch' from its individual
> documentary manifestations—and we interpret the individual
> documentary manifestations on the basis of what we know about
> the spirit of the epoch.[100]

The use that Mannheim makes of these positions is important. The
direction that his thought was to take was already hinted at in his
early discussions of the work of Max Weber, where he says that

> Weber postulates a mutual causal dependence among the various
> domains of culture and considers it necessary for purposes of the
> correct 'causal account' that the economic-material should at times
> be explained from the mental, and another time—as the occasion
> calls for—the spiritual from the material, with the reservation,
> however, that neither of these domains is wholly deducible from the
> other as if it were simply a function of it.[101]

The theory that Mannheim develops at this point

is an interpretive rather than explanatory one in the sense just defined. What it does is to take some meaningful object already understood in the frame of reference of objective meaning and place it within a different frame of reference—that of *Weltanschauung*.[102]

Mannheim argues, therefore, that

interpretation serves for the deeper understanding of meanings, causal explanation shows the conditions for the actualization and realizations of a given meaning.[103]

Overall, there is a need for both interpretation and causal analysis. The first stage in the analysis of a form of thought involves the formulation of the nature of the knowledge form through a process of interpretation. This is then related causally to particular groups. This is a process that will become clearer when Mannheim's analysis of conservative thought is examined in the final part of this chapter. It is now possible to draw the separate themes in Mannheim's sociology of knowledge together.

THE NATURE OF MANNHEIM'S SOCIOLOGY OF KNOWLEDGE

For Mannheim, competition is the central fact of human social existence. This is not the same as saying that human nature is inherently competitive, rather it is social life that has this characteristic. Competition is an essential fact of social interaction. This position is revealed at many points in Mannheim's work, and is most explicitly discussed in his essay on competition.

The reason why Mannheim argued for the centrality of competition is partly a result of the particular social and political situation in which he lived and worked. What appeared to be developing was a naked competition for power and political domination. As society was becoming increasingly conflictual the institutionalisation of particular social relations and ways of behaving was breaking down, making social competition more apparent. Marxism as an intellectual and political doctrine has effects on Mannheim's system here, but his views are far removed from Marx's stress on class struggle and even further away from the idea of the motor of change being the result of the tension between the forces and relations of production that is an alternate model of social change in Marx's work.

If it is accepted that competition is of central importance to Mannheim's thought, then his concern with *order* follows logically. This concern is expressed in different ways in different parts of Mannheim's work. Generally, synthesis is sometimes seen as coming out of the process of competition itself. Mannheim notes that

> We must now ask: Does competition at this stage only bring about polarization, or does it also produce synthesis?[104]

The reply is that

> we hold, in fact, that syntheses do arise in the process, and that precisely the syntheses play a particular important role in the evolution of thought.[105]

The idea of synthesis operates in various ways in Mannheim's work. First, methodologically, the sociology of knowledge has initially to 'particularise' showing the limited claims to validity of forms of knowledge and knowledge claims. Then it has to synthesise, developing from these particular claims, those truthful aspects that can be integrated to form the best approximation to knowledge of the truth to be gained at any particular time.

Second, Mannheim discusses the synthesis of different social sciences. Sociology is the key here; as compared with the limited and partial knowledges produced by the other particular social sciences, such as economics, politics and psychology, it can develop a theory of society as a whole, and therefore synthesise partial accounts. Relatedly, Mannheim also attempts to reconcile the different types of analysis produced within sociology itself. This is especially true of his later work, but it also occurs in his earlier writing.

Third, Mannheim attempts a political synthesis and his comments about ideology within the sociology of knowledge can also be seen as referring to the need to produce order and synthesis in society in the wider sense. This theme is reproduced in his general political/social writings, where he argues that unless competition is ordered, societal breakdown and chaos will result. It will be remembered that Mannheim had enough experience of societal 'collapse' in Hungary and

Germany for this to be a very real fear for him. Such degeneration is to be avoided through a system of an ordered democratic hierarchy. The precise structure of this differed in the succeeding phases of Mannheim's work. In his early Hungarian period he stressed cultural leadership; in the German, the sociology of knowledge was advocated as an aid to social order, and in the English period he maintained that planners should regenerate society through guided democracy.

Mannheim's advocacy of order and synthesis has become intertwined and confused with his account of the intellectual stratum. This is extremely misleading, but detailed analysis of this area will be left until chapter 3, when critics of Mannheim's theory of the intellectuals will be considered.

These ideas about competition and order stand at the heart of Mannheim's work. They are both derived from, and refracted through, the political and intellectual developments of his time.[106] Important aspects of this have already been mentioned, and now will be briefly summarised. Mannheim is concerned about the increasingly dynamic development of Western society, which is partly reflected in the doctrines of historicism and the uncertainty which these in turn produce. In addition, Mannheim oriented himself to Marxism, as both a political and intellectual doctrine. Despite this, he never became a Marxist, and produced a very different intellectual system. Marxism was also important for its political effects, as one of the most important movements that had to be taken account of in the formulation of a political and social programme.[107] Further, the intellectual background of his early Hungarian period remained important to Mannheim, producing especially his stress on culture and cultural regeneration.[108] Additionally, the political and social events of the Weimar period affected him greatly. At certain points Mannheim saw this as a new 'golden age', but he later recognised how the conflict of the period had opened the doors to the new totalitarian barbarism of the Nazis.[109] Finally, the concern of many English intellectuals and politicians for planned social change fitted in well with Mannheim's desire for directed order for the greater benefit of all.[110] These positions are at the base of Mannheim's more detailed sociology of knowledge.

I have argued that Mannheim adopts two forms of sociology of knowledge. First, there is a general theory. Here, knowledge is seen to correspond to society or societal development in a relatively untheorised fashion. Second, there is the more detailed, specific sociology of knowledge, which is most theoretically developed between the mid-1920s and the early 1930s. The distinctions between these two outlooks are not always clear and the theories interpenetrate and overlap.

Mannheim's writings on the nature of knowledge also show the effects of the specific and general theories that he adopted. In a general sense he related phenomena such as 'values' to the state and organisation of the social structure. In his more specific sociology of knowledge the concept of ideology is the storm centre, Mannheim sought to develop a concept of ideology (or replace it altogether by another), which did not have the pejorative connotations which he saw as being attached to it in Marxist thought.

The area of knowledge, especially, exhibits the marks of Mannheim's early hermeneutic phase. He always recognised that worldview was a term that could stand in for either style of thought or ideology and in the general sense made use of the methods of interpretation and formulation of world-views which was set out in 'On the Interpretation of *Weltanschauung*'. What changed as his work developed was the meaning of world-view itself. In the earlier period this refers to a rather a-social view of a period or age which is held to underlie all social life. In his more specific development of the sociology of knowledge, however, world-views are expressed through social groups. It is important to recognise that the tools for analysing these world-views can still have a great deal in common with those developed in the early hermeneutic writing. World-views, or styles of thought, can be formulated and recognised through the interpretation of cultural products and actions which are associated with the spokespersons of the groups which express particular concrete manifestations of world-views.

Mannheim did not think that all forms of knowledge were open to sociological analysis. Traditionalism and natural science are the most important forms which he exempted from sociological study in different ways. However, in the general sense, he argued that

> The author's philosophy has always been guided by the ideas of *Seinsverbundenheit*, i.e. by the idea that mental phenomena are related to the environment, the situation and the field, and do not exist in an abstract heaven.[111]

In the widest sense of the *specific* sociology of knowledge, Mannheim sees that knowledge corresponds to social groupings through the mechanism of commitment; in the specialised aspects of the detailed sociology of knowledge, political knowledge is related to social groups through interests. Mannheim also retains a role for interpretation on the part of the analyst, reflecting his earlier interests in hermeneutics. It is, however, only a prior stage to the work of the causal imputation of ideas to social groups. How these positions are worked out in practice can be made clear through the analysis of Mannheim's work on conservative thought.[112]

'CONSERVATIVE THOUGHT'

In his important work on conservatism Mannheim charts the development and character of early 19th-century conservative thought in Germany, as revealed in the writings of particular German conservative theorists.[113] One of the initial problems that confronts Mannheim is that of the demarcation of conservatism as a particular mode of thought. He has to decide what conservatism is and find a way of gaining access to it.

Mannheim begins his discussion by introducing the concept of a 'style of thought'.[114] This is used to indicate both the specific content of ideas and the forms in which the ideas are expressed. He stresses how successful this concept has been in the study of the history of art, which is used as an exemplar for the sociology of knowledge.[115] Mannheim draws on art history to formulate one of his main methods in the establishment of the nature of a style of thought. He maintains that there is a 'basic intention' behind a style of thought, which he relates to Riegl's category of the 'art motive'.[116] Mannheim stresses that this is not idealist, as intentions are 'ultimately born out of the struggles and conflicts of human groups'.[117]

For Mannheim access to styles of thought can only be gained indirectly, through the analysis of the writings of particular thinkers. This repeats the structure of argument produced in 'On the Interpretation of *Weltanschauung*', where the analysis of the cultural product is used to gain access to, as well as to define, the *Weltanschauung* of an age.[118] By 'Conservative Thought', however, Mannheim had developed his view of the nature of the social structure, and changes in the style of thought relate to the changing positions of particular social groups. However, at points, a degree of autonomy is given to thought itself, reflecting a continuing influence of hermeneutics. In the general sense, though, this position is increasingly subordinated to one which claims that each group has its own world-view.[119]

Mannheim concludes his introduction with a resumé of the general social context, examining the social situation in early 19th-century Germany and contrasting it with France and England. He stresses the importance of the French Revolution and its effects on the other European states, where, he argues, its aims were translated into different areas of life. He quotes approvingly Marx's view that the French Revolution occurred on a philosophical plane in Germany and stresses the influence of Burke's writings on German conservative thought.[120]

For Mannheim, the specific manifestation of conservatism at this point in German history is, in part, due to its opposition to the rationalist mode of thought. This rationalism is itself defined by its difference from, and opposition to, other forms of thought, notably 'Aristotelian scholasticism' and 'the philosophy of nature of the Renaissance'.[121] Rationalism stresses Reason and general study. One of its results is quantification of the use of mathematics as an exemplar. The development of this mode of thought is related to two processes—the development of commodity production, and the consequent rise of the bourgeoisie. Mannheim terms the latter a 'sociological factor' and stresses it in his analysis.[122]

Mannheim argues that the 'conservative' attitudes which existed prior to this rise of rationalism, in feudal society, became latent for a period, before being taken up and worked upon by the later conservatives expressing a reflective political ideology. These latent attitudes were to some extent carried in the form of romanticism, this being one of the sources of modern conservatism.[123]

Conservatism is also, to some degree, an outcrop from traditionalism. As has already been noted, Mannheim thinks that traditionalism is a universal instinct. Conservatism is not the same as traditionalism, but develops from it, building on the desire for stasis. There are many difficulties with this argument, as Mannheim never offers any convincing evidence to show that human beings are traditional by nature. This is pertinent to the general analysis of Mannheim's thought, but paradoxically, does not affect his discussion of conservatism to the same degree, which can be separated from his philosophical anthropology. The existence of traditionalism is not used to explain conservatism. Conservatism can only be properly understood as a sociological phenomenon, which has a particular and traceable history, something that traditionalism, as a psychological trait, cannot have. The relationship is summed up by Mannheim in the following fashion:

> To put it briefly, the development and widespread existence of conservatism, as distinct from mere traditionalism, is due in the last resort to the dynamic character of the modern world; to the basis of this dynamic in social differentiation; to the fact that this social differentiation tends to draw the human intellect along with it and forces it to develop along its own lines; and finally to the fact that the basic aims of the different social groups do not merely crystallize ideas into actual movements of thought, but also create different antagonistic styles of thought. In a word—traditionalism can only become conservatism in a society in which change occurs through the medium of class conflict in a class society. This is the sociological background of modern conservatism.[124]

Mannheim argues that German conservatism can be studied as a 'unit' and from the point of view of its genesis. These currents run through Mannheim's analysis of the basic 'intention' and the 'key problem' of German conservatism.[125] With respect to basic intention, Mannheim notes the concentration on the 'concrete' in conservative thought and how it begins from the immediately given rather than the 'possible'. This contrasts with transcendent thought.[126] Additionally Mannheim describes the particular meaning that conservatives accord to property, which, in contrast to 'bourgeois' ideas, confers duties on, as well as rights to, its owner.[127] Furthermore, conservatives accord a particular meaning to liberty and people are seen as being inherently unequal. However, this view can lead to the 'dangers' of individualism and 'anarchistic subjectivism' in conservative thought, and to combat these conservatives developed more holistic categories such as the state and the nation.[128]

In stressing the manner in which conservatives experience the present in terms of its being a product of the past, Mannheim produces analyses of the conservatives' experience and understanding of both space and time. He examines the way in which the conservative collapses time into space, so that the past is seen as a part of the present. This concentration on the 'spatial' existence of structures is paralleled in socialist ideas. The nature of these structures differs, however, with conservatives seeing them as 'organic' and 'proletarians' as 'agglomerations'. Consequently, Mannheim summarises the 'basic intention' of conservatism as follows:

> To see things authentically as a conservative, then, is to experience events in terms of an attitude derived from social circumstances and situations anchored in the past.[129]

This forms the core of 'authentic' conservatism and the base for 'modern' conservatism. Looking at the theoretical core of conservative thought, Mannheim structures his argument around the consideration of what conservatism is not. Conservatism is seen as being opposed to natural-law thought, and here he shifts to analysing the more conscious, coherent, modern form of conservatism. Mannheim stresses the attack on the different aspects of the idea of Reason with ideas centred around History, Life, the Nation, the irrational nature of reality, a particular form of individuality and the organism. He argues that the rationalist concept of reason is replaced by more 'dynamic' ideas, which stress 'life' and especially 'history', this tending to some of the later developments in German philosophy and especially to historicist doctrines.[130]

Mannheim then moves into a more detailed discussion of particular German conservatives and their ideas. The role of the intellectuals is especially important here, and Mannheim emphasises the manner in which they should be seen as 'selling their pens' to one group or another.[131] The social position of the intellectuals does not bind them to any group, and they can therefore take up another group's interests, 'knowing' and expressing them better than the group itself. The struggle of romantic conservatism against the rationalism of the bureaucracy and later against that of the bourgeoisie is traced and it is with the details of this that Mannheim is much concerned.

'Conservative Thought' brings out some of the main themes of Mannheim's sociology of knowledge. He considers both the general and the specific referents of knowledge. He thus discusses both general social crises and very broad movements, as well as the specific groups and classes that are represented by the particular authors that he considers. Conservative thought is seen as being expressed by various groups in opposition to the ideas attached to the bourgeoisie. In the area of knowledge, Mannheim also makes use of a dual conception, shifting between the specific, consciously articulated conservative 'ideology' or world-view and the general ideas which form the base and underlying source of these specific ideas. These forms of knowledge correspond to the social structure, and specifically can be seen as an outcrop from the generalised competition for power between different social groups.

In the more analytical sense, it is possible to divide the argument in 'Conservative Thought' into 'explanatory' and 'interpretive' realms. On the explanatory level Mannheim sees that there is a particular conservative style of thought, which can be used as a resource in different ways at particular moments in history. Depending on the nature of particular occurrences and events, such as the French Revolution or the rise of the bourgeoisie, explicit conservative statements will be produced. These may have the effect of modifying aspects of the conservative style of thought, but will leave its essential

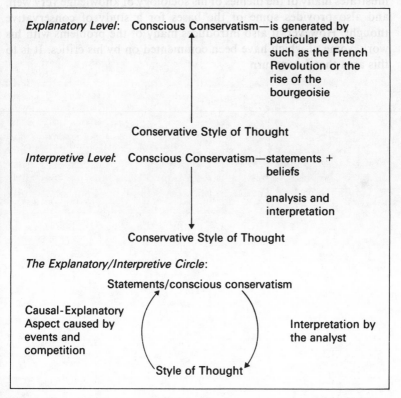

Explanatory Level: Conscious Conservatism—is generated by particular events such as the French Revolution or the rise of the bourgeoisie

Conservative Style of Thought

Interpretive Level: Conscious Conservatism—statements + beliefs

analysis and interpretation

Conservative Style of Thought

The Explanatory/Interpretive Circle:

Statements/conscious conservatism

Causal-Explanatory Aspect caused by events and competition

Interpretation by the analyst

Style of Thought

FIGURE 2.5 *Explanatory and Interpretive Arguments in 'Conservative Thought'*

structure intact. The statements at the level of conscious conservatism are a manifestation of the essential level of the conservative style of thought.

This is only one side of the analysis, however, and the initial problem that Mannheim deals with is the interpretive one: how is the conservative style of thought to be known in the first place? The solution involves the grouping together of conservative statements, by contrasting them with what they oppose, then showing how these statements cohere in the conservative style of thought. The style of thought is known through the explicit documents which express it.

These arguments can be represented in the diagrammatic form shown on page 63.

While Mannheim's analysis of conservative thought is not always as clear as might be desired, it does possess a general logic which illustrates many of the themes of his sociology of knowledge very well, and also provides some of the bases for a study of conservative thought. However, it also introduces many of the problems with his work, some of which have been commented on by his critics. It is to this area that I now turn.

Part II
Towards the Contemporary Sociology of Knowledge

3 Problems in Mannheim's Work

In the first part of this book I set out the main elements of Mannheim's sociology of knowledge and in the course of doing so introduced some of the fundamental issues in the sociology of knowledge. In this chapter I discuss the major problems in Mannheim's work. In general I argue that few of the conventional criticisms expose serious flaws in Mannheim's perspective, and that much contemporary writing in the sociology of knowledge and sociology of science is close to his approach in several respects. However, this does not mean that Mannheim's writings are free from difficulties and I discuss these in the second part of this chapter. This critique is carried out constructively, in the sense that I retain a general outline for the sociology of knowledge derived from Mannheim's work, which is developed in greater detail in chapter 4.

CONVENTIONAL CHARACTERISATIONS AND CRITICISMS

Mannheim has been very widely criticised over the past 50 or 60 years. These criticisms can be related to the theoretical position of the critic. There are three main schools of thought. First, there is a view dominant in the sociological literature which argues that Mannheim adopts, to some degree, a perspective derived from Marx (Mannheim as Marxist). Second, there are writers normally classified as Marxist who see Mannheim as typical *sociologist*, perverting rather than conforming to Marx's insights. This perspective is discussed under the heading of Mannheim as sociologist. Third, there are those who think that Mannheim does not adopt a causal or deterministic approach and that insofar as sociology and Marxism are dominated by these trends, he is neither Marxist nor sociologist (Mannheim and Hermeneutician). In the rest of this section these characterisations are discussed in turn. The section is concluded by discussion of two common areas of criticism of Mannheim: relativism and the intellectuals.

Mannheim as Marxist

In sociological writing on Mannheim the dominant view is that he 'extended' Marx's insights in several different directions. Many commentators have argued that he expanded Marx's theory of class to include other groups. In Mulkay's words, 'Mannheim tried to extend the Marxist notion of the "existential base" to cover generations, sects and occupational groups'.[1] From the sociological viewpoint Mannheim is often seen to accord primacy to class as a social referent of knowledge, despite his attempt to include other groupings. However, within this general perspective there are different emphases, for example, Remmling maintains that, 'Guided by Marx's conception of class, Mannheim argues that both classes and generations received their unity in the first place from the objective fact of 'social location'.[2] Another analyst has contended that 'Mannheim did not develop a theory of social stratification, even though he leaned toward an acceptance of the Marxian class concept'.[3]

An additional way in which Mannheim is held to have extended Marx's insights is through the generalisation of the concept of ideology. Mulkay argues that Mannheim 'supplemented the concept of "ideology" with an associated concept of utopia'.[4] Remmling adopts a similar view, seeing Mannheim as widening 'Marx's total but special concept of ideology into his own vision of ideology which is not only total but also general'.[5]

A further aspect of the presentation of Mannheim as a Marxist is the idea that he translated Marxist political positions and attacks on other forms of thought into social analysis. So, for example, Coser writes that

> Mannheim undertook to generalise Marx's programmatic orientation 'to enquire into the connection of ... philosophy with ... reality' and to analyse the ways in which systems of ideas depend on the social position—particularly the class position—of their proponents. Mannheim transformed what to Marx had been mainly a tool of polemical attack against his bourgeois adversaries into a general instrument of analysis that could be used as effectively for the study of Marxism as for any other system of thought.[6]

Interestingly, this is strikingly similar to the critique made of Mannheim by Marxist writers, who see him as blunting the sharp edge of Marx's critique of capitalist society by the use of classificatory and typological concepts. In this respect these writers see Mannheim as acting as a typical 'sociologist' rather than as extending Marxist principles.

Mannheim, in addition, is also seen as adopting the Marxist method for the imputation of ideas to social classes,[7] seemingly following Marxists such as Lukács. Similarly Kettler has argued strongly that Lukács' *History and Class Consciousness* must be seen as having a fundamental prompting effect on the subsequent development of Mannheim's sociology of knowledge.[8] Kettler argues that 'Lukács undertook to explode the barrier between the social function and intrinsic value of cultural products which writers like Mannheim had carefully maintained, and he did so in terms likely to be authoritative or at least persuasive for Mannheim'.[9] Kettler's arguments about the influence of Lukács on Mannheim's development are multifaceted. Other commentators simplify the relationship and Mannheim is held to allocate the intellectuals the role to be performed by the proletariat in Lukács' theoretical and political scheme.[10]

The essence of the argument that Mannheim is a Marxist is as follows. Mannheim is held to concentrate on the effect of class on the production and utilisation of knowledge, even though he extended Marx's work by looking at other social groups, developing his analyses of these forms from Marx's method. Seemingly, for these commentators, 'class' is a Marxist concept and the presence of it is sufficient to characterise a system of thought as Marxist.

Furthermore, Mannheim is seen to have refined Marx's theory of ideology to include utopias and remove polemic. Thus, it is claimed, Marxism itself may be analysed using the insights of the sociology of knowledge—it is not exempt as a science in the way that Marx claimed. Mannheim is thought to have been fundamentally influenced by Lukács and to have allocated the intellectuals a role similar to that filled by the proletariat in Lukács' scheme.

This type of characterisation of Mannheim can easily be turned into a critique of his sociology of knowledge. It would be possible, for example, to argue that Mannheim provides no warrant for treating class as the most important social group to which to relate knowledge and that, like Marx, he pays too much attention to formalised sets of political ideas and too little to everyday life. It might also be argued, for example, that Mannheim describes in too mechanistic a fashion the relationship between knowledge and social structure, reducing this to simple cause and effect.[11] Finally, the position ascribed to Mannheim on the intellectual stratum may be thought to be too simplistic, failing to account for the ways in which the intellectuals are politicised and act on behalf of other groups at particular points in history. This is seen to be true especially in the period of Weimar Germany.

Several points can be made in criticism of the view that Mannheim simply extended Marx's insights in different directions. However, to give these analysts their due, there are several parts of Mannheim's work where he asserts the importance of Marx to the sociology of knowledge. For example, he states that

> the sociology of knowledge actually emerged with Marx, whose profoundly suggestive *apercus* went to the heart of the matter. However, in his work, the sociology of knowledge is still indistinguishable from the unmasking of ideologies since for him social strata and classes were the bearers of ideologies.[12]

In response to this it is important to recognise that authors are not always the best interpreters of their own work and attention should be paid to the structure of Mannheim's sociology of knowledge rather than to what he says about it. Further, Mannheim also mentions many other authors as being influenced on the development of the sociology of knowledge.[13] In addition, even in the text from which the above quote is taken, Mannheim also comments that

> Competition controls not merely the course of political and social events, but furnishes also the motor impulses behind diverse interpretations of the world which, when their social background is uncovered, reveal themselves as the intellectual expression of conflicting groups struggling for power.[14]

In accord with this the main criticism that can be made of the characterisation of Mannheim as a Marxist is that he did not use class in the same sense, or within the same type of theoretical system as Marx. For Marx class only has meaning within a developed political economy and is understood in relation to the economic system. However, in Mannheim's work classes are actors in a competitive struggle for power. They are essentially political actors, having their basis in the competitive nature of all social life.

Furthermore, it is implausible to suggest that Mannheim extended the theory of ideology from Marx, for as many commentators have pointed out, it is difficult to find one coherent theory of ideology in Marx.[15] This has led to many of the debates about the nature of the use of ideology in Marx's work within the context of the attempts to construct a general theory of ideology.

The characterisation of Mannheim as a Marxist fails to consider those places in his work where he is explicitly critical of Marx. Comments of this kind are dotted throughout his work.[16] In addition, it is clear that Mannheim had a particular view of Marx and Marxism, as economistic and mechanistic. Mannheim retained many aspects of the view of Marxism that he had adopted in his early Hungarian years.[17] For Mannheim, Marxism is to be superseded rather than generalised or extended. Finally, it should be noted that Mannheim's work exhibits an essentialism which is far removed from Marx's materialism. Mannheim often reduces social structure and thought to essences of action and competitive struggle.

Taking account of these points, it is clear that Mannheim did not develop Marx's work in any straightforward sense. His work possesses a very different theoretical structure and set of aims. This leads directly to the main alternative view of Mannheim: that he is a typical sociologist.

Mannheim as Sociologist

The characterisation of Mannheim as a sociologist by Marxist writers,[18] paradoxically, has certain points in common with the characterisation of him as a Marxist. These writers often see him as starting from Marxist beginnings, which are then deformed rather than extended or generalised. Any extension that Mannheim does carry out involves the perversion of Marx's insights. This means that Mannheim is, for these writers, parasitic upon Marxism in a typical sociological fashion. In addition he is held to neglect social critique by transforming a political perspective into a tool or method of analysis.

Lukács argues that Mannheim's work is problematic in that it is unable to provide an account of the differences between true and false consciousness. For Lukács Marx's theory of historical materialism 'involved a "false consciousness" as a complementary pole for correct consciousness'.[19] Mannheim's supposed inability to distinguish true and false consciousness can be seen as a part of the relativism which is often identified as one of the prime difficulties in his work. This criticism is produced from several perspectives, and is discussed fully later in this chapter.

In addition to removing the distinction between true and false knowledges, Mannheim is held by these critics to eliminate Marx's dialectical standpoint. For Lukács this is the root of the failure to appreciate that Marxism entails a strict view of true knowledge. In historical materialism

> the relative and the absolute mesh in a dialectical reciprocal relationship and . . . this gives rise to the approximate character of human knowledge, for which objective truth (the correct reflection of objective reality) is always an inherent element and criterion.[20]

Adorno's critique of Mannheim's sociology of knowledge adopts a similar position. Adorno contends that 'the distortions of the sociology of knowledge arise from its method, which translates dialectical concepts into classificatory ones'.[21] This is a critique of the intellectual methods and characterisation of the world used by the sociology of knowledge. Contradictions are ironed out and the 'picture of the whole becomes harmonious'.[22] Horkheimer thought the same, attacking the 'notion of "social relatedness" as undialectical without a critique of social existence itself. Lacking this analysis Mannheim had regressed back to Hegel's metaphysical notion of Being in his *Logic*'.[23]

Adorno develops this theme arguing that the attempt to translate dialectical concepts into classificatory ones has particular and inadequate results. The sociology of knowledge becomes concerned with the formulation of general laws in a positivistic sense. 'The sociology of knowledge characterizes stubborn facts as mere differentiations and subsumes them under the highest general units: at the same time, it ascribes an intrinsic power over the facts to these arbitrary generalizations, which it calls social laws'.[24] Adorno thinks these laws 'hypostasized' and 'extravagant'.[25] The problems introduced by the undialectical nature of Mannheim's method are revealed in his use of examples. These are seen as arbitrary and politically neutralist: 'Examples function as convenient and interchangeable illustrations; hence they are often choosen at a comfortable distance from the true concerns of mankind today, or they are pulled, as it were, out of a hat'.[26] Adorno captures his meaning here in the following memorable phrase, 'Sociology originated in the impulse to criticize the principles of the society with which it found itself confronted; the sociology of knowledge settles for reflections on hunters dressed in green and diplomats in black'.[27]

Adorno attacks the politics he sees as entailed by Mannheim's method. Again, it is useful to note that this repeats, in a slightly different form, one aspect of the characterisation of Mannheim as a Marxist by sociological writers. It will be remembered that Mannheim was seen as extending and generalising Marx's theory of ideology with the concept of utopia and subjecting all forms of political knowledge to sociological analysis without exempting any as scientific or true. Jay notes that

> To Horkheimer there was no real connection between theory and practice in Mannheim's thinking. Whereas Marx had wanted the transformation of society, Mannheim was only interested in the salvation of a totalistic view of cognition. In the language of an article Horkheimer was not to write until several years later, the sociology of knowledge was thus a 'traditional' rather than a 'critical' theory.[28]

In this sense Mannheim's work could not be really critical of the society from which it developed as it does not reach the problems of existence at the heart of capitalism.

Mannheim's failure to come to grips with the essentials of capitalist society and existence is revealed by his 'radical elimination of economics from sociology'.[29] For Lukács this is manifested in Mannheim's theory of competition, which is general rather than economic in focus. This reinforces the idea that Mannheim produced a very different conceptual system rather than simply attempting to extend (and hence deform) Marx's original insights.

Mannheim's Marxist critics also criticise his views on the intellectuals. For Adorno Mannheim holds a 'reverence for the intelligentsia as "free floating"'.[30] This he links to Mannheim's sociology of planning where solutions to crises are to be directed from above.[31] Adorno criticises this idea of the 'free-floating intelligentisia' as he thinks that 'the very intelligentsia that pretends to float freely is fundamentally rooted in the very being that must be changed and which it merely pretends to criticize'.[32] In Adorno's words, 'The sociology of knowledge sets up indoctrination camps for the homeless intelligentsia where it can learn to forget itself'.[33]

The Marxists contend that Mannheim's attempt to extend Marx's work on ideology fails because it eliminates the critical and political edge that is central to Marxism. For the Marxist this is a typical sociological operation, as in a general sense sociology is a bourgeois deformation of Marx's insights.

The fundamental problem with this characterisation is that it fails to specify what sociology actually is. It relies on an overly rigid separation of Marxism from sociology, which is difficult to maintain, especially in the current intellectual climate where disciplinary boundaries are becoming increasingly fluid.[34]

Once this general point is made, however, it is clear that the Marxist critique of Mannheim's work does develop some useful points. Most important is the neglect of the importance of the economic structure. For example, Mannheim does not provide an explanation of the competition between groups and classes except by contending that this is an *essential* feature of human associative life. In this sense, Mannheim is as unsociological as he is unMarxist.

Mannheim as Hermeneutician

Accounts which see Mannheim's work as an exercise in hermeneutics are less common than those which characterise him as a Marxist or a sociologist.[35] Bauman characterises Mannheim's work as a movement from a more hermeneutic viewpoint to a causal, sociological approach,[36] contending that Mannheim separated the natural from the cultural sciences in typical hermeneutic fashion. Simonds concurs, arguing that the analyst working in the cultural sciences studies meanings and

> Mannheim's sociology of knowledge represented an attempt to do justice to the meaningful nature of social thought thereby surrendering the aspiration to establish 'objective' (in the sense of intersubjectively communicable) knowledge about social phenomena. He was concerned, above all else, with developing a method of social study that would permit both hermeneutic adequacy and intersubjective validity.[37]

For Simonds Mannheim is concerned to *interpret* and *understand* the meaning of social life: 'The sociology of knowledge undertakes to secure the understanding, not the explanation, of thought'.[38] For Simonds all of Mannheim's sociology of knowledge is to be seen in this way; in his view Mannheim does not attempt to relate meanings to non-meaningful social existence as social existence is itself to be seen as meaningful. Mannheim relates one set of meanings to another. The analyst seeks to understand and interpret the meanings in different areas of social life, joining them together to provide a coherent account.

Such views which interpret Mannheim's work as an exercise in hermeneutics rely on the analysis of 'On the Interpretation of *Weltanschauung*'. As I have already noted, this is Mannheim's most hermeneutic work and while he does retain some of its methodological propositions in his late work,[39] more deterministic methodologies emerge more clearly.

It is also the case that by taking account of the development of Mannheim's thought it is possible to explain its character after his move to England and his abandonment of the attempt to produce a detailed sociology of knowledge. The characterisation of Mannheim's sociology of knowledge as hermeneutic in its entirety makes his subsequent development seem like a very large break with what had gone before and such a disjuncture does not exist.

As a final comment on the hermeneutic interpretation it is important to note that it relies on a strong separation of hermeneutics from causal sociology. However, as has been recognised since Weber, and reiterated by such as Giddens,[40] sociology should try to interpret, understand and explain. In this respect Mannheim's sociology of knowledge remains of contemporary importance. I now wish to consider in turn two areas where Mannheim is thought to be most seriously deficient by a variety of critics: in his relativism and his characterisation of the intellectuals.

Relativism

Critiques of Mannheim's work that castigate him for relativist assumptions and implications abound. Of all the points made against his work this is the most common. Essentially the argument is as follows. Mannheim is held to believe that all thought is socially determined: knowledge is related to a social group. For many critics this means that what Mannheim is saying is that belief is *relative* to the social location of the social actor, who is constrained by the membership of particular social groups which determine the form and content of the particular ideas adopted. However, if beliefs are relative to social position, then they are in some sense *unobjective* or *partial*. This, in turn, means that Mannheim's own views are unobjective, as they are relative to his own social location. Why, asks the critic, should we accept Mannheim's view rather than any other?

A danger often alluded to here is that this type of position leads society to the edge of (and ultimately deep into) the abyss. One set of ideas and their consequent practices are as correct as any other and hence there may be a breakdown in morality in society as all beliefs and practices are equally legitimated, there being no method for the evaluation of true and correct beliefs. Of course, there is a large philosophical debate around such issues, and it is not clear that there is any necessary relation between the evaluation of the truth of an idea and the morality of a set of practices that might be held to stem from such an idea. For example, one may hold that fraud is a crime (a notion that may be related to a particular system of private property and hence socially determined) without needing to conclude that all people convicted of fraud may be executed! This point aside, however, it is clear that many of the worries about certain relativist implications of Mannheim's sociology of knowledge stem from a concern with the political and social development of Germany in the 1920s and 1930s.

The main point here, however, is that Mannheim is often seen as maintaining that because beliefs or sets of ideas are socially caused, they are by necessity *flawed* or *limited*. There is some warrant for such an interpretation of Mannheim. It has been maintained, for example, that in his earliest period of attention to the issue of relativism, Mannheim argued 'that to say of a belief that it is causally related to social structure is to say that it is false or partial'.[41] Certainly Mannheim produces such a position in his discussion of ideology.[42] However, simply to suggest that Mannheim's sociology of knowledge is to be rejected because of its 'relativism' is problematic for three sets of reasons.

First, it has to be considered whether Mannheim's work is indeed relativist in the senses conveyed by his critics. Second, there are many different forms of relativism which Mannheim's critics have often failed to distinguish. Third, the fact that Mannheim's work may be relativistic may not necessarily matter. Many contemporary writers in the sociology of science *proudly* proclaim themselves relativist, seeing this as a virtue rather than a vice. Paradoxically, they see Mannheim as insufficiently relativistic because he refuses to subject natural science and mathematics to a full sociological analysis. As Barnes and Bloor maintain,

Even the sociologist Karl Mannheim adopted this dualist and rationalist view when he contrasted the 'existential determination of thought' by 'extra-theoretical factors' with development according to 'immanent laws' derived from the 'nature of things' of 'pure logical possibilities'. This is why he exempted the physical sciences and mathematics from his sociology of knowledge.[43]

If the arguments of such writers are taken seriously it is possible to argue that, to a good degree, the issue of relativism is still an open one, and that the sociologist of knowledge should not necessarily be overly detained by a concern with it.

It has been argued that while Mannheim is much concerned with the issue of relativism, his position is not static and his critics have oversimplified it and in the course of so doing, accused him of crimes that he did not wholly commit. For Abercrombie there are three distinct stages to Mannheim's thought concerning relativism.[44] In the first stage Mannheim virtually accepts relativism. However, he becomes aware of the dangers that may be involved and consequently develops his famous concept of 'relationism'. In this period Mannheim has rejected the idea that there is an absolute truth. This phase is itself subject to development and in its later stage 'relationism often seems to be the same as the sociology of knowledge, in that systems of belief should be related to each other and to the social structure'.[45] In the last period of his discussions of relativism Mannheim transforms the issue by focusing on the role of values in the determination of beliefs. It is not Mannheim's penchant for relativism that is a particular problem but his earlier view that socially caused thought is inevitably partial. Moreover, even if this latter view is not accepted Abercrombie shows how Mannheim attempted to grapple with the issue of relativism, that he may have been aware that it is problematic, even if not fundamentally debilitating, and that he needed to do something about it.

Simonds, on the other hand, clears Mannheim of any charge of relativism. He separates the sociological analysis of meaning from that of truth and falsehood and maintains that in *Ideology and Utopia* Mannheim claims 'that the social connectedness of an idea *cannot* be taken to imply its falsehood'.[46]

At this stage, then, it is possible to see that if Mannheim is guilty of relativism, he is not unaware of such difficulties and that his views on the subject are rather more complex than those often ascribed to him by his critics. However, it should be noted that there are several different types of relativism, which should be separated before the argument can proceed in any more detail.

It has been argued that there are five forms of relativism.[47] These are 'moral relativism', 'conceptual relativism', 'perceptual relativism', 'relativism of truth' and 'relativism of reason'. In 'moral relativism' the grounds of moral belief are held to be relative to a particular position. 'Conceptual relativism' holds that different people classify their world in different ways. Much of the evidence often quoted for such a position is anthropological in nature. For example, different cultures are held to categorise animals in different ways.[48] This becomes a full blown relativism 'with the idea that neither reality itself, nor men's relation to it, nor the constraints of rational thinking set limits upon the content or form of such schemes'.[49]

The third type of relativism is 'perceptual relativism'. Here it is the perception of reality that is held to be relative to the situation of the knower. It also leads to the idea that language differences and language itself have an important role to play in relativism. The fourth type of relativism and 'the crucial further step is the claim to relativize truth'.[50] Here there is a break away from the idea of a single world-wide and culturally independent truth. The final type of relativism is that of reason. The central idea here is 'that what warrants belief depends on canons of reasoning, deductive or non-deductive, that should properly be seen as social norms, relative to culture and period'.[51]

In addition to identifying these major forms of relativism, it is important to consider what belief is to be seen as relative *to*. Five factors have been identified as sources of the relativity of thought.[52] First, there is the possibility that 'beliefs vary with natural environment'. Second, the human apparatus utilised for perception may be a source of relativism. 'Thirdly there is social context, which has often been proposed as a source of variation in beliefs, notably when constructing a theory of ideology'.[53] Fourth, language can be seen as important and, finally, thought may be relative to a wider context, such as a 'form of life' or, though Hollis and Lukes do not see it in this light, to a culture.

Mannheim does not subscribe to a moral relativism and in much of his work he seeks to combat the effects produced by those adopting such a position. At times he flirts with both conceptual and perceptual relativism, but still generally holds that there is a common element, hence his use of the term perspective. He thinks that different groups may produce different perspectives on the same object—akin to viewing it from different angles. Many of Mannheim's critics see him as subscribing to a relativism of truth. However, it is by no means clear that Mannheim adopts such a view, as he prefers to formulate a different version of truth, one that is more dynamic and suited to the requirements of the age, than the older static version, rather than reject the idea of a unified truth altogether. Mannheim has relatively little to say on the possibilities of relativism of reason.

As far as the sources of relativism are concerned Mannheim, in *Ideology and Utopia*, is chiefly interested in the social context. He is little concerned with other possible sources of relativism. However, he does address one possible base that Hollis and Lukes omit: the historical situation of the actor. Indeed, in his historical phase he comes close to accepting a full-blown historical relativism, despite having recognised the dangers of such a position in his hermeneutic work.

Writers associated with the strong programme in the sociology of knowledge have been clear advocates of a particular relativist strategy. For example, Barnes and Bloor claim that relativism is, in effect, a 'good thing' and to be embraced within any attempt to study knowledge sociologically from a scientific perspective.[54] They make three initial claims. First, 'that beliefs on a certain topic vary'; second, 'that which of these beliefs is found in a given context depends on, or is relative to, the circumstances of the users'; and, finally, 'that all beliefs are on a par with one another with respect to the causes of their credibility'.[55]

Barnes and Bloor are not the only contemporary sociologists of scientific knowledge to be making relativist claims. Many in the field would probably accept such a position, for example Collins, who argues that the study of scientific knowledge should proceed in accord with the canons of the Empirical Programme of Relativism (EPOR).[56] EPOR consists of three stages:

(1) Revealing the openness of scientific results;
(2) Examining the social processes scientists use in closing debates over results;
(3) Studying the relation of these processes to social forces beyond the immediate social community of scientists.[57]

Collins' approach to the issue of relativism is sociological and empirical rather than philosophical, and he

> is not committed to saying that people can believe just anything, far less is he claiming that scientists make the wrong choices. He is simply insisting that there are always insufficient cognitive grounds for reaching any conclusions and that various social mechanisms may eventually enforce the closure which cognitive factors cannot make.[58]

The point of introducing these examples of relativist claims in the contemporary sociology of scientific knowledge is not to show that relativism is necessarily to be adopted in the sociology of knowledge, but that it has been so by practitioners of that discipline and despite much debate about its merits continues to be so. This should alert any commentator to the point that in many respects this is still a relatively *open* issue. It is at this point that the sociologist of knowledge should stop and think about the wisdom of entering into the details of such a debate. Sociology has paid too much attention to the debates of philosophers and their prescriptions for how sociologists should proceed.[59] This does not mean that sociology should be unreflexive or pay no attention to philosophical debates and issues; indeed it is to sociology's credit that it continues so to do in a contemporary social climate which discourages such awareness. However, it does mean that the sociologist of knowledge should not be overly concerned with philosophical issues, as has been the case in the past. The criticism of Mannheim's relativism is a very good example of the fixation on a particular issue of this kind.

While much of the debate about new sociologies of knowledge has focused on philosophical and theoretical issues, the most glaring omissions and problems in many of the contemporary relativistic sociologies of knowledge lie in their inadequate theories of *social structure*. Most of these approaches simply do not tackle this very significant aspect of a sociology of knowledge at all, often making overly 'culturalist' assumptions about the nature of the social stucture, to which scientific knowledge is held to be related.[60] Where these studies are often important is in the generation of evidence about particular cases and controversies in science. These may then be used as a resource in a sociology of knowledge which operates with a rather different set of principles.

Intellectuals

In the conventional view Mannheim is seen to argue that the socially unattached intelligentsia can reconcile competing claims to the truth and will lead society away from fundamental conflicts. For example, it has been argued that for Mannheim, in the German edition of *Ideology and Utopia* 'the fact that a conception comes out of the brain of a socially unbound intellectual is the guarantee of its validity'.[61] The criticism of this imputed position is obvious. It is that historically intellectuals have not played this role but have, on the contrary, represented particular interests, acting as mouth-pieces and synthesisers for other people's views, rather than utilising the potential of their own position to reach a true understanding, which had hitherto been obscured by interests and confusions.

The conventional view totally misrepresents what Mannheim really thought about the intellectual stratum. As Heeren has argued, Mannheim's views on the intellectuals can be divided into four stages. In the material he produced up until the publication of the German edition of *Ideology and Utopia* in 1929 Mannheim is relatively unconcerned with the intellectual stratum and when he does speak of them 'the intellectual is seen as a mere spokesman [sic] for the interests of the class with which he is associated'.[62] It can immediately be seen that this contradicts the view normally imputed to Mannheim. It also demonstrates that it is important to study the *development* of Mannheim's thought, as a misleading characterisation may be gained by concentrating on one period or text.[63]

A view close to that conventionally ascribed to Mannheim appears with *Ideology and Utopia*, where intellectuals are seen to possess the *potential* to perform an intellectual and political synthesis. It is important to stress that this is only a potential; whether this is realised or not may be a conjunctural issue. Mannheim, in *Ideology and Utopia*, contends that intellectuals can become 'party functionaries'[64] and that even here, where he perhaps comes closest to the position ascribed to him, Mannheim does not fully adopt it.

Mannheim did not retain his position in *Ideology and Utopia* for very long as by the early 1930s he was playing down the idea of the mission of the intellectuals.[65] Heeren also notes that in his later works Mannheim becomes much more pessimistic about the intellectuals realising the limited potential that they possess for social enlightenment. Heeren destroys the conventional view.

By contrast, Mannheim often recognises the way in which the intellectuals, due to the fact of their education and social location, *may* play particular roles in different historical and social situations. For Mannheim the intellectuals may be either 'an autonomous grouping without any strict social ties with other groups', or be 'more or less tied to social classes articulating the interests of those classes'.[66] It is also the case that they may fall between the two. It is possible to speak of a relatively autonomous intellectual stratum, remaining true to Mannheim's wish to speak of a *'relatively* classless stratum'.[67]

Contemporary writers on the intellectual stratum have adopted such a position. An example of this can be found in Raymond Williams' attempt to develop a materialist theory of culture.[68] For Williams there is a problem of definition of intellectuals, for, as he notes, 'the category "intellectuals", typically centered upon certain types of writers, philosophers and social thinkers, in important but uncertain relations with social order and its major classes, is in fact a very specific historical formation, which cannot be taken as exclusively representative of the social organisation of cultural producers'.[69]

After noting that everyone in society is, in some way or another, a cultural producer and that therefore a stratum of cultural producers or intellectuals can never be completely separated from other groups in society, Williams characterises the position of intellectuals (or cultural producers) in terms of a concept of 'relative autonomous distance'. Hence, the degree to which a group of 'relatively autonomous' intellectuals is recognised in a society 'is a function of the distinction of cultural production "as such", at certain relative distances from the still quite general and fundamental processes of social and cultural production and reproduction'.[70] This leads Williams to maintain that attention must be paid to the different places and roles of the intellectuals in different historical and social situations, and he discusses the bases of the relative autonomy of the intellectual stratum such as it exists in an attempt to sociologically underpin what he sees as the 'Weber-Mannheim definition' of the intellectuals and their role.[71] The relative autonomy or relative uncommittedness of the intellectuals is based on three main sociological factors for Williams; these are, first, 'the specific condition of asymmetry between a capitalist market and a bourgeois social order'; second, the location of the intellectuals in universities, where to some degree critical and independent work is possible; and, finally, on 'alternative' and 'oppositional' organisations which can operate as bases for intellectual production.[72]

It can be seen, therefore, that Mannheim's theory of the intellectual stratum, once it is recognised as the nuanced and complex account that it is, can serve as the starting point for an analysis of the intellectual stratum within contemporary society. Mannheim's critics have again been too quick to reject (or attempt to reject) his formulations instead of working with them within a different framework to provide a developed and detailed account.

A focus on the intellectual stratum is important in a methodological as well as an empirical sense in the sociology of knowledge as the intellectuals act as a 'mechanism of transmission'.[73] As 'it is the intellectual stratum that articulates and gives shape to bodies of belief, and is then also responsible for their transmission to society at large',[74] one way in which the sociology of knowledge can study the spread of ideas in society is to look at the role of the intellectual stratum. Of course, there are dangers here as the sociology of knowledge's focus can become overly centred on the intellegentsia. However, a consideration of the intellectual stratum which takes into account and attempts to discuss the exact nature of their position and their possible contingent attachments to the groups and classes must obviously be a part of any developed sociology of knowledge.

So far in this chapter I have considered criticisms of Mannheim from various positions. I have concluded that very few of these are totally convincing and that many miss the mark by a long way. I have also argued that while Mannheim's work is of contemporary relevance, it does contain flaws and is in need of development and it is to these themes that I now turn.

MANNHEIM'S SOCIOLOGY OF KNOWLEDGE: A CRITIQUE

In the rest of this chapter I criticise Mannheim's discussions of the social, knowledge and determination. These criticisms are used to clarify the issues to be considered further in chapter 4 of this book, where the beginnings of a contemporary, developed sociology of knowledge are outlined. Generally I argue that, while Mannheim's sociology of knowledge is flawed, it does provide a basis for the fuller development of the discipline. In the course of this discussion I introduce some of the concepts and categories which are fully analysed in the next chapter.

The Social

I have argued so far that Mannheim sees the social as consisting of groups and social locations which exist in relationships structured by the principle of competition. It is clear, therefore, that for Mannheim the possible effects of this competitive struggle are a problem. If groups are involved in a fundamental and continuing set of competitive relations then the ordering of the social is difficult, but necessary. Mannheim becomes concerned with a problem of order. The competition between groups needs to be contained or society will fall apart. One important aspect of Mannheim's concern with order is the attention that he pays to the idea of synthesis in his sociology of knowledge.

Mannheim argues that a 'true' interpretation of the world may be obtained through the dynamic synthesis of several different 'partial' perspectives.[75] The gaining of the correct view of reality is a matter of the creative arbitration between different extant views. There are several problems and issues associated with the use of synthesis in Mannheim's sociology of knowledge.

First, there may be no need to synthesise perspectives, as one particular 'world-view' may be correct, or at least correct in all its essentials. There is no *a priori* reason why it should be accepted that all views are inherently incomplete or skewed. If such a view is to be adopted it requires rather more development than Mannheim accords to it. In addition, and relatedly, it is often the case that one 'world-view' can be evaluated in terms of another. Mannheim recognises this. However, he still wishes to see this as a process of synthesis, which implies a much more orderly operation than may actually be required.[76]

Second, Mannheim's stress on synthesis introduces the issue of interpretation and especially that of the relationship between the whole and parts in the hermeneutic circle or spiral. In his discussion of the 'Interpretation of *Weltanschauung*', it is not immediately clear if the *Weltanschauung* includes or underlies the cultural products which are analysed to gain information about it. In a general sense the recognition that something is partial implies or assumes a notion of a whole. Mannheim does not admit to having such a view, preferring instead to see his own perspective as the resultant of previous approaches rather than as something prior to them.

Third, it well may be that some sets of concepts exclude others, and therefore that synthesis is impossible. One example of this is the manner in which Mannheim wishes to relate the different social sciences together in his later work.[77] While there is some confusion over whether sociology oversees all the other social sciences or is, to a certain degree, a resultant of them, generally Mannheim seems to think that a social science such as psychology can be integrated with the overall theory of society produced in sociology.[78] In a sense sociology is neutral. However, this neglects the ways in which the place of the social is theorised within psychology and the space the individual is allocated in sociology, which may not in fact coincide. The integration is likely to be more difficult and acrimonious than Mannheim imagines.

Fourth, Mannheim's use of synthesis links back to the more general bases of his account. His views on political developments and the construction of theory often suppose a smooth synthetic development, in which all parties will eventually see the light (from Mannheim's torch) and reconcile their differences. While in certain of the later planning works Mannheim does make the point that in the future society there will be areas of planned disagreements, even this assumes that agreement can be reached over which areas are to be left open to disagreement. This is unlikely, as different groups might not want to accept things that Mannheim thinks there should be no disagreement about. Mannheim has little notion of *fundamental* differences in the political/cultural, or theoretical, realms. This is very surprising given his general stress on the centrality of competition between social groups, and shows how Mannheim believes that in the long run the competitive relations between social groups which lie at the heart of the social may be ordered into a pattern of hierarchial relations.

Mannheim's stress on synthesis and ordering must be rejected. There is no need for a contemporary sociology of knowledge to integrate and evaluate the different views produced by different groups to produce a synthetic view of the truth. It is enough to show how those views are produced and utilised by different groups. It is also unnecessary to follow Mannheim's more political use of synthesis and ordering contained in his views on the nature of social life in Western democracies. It is the clashing of different ideas against each other that contributes to the vitality and development of contemporary societies. There is no need for an ordering or integration of such views and approaches. It can be seen therefore that both Mannheim's intellectual and political uses of the concepts of ordering and synthesis are to be omitted from any contemporary sociology of knowledge.

If there are problems with Mannheim's positions on order and synthesis, the use made of competition is even more difficult. He provides little theoretical justification for the importance of competition. Of course, this is often a problem with accounts which assume that there is an essence to human associative life or human nature.

Mannheim's work betrays the search for essences in the development of history, leading him to stress the smooth unfolding of the historical process. An example of this can be found in his discussion of utopias, where some very different types of position are reduced to an essence of utopianism, which is so broad a category that many different things can be fitted into it.[79] Mannheim's work falls into the trap of oversimplifying and smoothing out the development of history and also of seeing it leading up to the present day in an unproblematic way.[80]

Mannheim uses competition as a principle of the structuring of the relationships between groups. It is, however, unclear why groups should compete with one another at all. This is not only a problem for Mannheim, however, and it centrally concerns the issues of the structuring of the social, and what groups are important for the sociology of knowledge. It is one of the central problems of sociology that what is meant by the social and how it is structured are different in nearly every form of the discipline.[81]

The sociology of knowledge has tended to follow, in very general terms, a concentration on 'class' as the fundamental grouping or property in the societies that are analysed.[82] Class is the most popular category that has been used as the 'social base' in the sociology of knowledge and, to take an example, the development of liberal/rationalist thought is taken as consequent upon the rise of the bourgeoisie.

The most important problem with many class-focused explanations is their lack of understanding of the base of class itself. A class-centric view tends to neglect the reason for the existence of classes and why they might exist in a relationship of struggle. This is where the fundamental difference between a Marxist approach and one that is more centred in the utilisation of the notion of class as a form of grouping lies. Marx can explain the existence and rise and fall of classes from his theory of the development of different modes of production.[83] This type of 'mode-theoretical' approach has so far been relatively under-used in the sociology of knowledge.[84]

A class-centric view can also run into difficulties in the empirical analysis of bodies of knowledge. In the discussion of liberal-rationalist thought, for example, it is useful as a working hypothesis to see that it is related to the rise of the capitalist bourgeoisie. However, the relevance of this sort of analysis is less clear when due to the difficulty of showing that conservative thought has a particular social class base, as is shown by Mannheim's analysis, where disparate groups are seen as upholding conservatism.[85]

It should not be thought, however, that a structural Marxism can provide a complete explanation of the relationship between classes and other groups in contemporary societies; these types of Marxism have been especially problematised by the insights produced by contemporary feminism. Many of these issues will be mentioned in the next chapter. At this point it is sufficient to indicate that the feminist critique has problematised the whole conception of class as normally used in the social sciences. Delphy, for example, sets this out when she examines the manner in which womens' class positions have been located in relation to those of their husbands (where the woman is married), so that 'the absence of an occupation is seen to be the same as the absence of a place of one's own in the class structure'.[86] Even more importantly, she argues that women are a part of a different class system.[87] Delphy's propositions are obviously debateable, and have been contested by other feminist theorists.[88] There is still, however, a tendency within such disciplines as the sociology of knowledge to neglect this sort of literature, which casts radical doubts on the whole definition of class. An important way that women can be taken into account is in the theory of social structure. In effect the sociology of knowledge needs a theory of the articulation of capitalist and partriarchal structures as much as does other sociology.[89]

Many of the ideas generated and utilised in capitalist societies are not directly class or gender related. This has been increasingly recognised in many branches of contemporary sociology, and has been most interestingly developed in urban sociology. Here a distinction has been made between production- and consumption-based social cleavages. An example of the latter is the differences in housing provision. It should be recognised that social position in the housing market may potentially have a strong effect on people's beliefs.[90]

However, it is necessary to examine the *causes* of consumption cleavages and struggles. An exploration of this issue is obviously beyond the scope of the present book, but it should alert the sociologist of knowledge that struggles over consumption may have an important part to play in the generation of ideas.

The other centrally significant social cleavage that must be considered in the contemporary sociology of knowledge is race. Distinctive racial experiences and groupings have important effects on the generation of forms of thought. This is clear in the example of religious belief systems, for example. A case in point is the development of Rastafari in contemporary British society.[91] It is easy for the sociologist of knowledge to demonstrate how the influence and spread of Rasta ideas can be related to the position of young blacks in British society. In a developed analysis it can also be shown how many of these ideas have, at least partially, been gleaned from the influence of Rasta on reggae artists and consequently on reggae music. These ideas have then often been communicated to, or picked up by, white people and more particularly white recording artists and consequently come to have a wide currency. A set of beliefs appeals to a particular group in British society and is transmitted to other groups through a musical medium. Again it is clear that the situations and discourses of different racial groups must be related to more general situations and fundamental structures which generate particular struggles.[92]

Up to now I have criticised Mannheim's view of synthesis and his concentration on competition. I have introduced the groups to which knowledge must be related, focusing on class, gender, consumption cleavages and ethnic groups. Some analysis in the sociology of knowledge has also attemped to link the generation of knowledge to a particular event in a society at a certain time. This is a common theme in much of the writing in conservatism, where the importance of the French Revolution is most often stressed.[93] There are problems with this type of approach, and of particular importance is the lack of any real explanation of the persistence of the form of thought after the direct event to which it was a response has been taken for granted or ended. It is also clear that an *explanation* for the occurrence of a particular event is necessary so that the different interests behind the reasons for particular discursive expressions can be interrogated.

I have used the critique of Mannheim's view of the social in his detailed sociology of knowledge to introduce the types of cleavages and groups to which belief should be related in the sociology of knowledge. It should be noted, in addition, that Mannheim's work contains another view of the social; this can be termed a *broad view*, where there is less discussion of the make-up of the social. Values, for example, are related rather generally to society in his later work, as well as in some discussions in the detailed sociology of knowledge. The lack of a detailed discussion of the social here reflects a general tension in Mannheim's work between detailed historical analysis and typologising. Mannheim argues that sociology can be both a typologising science and also take account of the historical development of society, seeing these as different parts of the sociological enterprise.[94] He divides sociology up into several different branches, which have different methods and subject matters. The results of these studies are then synthesised within sociology as a whole.[95] As Adorno points out the feasibility of this is debateable. At times the typologies do rather take over the analysis and are in tension with the developed historical sense of much of Mannheim's work. This can be seen in the manner in which the development of capitalism in England is utilised as an ideal type of development of capitalism as a whole. Here Mannheim assumes that the historical way in which capitalism developed was the same in every country and that this can be assimilated to the English case.[96] There are many dificulties with this type of procedure, but importantly it can be seen how it obstructs the detailed historical analysis.

The nature of the relationships between history, empirical studies and theory is an issue for sociology in general. However, it is especially relevant to the sociology of knowledge, as this has been prone to high-level generalisations. Generally, there is a need for substantive study in the sociology of knowledge.[97] Mannheim recognised this, and his best attempt in this direction is 'Conservative Thought', which has been detailed in chapter 2.

In accord with the relative neglect of substantive study, there is also a tendency for the sociology of knowledge to think about history in terms of epochs. While in some senses this is unavoidable, given the nature of the subject and of the historical process, it should be recognised that these are generalisations.

In summary, Mannheim's view of the social suffers from the assumption about competition that lies at its heart. This cannot be accepted as a structuring principle and leads to confusions in the specification of the relationships between the groups to which knowledge is to be related. The task of the sociology of knowledge is to show which groups are important, how they are related together, and why this is so. Mannheim's work is useful for its stress on the way in which groups exist in relations of political struggle, and for the manner in which knowledge is related to a plurality of groups. However, the relations between these groups must be specified and further investigated. In these respects Mannheim's work is a starting point, and it provides a framework from which to begin analysis in the sociology of knowledge.

Knowledge

As I showed in the previous chapter, Mannheim suggests that the sociology of knowledge should embrace a range of different concepts of knowledge. However, the most important category that he addresses is that of ideology. Mannheim uses this concept in several different senses. At times he mobilises it as a general description of a coherent body of thought, while at others referring to the ideas produced by ruling groups. In addition Mannheim develops other concepts such as style of thought and world-view.

Mannheim's work prompts the conclusion that a sociology of knowledge is significantly different from a theory of ideology and that the relationships between the two need to be spelled out in a detailed and analytical fashion. In chapter 4 I shall argue that the sociology of knowledge cannot be assimilated to the study of ideology (or ideologies) in society. However, this is only the first stage of analysis, as the differing theoretical objects of study of the sociology of knowledge need to be specified and differentiated. In this discussion I wish to limit the scope of the concept of ideology. A further point that should be stressed here is that to limit the concept of ideology is not to eliminate it. One of the most worrying things about the development of sociological analysis over the past few years is the tendency for concepts to be utilised and then dropped in an almost indecent rush. Ideology is one such sufferer.

Mannheim is correct to be concerned about the category of ideology and the difficulties of an over-generalised use of it. However, he never provides a clear jutification for the procedures that he adopts. The different categories of knowledge to be studied by the sociology of knowledge need to be specified and the relationships between them formulated. This is, again, an issue that Mannheim introduces, but does not elaborate adequately. The sociology of knowledge needs to theorise and specify the differences between the specific ideological level and the more general style of thought or

Weltanschauung. This is another aspect of Mannheim's analysis that is further developed in his essay on 'Conservative Thought', where he argues that specific statements of conservative ideas are formulated from the resource of a more general style of thought in response to particular situations and events at certain times. While the specific expression of conservatism may differ due to the precise struggle that is being engaged in at any point in time, the resource and base for this struggle is relatively unchanging, though, of course, added to by the experience of the results of previous conflicts.

Mannheim's work also introduces a related, significant issue in the area of knowledge; that of how to constitute the object of study. In some areas this object is seen as relatively unproblematic, as in some studies of literature, television programmes, films or painting and in the analysis of natural science, where often the category of science is rather assumed as a given theoretical object.[98] This type of study tends to neglect some of the difficulties that are involved in the analysis of commonsense forms of thought, political forms of thought, such as conservatism, and, of course, of such phenomena as 'sexism' and 'racism'. In an important sense these have to be 'constructed'. Mannheim is much exercised by this sort of problem, as can be seen in his essays on 'Conservative Thought' and competition. Work must be done by the analyst to produce a viable object of study as this is not always immediately apparent in all its detail.

Another issue raised by the consideration of the nature of knowledge and ideology in particular is that of the materiality of ideology. This has been signified in debates on ideology by the discussion as to whether ideology should be seen as 'ideas' or 'practices'. The focus on ideas should be retained, as the concept of practice in this area only leads to a displacement of traditional issues. Also, to some extent, this is a false dichotomy and as Lovell notes, 'in whatever form it appears, ideology may always be expressed in terms of a body of ideas, and I wish to argue that it is certain substantive properties of these ideas which allow us to refer both to them, and to the institutions and practices in which they are produced, as ideological'.[99]

The main problem with Mannheim's use of different categories in the area of knowledge is that he never properly specifies either their nature or the relationship between them. He does provide a basic structure which may be built on, that is, one stating a relationship between a more general level and its more specific manifestations. However, this needs further development within the context of contemporary work on ideology and discourse. Some pointers in this direction will be offered in the next chapter.

Determination

Mannheim's less detailed view of the sociology of knowledge is particularly reflected in his theory of determination, where in a number of places here he returns to a correspondence theory. Forms of knowledge are seen to 'correspond' to a particular society. There are several difficulties in this approach.

There is a lack of detail and specificity about the meaning of 'correspondence'. This is compounded when the terms function and constellation are used used more or less interchangeably with it. It needs to be asked how this relation operates. Classically Marxism has used the idea of interest here. Mannheim is dissatisfied with this, and replaces it with the more generalised 'commitment'. However, he fails to specify this in enough detail.

It is also important to consider the vehicle or route of this determination. One way of looking at this is through the role of human agency and practice. Mannheim places a good deal of stress on this area, which can be seen as a part of his leaning towards a Weberian type of action theory, though, especially in his later work, he becomes much more interested in the role of social interaction and has much to say about the work of Mead.[100] This immediately brings in the issue of structural determination versus human action and the relative weight to be given to each.[101] Mannheim is rather unclear on this issue.

The precise nature of the relationship between ideas and social groups is not always obvious. At times Mannheim adopts a genetic account, seeing that ideas are produced by a particular group and exist within it. However, he often combines this with an account of how particular ideas are 'picked up' by other groups from those which formulated them.[102] He makes this point so often, and with such force, that it can only be an attempt to combat a naive geneticist interpretation of his work. This anti-geneticism at times produces an account where an ideological cloud is seen to float above the groups in the social structure. Groups then 'reach up' and 'pick out' ideas from this as it suits them in the course of political struggle over power.

Conclusion

There are two main issues to be considered in each of the three dimensions of the sociology of knowledge, the social, knowledge and determination. The nature of the components of the social and how they are related needs to be discussed. The form of knowledge needs consideration, along with the more technical difficulty of the separation of one ideology or discourse from another. The character, and substantive operation of the relationship between knowledge and social structure, require study.

In conclusion, Mannheim has both a broad and a detailed view of the nature of the sociology of knowledge. The broad view is of less interest and consists in the relation of knowledge to society in a relationship of correspondence. Mannheim's detailed sociology of knowledge relates knowledge to social groupings structured by competition, both through a functional type correspondence theory and by utilising a generalised interest-based type of account. The fundamental problems with this theory are that the principle of competition is arbitrary and does not provide a real mechanism for the clear relating of groups to each other in a structural sense. In the area of the knowledge form Mannheim attempts to break out from a generalised use of ideology, but does not succeed in formalising the relationship between the different categories that he adopts at different points in his work. Again, in the area of determination Mannheim's correspondence perspective is insufficiently theorised, and he fails sufficiently to consider the mechanisms through which determination operates.

It has been shown how the issues that Mannheim considers develop both out of his own thought and from the intellectual and political issues of his time. It has been demonstrated that many of his own solutions to these problems cannot be accepted, though they do provide a starting point from which a more adequate sociology of knowledge can be developed.

Mannheim's stress on the relationships of groups and their creation and use of knowledge in competitive struggle can be taken as a starting point for the analysis of the production and utilisation of different forms of knowledge. While his idea of competition is deficient, the concepts of social location and group are important within a different framework. In this respect the distinctions that he draws between potential and actual consciousness within the category of generation may also have wider ramifications. In the realm of knowledge Mannheim fails to theorise ideology in the context of a set of categories. However, he retains a role for both interpretation and ideas of causality, which is of central importance. In the field of determination Mannheim's account of the relationship of all forms of knowledge to commitment is thought provoking, but again is insufficiently developed and needs to be updated.

4 Mannheim and the Sociology of Knowledge Today

In this book so far I have outlined Mannheim's sociology of knowledge, the criticisms made of it by other writers and the central points of my own critique. My main interest is in the detailed sociology of knowledge which he developed in Germany between 1924 and 1929. However, as I have argued, this approach can only be understood in the context of Mannheim's work as a whole. Hence, chapter 1 examined the corpus of Mannheim's writings, locating the sociology of knowledge within this. From this it was possible to see that his detailed sociology of knowledge was supplemented at different times by a broader outlook and that, indeed, these perspectives were often intertwined. In chapter 2 these strands were separated and the bulk of the discussion centred on the detailed sociology of knowledge. The analysis was split into a consideration of the three fundamental areas of the sociology of knowledge, namely the social, knowledge and determination.[1] Mannheim thought that human social life was inherently competitive, social groups of varying types being involved in competition principally over political power and positions of dominance. Certain social locations and categories were held to be particularly important and space was devoted in particular to Mannheim's ideas on generation and class.

In the course of this competition for power and influence groups, Mannheim contends, often draw upon particular conceptual resources. At different times he describes these as *Weltanschauungen* or styles of thought, and in discussing this level I have most often used this later term. Styles of thought can act as repositories which different groups can raid to formulate particular expositions/expressions of a perspective, belief system, ideology or utopia at any particular historical moment. Such a differentiation between the surface and the deep, or between the particular and the whole, was fundamental to Mannheim's social and philosophical views from his earliest writings, being very clearly expressed in his early, hermeneutic essay 'On the Interpretation of *Weltanschauung*',[2] for example. This structure of argument and description of the relation between levels of knowledge is carried through to Mannheim's detailed sociology of knowledge; however, in the course of this development Mannheim's work becomes much more sociological. In the early work the ideas of group struggle and competition and of the attachment of styles of thought and ideologies to social carriers was not developed at all.

In Mannheim's view not all forms of thought were to be analysed sociologically, and, as I have discussed, he excepts natural science and 'traditionalism' from such analysis. In this respect, Mannheim differs from many contemporary types of social study of knowledge, which have increasingly focused their attention on one of those areas that Mannheim omitted, becoming studies in the sociology of scientific knowledge.[3] In this respect these approaches have attempted to focus on what they have perceived to be the hardest cases for study.[4] Mannheim's study of conservative thought provides an example of how he split the different levels of knowledge, and this has been examined in a good deal of detail.

In the realm of determination, on one level Mannheim makes use of concepts such as correspondence and function. He is less convinced about the efficacy of Marxist theories of interest and, consequently, develops the idea of commitment. Groups made up of people structured by social location formulate and reformulate sets of ideas in accord with their commitments in the competition for power and dominance which is inherent in social life. Groups are social actors in the competition for resources and dominance. Mannheim's view is dynamic and focuses on the actions of social groups. Methodologically Mannheim retains a significant role for interpretation. While it would be incorrect to see Mannheim's work as wholly an exercise in hermeneutics or interpretive sociology, he does, nonetheless, employ an important interpretive slant in his detailed sociology of knowledge.[5] Again the example of the study of conservatism is of particular importance as it illustrates the interpretive and causal/explanatory elements of Mannheim's later sociology of knowledge.

In chapter 3 I examined some of the more conventional criticisms of Mannheim's work. It was shown how these could be grouped into positions which see Mannheim as a Marxist, a sociologist or a hermenutician. I argued that all these approaches were flawed in their main arguments, even if some of the points they make are pertinent. For example, Mannheim does place a good deal of emphasis on social class groupings in the struggle for political power; however, this does not make him a Marxist. Similarly, it might be possible to agree that some of Mannheim's approaches are typically sociological. However, there is nothing wrong with this and, indeed, the gap that is held to exist between Marxism and sociology by Mannheim's Marxist critics does not exist in this way. I also mentioned that much attention had focused on Mannheim's supposed problems with relativism and his description of the intellectual stratum. I showed how, to a large degree, relativism is a false issue for the sociologist to be overly concerned with and how Mannheim's views on the intellectual stratum are by no means as naive as those commonly imputed to him. Indeed, it is very easy to see how Mannheim's views on the intellectuals could be used as a basis for current research on this social category. Instead of writing off Mannheim's views, analysts should pay more attention to their possible uses.

It was in such a spirit that Mannheim's work was criticised in the second part of the previous chapter. I have sought to elucidate the structure of Mannheim's argument and show its weaknesses. In this chapter I will explore the directions in which Mannheim's work can be developed in the light of contemporary research. So far this book has interpreted and criticised Mannheim. However, it is also necessary to consider where Mannheim is correct, why his work is useful and how it can be utilised in contemporary research. If anything is to be stressed as *the* point of this book it is this. Many of the valuable commentaries on Mannheim's work that have appeared over recent years have contained interesting and sophisticated interpretations which have taken analysis forward in a way that has been very productive. However, they do not address Mannheim's contemporary relevance in enough detail.

Mannheim is important, not just historically, but for providing the most important source for the contemporary sociology of knowledge and as a mechanism for bringing together the disparate strands of analysis that are being produced in the current, stimulating period of activity in this field. Such an organising perspective is necessary as much of the work in the sociology of knowledge is taking place in relatively separated areas and needs to be brought together. This chapter will point the way forward for such an analysis. I will introduce important examples from the contemporary sociology of knowledge and show how they can fit into an enhanced Mannheimian perspective. However, this chapter does not develop my own views on the sociology of knowledge in full detail.[6] Rather, I provide some pointers to the structure of approach to be used and introduce some concepts and distinctions which I hope are helpful theoretically and empirically. The full specification of the details of this perspective and its use in substantive analysis is a matter for another discussion and one which I hope to provide at a later date.[7] In common with the structure used so far I develop my analysis through consideration of the social, knowledge and determination. I begin with the social.

THE SOCIAL

It is important that a sociology of knowledge developed in the current context retain elements from Mannheim's stress on how groups are related through processes of competition for domination and re-sources. However, it is clear that Mannheim's own concept of competition should be rejected, as he provides no explanation of why groups compete. In Mannheim's view groups compete because the essence of social life is competitive. Such a claim, as I have stated, rests on no empirical evidence and is never theoretically grounded in Mannheim's account. However, Mannheim does provide a base for a contemporary theory of the social, provided that his concept of competition is recast taking account of contemporary views on the structuring of struggle. Knowledge and sets of beliefs are indeed produced and utilised in the course of struggles for power, but I would claim that any such struggle for power is not based in essential characteristics of human social life or in inherent human nature, but is socially determined, having its basis in the structural components of social life.

In what follows I address, in turn, three issues that are raised by this focus, derived from Mannheim, on the structuring of the social into struggle between social groups. The three issues are: first, why do groups struggle?; second, which are the most important groups and how are groups in struggle related?; and, finally, how do groups struggle?

Why do groups struggle?

A stated above, Mannheim assumes an 'essence' of competitiveness. I want to stress the importance of the structuring of the struggle for power. I should stress from the outset that in maintaining this I do not mean that the sociology of knowledge should concentrate on how the

social is structured by the struggle for political power as conventionally interpreted. If such were the case, it would focus on the creation
and utilisation of political ideologies in the normally understood
sense.[8] Power is manifested in many areas that are at first sight free
from power relations in the traditional use of the term. Recent
sociological investigations have revealed the extent of power relations
in science and gender, for example.

Much contemporary research on natural science has stressed how
scientific discovery and research are related to power structures and
struggles. Scientific research is not disinterested pursuit of knowledge
for its own sake, but relates to social struggles. Many studies have
shown the extent of this.[9] In research carried out on small research
groups in biological science, it was found that the relations between
co-operation and competition in scientific research are varied and
complex, but that they underpin the process of academic research at
different levels. Struggles over resources and the co-operation that
results from the need to overcome difficulties have particular effects
on the nature of scientific knowledge produced in the research
context. In this sense it can be clearly seen how knowledge production
and use are, even in this seemingly relatively neutral sphere, inherently related to social struggles.[10]

To take another example, it is clear that the production of ideas
relating to the relationship between the sexes is related to social
struggles. Again, this has been relatively hidden from academic
analysis until recently. It is clear that beliefs in this area result from
the structuring effects of the struggle between gendered social groups.

In general, then, it is important to recognise that forms of belief are
produced through the struggles of social groups. However, it is even
more important to notice that this is only the first step in the analysis
of the relationship between knowledge-producing groups. Groups
struggle, but they struggle for reasons. Hence, the struggles need to be
explained. It is here that Mannheim's account is particularly deficient.
Groups in our society struggle not because of some inherent desire for
power, or because of the structuring effects of power itself (hence the
accounts provided by such as Foucault are wide of the mark), but
because our society is structured in particular ways. It is possible to
recognise the structuring effects of power, and indeed to stress this in
any analysis; however, it is important that the sociologist of knowledge consider how power is related to social structures. In this way it
is possible to account for group struggle.

It is important that the material bases of power and struggles that produce forms of knowledge are considered. In some variants of the sociology of knowledge this has been termed the 'social base problem'. For example, it can be argued that Mannheim selected class and generation as the most important social bases of knowledge, with the relationship between them being structured by competition. In the next section I will examine this level of the social structure further. However, at the moment I wish to concentrate on a consideration of why the groups that are selected at the next level of abstraction are in a relationship of struggle.

The main point to be made here is that struggles of social groups are structured by the relationships between dominant forms of production and control. An increasing amount of evidence has shown how, in contemporary Western societies, relationships between social groups are, at the most fundamental level, determined by the relationship between capitalist and patriarchal structures. The relationship between these two should be used in the contemporary sociology of knowledge to explain social relationships at other levels of the social structure, as well as in the consideration of broad changes. It is only through the sophisticated and cautious application of general concepts that the complexity of society can be understood.

Abercrombie, Hill and Turner have defined capitalism in the following fashion:

> Capitalist economic organization involves the production and exchange of commodities with the aim of accumulating a surplus value, that is, profit, with some part of this profit being re-invested in order to maintain the conditions of future accunmulation.[11]

They write further that capitalism has several 'distinctive features as a mode of production'. These are, first, that 'it uses commodified labour which, like other commodities, may be traded on the market'; second, that 'labour is separated from the means of production and subsistence, which makes it dependent on others for its own survival; and, finally, that 'capitalism functions with exclusive property rights in the means of production and the products of the labour process'.[12]

It is, of course, the case that capitalism takes various forms. Most often a competitive form has been contrasted with a 'monopoly' or a 'late' variant. Recent work has discussed a 'disorganised' type.[13] In any further analysis of the structure of the social in the sociology of knowledge these distinctions will need to be considered and elaborated further. At the moment it is sufficient to highlight the structuring properties of capitalist organisation. This is something that Mannheim recognised at points but tended to downplay, probably because of his antagonism to Marxist positions.[14] However, it is important to recognise that one does not have to be a Marxist to stress the important structuring effects of capitalism: Max Weber is only one of the sociologists who have drawn attention to its importance.

The rediscovery of the structuring properties of patriarchal social organisation is, by contrast, a relatively recent phenomenon. Despite its use in the social theory of the late 19th century[15] and by sociologists such as Mannheim in the 1930s,[16] this concept has only been revived with the resurgence of the women's movement since the late 1960s. There has been much debate over it,[17] but no convincing arguments have been produced to prevent its use. Patriarchy is an important structure in contemporary society and can be defined

> as a set of social relations between men, which have a material base, and which, though heirarchical, establish or create interdependence and solidarity among men that enable them to dominate women.[18]

Hartman, for example, has analysed in a sophisticated fashion the articulations between capitalism and patriarchy in the economic realm,[19] using these concepts in a historical frame. This sort of analysis needs to be reproduced in the ideational or cultural sphere, where the relations between groups in struggle are seen as structured by capitalism and patriarchy.

To reiterate, it is important that the relations between such structures are stressed, as they provide a first level of explanation in the sociology of knowledge. Analysis is moved away from description to explanation. Mannheim neglects this important structural level and it is important that the contemporary sociology of knowledge address it. The relations between these structures provide the context in which the struggles between important social groups can be understood. It provides a way of explaining which groups are important and why.

Important groups and groups in struggle

Mannheim's discussion of social location identifies those groups which he thinks are of particular importance as bases for knowledge.

The details of his account here have been set out in chapter 2. However, despite his empirical stress on class and his more theoretical exposition of generation, Mannheim does not *explain* why such groups are of particular importance. It is obviously possible to infer explanations from his considerations of these groupings, relating these to the intellectual and political context of his work, but such an exercise can only be taken so far, and is of limited use in specifying how the sociology of knowledge should operate in the current context, beyond making the obvious point that the discipline must pay attention to important developments in contemporary societies.

Mannheim's lack of explanation as to why certain groups are invested with importance obviously relates to the deficiencies of his account of the structuring of such groups. His work on groups is flawed due to the inadequacy of his emphasis on competition. The contemporary sociology of knowledge should stress the importance of capitalist and patriarchal structures in explaining why particular groups demand attention and analysis. The most important social groups in the current situation are those structured by class, gender and race. The relationships and struggles between these groups are ultimately related to the structuring context of capitalism and patriarchy.

Classes are defined by their relationships to the dominant forms of production though in common with most sociological accounts, I use occupation as a shorthand for class location. Marxists have stressed the importance of class to the production and utilisation of forms of belief. For example, McCarney has argued, from a study of Marx's work, that 'The ideology of a class is the set of representations that serve its particular interests'.[20] McCarney, in rejecting any account which would attempt to relate ideas to class in a direct or simple way, focuses on class *struggle*:

> to follow Marx in dealing with the ideological it is not enough to insist on the vital importance of classes. The context within which it has to be located is specifically that of class struggle.[21]

It is important to follow this direction, as it stresses the *relationship* between classes. The danger with some accounts is that 'struggle' becomes the sort of touchstone that 'competition' is for Mannheim. Class struggle tends to become abstracted as a process, having its own logic removed from the social context in which it is contained. Here it is also important that the struggle is related to the dominant forms of production and domination, so that an explanation of why particular class groupings are struggling can be pursued. It should not be thought that this implies that the behaviour of classes and classed actors can be directly inferred from the relationships between the capitalist and patriarchal structures; rather, these provide a context for the relationships between classes which produces a set of pressures to produce and utilise particular forms of belief.

Class is not the only important social category and, as I have mentioned in the preceding chapter, gender is also central. The importance of the study of women and gender in the context of ideas in the general sense has been brought out in many ways. One example is the reconsideration of novels and writing from a 'gender' perspective. This has produced new interpretations of texts.[22] Other work has studied less formal bodies of belief and knowledge. McRobbie's work on female youth subcultures is a pioneering example of this.[23]

Furthermore, feminist influenced forms of sociology have challenged the categories that sociologists have used in their studies of society.[24] For example, the feminist critique of conventional sociological and Marxist theories of class illustrates the contentious nature of this concept and, more importantly, how gender groupings cut across and through class categories. There is now a developing literature on the relationship between class and gender, which has addressed the issue of labour market segmentation and segregation in particular.[25] It is clear that such a perspective must be utilised in other realms of substantive investigation and the sociology of knowledge is no exception. It is also important to stress the division of the social along racial lines, which again cuts across class and gender.[26]

The complexity of society must be recognised. The social cleavages identified so far interact, placing any individual in contradictory social locations. The sociology of knowledge can only separate and order the importance of these different aspects of social location in particular cases. In one situation it may be the case that gender stuggles and location are more important than class or race ones and that these have priority in determining the nature of belief and knowledge produced and utilised. Again it is important to stress struggle over resources and power: groups produce belief or adopt beliefs in accord with their social locations in order to filter their aims in particular contexts.[27]

As is clear, I wish to stress how social groups should be categorised along class, gender and racial lines, seeing these cleavages as ultimately determined by the relationship between capitalism and patriarchy. I stress struggle, developing Mannheim's concept of competitive struggle. The structured relationships between class, gender and race produce many particular social locations in the Mannheimian sense. Social groups are clusters of social locations structured along class, gender and racial contours. For example, a social group such as a rugby club in the South of England is likely to be male, white and of particular class composition, containing relatively few industrial manual workers. In South Wales it will probably be male, white and contain more manual workers. The group structure itself may have particular effects on the beliefs and practices of its members. This will be the case with any voluntary organisation. To continue with the rugby club example, in such a context beliefs about masculinity may be evolved, with the maleness of the group being dominant over class and ethnic considerations. The club itself may be defined, by its members, in terms of male exclusively and bonding. It may be the case that maleness and masculinity are being defended, being under attack from groups of women and other groups of men, male pride being tested in the match itself. Many sports and games which take up much of men's leisure time can be seen in such a light, as can other aspects of male culture and beliefs.[28] Many other specific social groups of a more informal type may also be looked at in this light. The forms of knowledge produced will be specific to the particular situation, but analysts will need to pay attention to the general social cleavages and structures before an analysis can be fully developed. Hence, by drawing on Mannheim's perspective and showing where it needs to be developed I have detailed the most important social groups and cleavages and how these are related in struggle in a structural context.

The manifestation of group struggle

So far I have maintained that groups struggle mainly along class, gender and racial lines in the context of capitalist and patriarchal structures. Groups produce and utilise beliefs and sets of ideas in the struggle for power. I have developed this perspective from Mannheim's suggestive framework, but have placed his idea of competition within a different, contemporary, context. I have, consequently, suggested answers to the issues of why it is that groups struggle, what the most important social groups are and, connectedly, the question of how such groups are related. I now wish to consider briefly the question of *how* groups struggle, in the context of the sociology of knowledge. The basic premise of my argument here is that, apart from violence, one of the most important ways that groups struggle is through the production of sets of ideas.

It is possible to recognise how group struggle is expressed and structured by forms of belief and knowledge. For example, much of the recent literature in the sociology of scientific knowledge has taken such an approach. Scientific controversies, where explanations and theories are opposed, are related to the social positions and wider sets of beliefs of the parties to the controversy. Fundamental struggles between groups are expressed in esoteric forms of knowledge, as well as in more 'political' beliefs. Such struggles between groups involve competing responses to particular events and alternative definitions of them. A good example of this process is contained (though in a buried fashion) in Raymond Williams' *Culture and Society*.[29] This book examines the ideas expressed by groups involved in struggle over the definition and meaning of a set of events in a particular context, and is worth exploring in some detail.

On first analysis *Culture and Society*, perhaps Williams' most famous work, is a chronologically arranged discussion of a number of responses to the English industrial revolution and the subsequent development of parliamentary democracy. Williams' argument is ultimately united by his use of the concept of 'culture' and its formation through particular authors' repsonses to their perceptions of 19th-century events. This means that Williams tends to run rather different types of response and position together. Indeed, several different strands to the 'tradition' identified in *Culture and Society* can be identified. These are forms of knowledge organised in texts which are related to the social location of the writer, who 'represents' a particular social group.

The first of these positions idealises the past or seeks to preserve the present set of social arrangements. The approved social and political values need to be secured through the formation of an elite group. This is a well defined current in Williams' analysis, running from Burke through Coleridge, Carlyle, Newman and Arnold to the Leavises and T. S. Eliot in the 20th century.[30] This form of thought affects others such as utilitarianism, through J. S. Mill's analysis of Bentham and Coleridge, and Fabianism through Shaw and Ruskin.[31]

A second form of response or set of beliefs can be found in 'fictional' forms of writing. Williams' focus falls first on the 'romantic poets' such as Shelley, Wordsworth and Keats. In discussing these authors he stresses the connection between individual feeling and social comment in their writings. The core of this mode of response is, however, found in the 'industrial novelists'. Here Williams considers the novels that deal with the 'State of England' question in the 1840s, discussing *Mary Barton* and *North and South* by Elizabeth Gaskell, *Hard Times* by Charles Dickens, *Sybil* by Benjamin Disraeli, *Alton Locke* by Charles Kingsley and *Felix Holt* by George Eliot.[32] Williams evaluates the quality of the authors' response to a particular situation and the degree to which it is based in authentic personal experience. This means that, for Williams, Mrs Gaskell was able to produce a truer picture of the industrial working class than some of the other authors, simply through living in Manchester. Ultimately, however, her own social position and experience led her to perceive the working class as potentially a mob: a common theme in all these novels.[33] These authors often perceive that the working class is being unjustly treated and fear a violent reaction. They seek to avert this by pleading for 'responsible' leadership and guidance of the working class: a theme especially prominent in *Felix Holt*. It is apparent that in stressing such a theme these writers are led towards the positions advanced by the first group of authors, having in common the call for a stable hierarchy of classes.

There are significant differences between the groups and the positions, however, as the second attempts to depict and illustrate the situation of the working class, appealing to the 'responsible' element within it, whilst the first, more generally, argues the need for a relatively separated elite, possessing the correct ideals, to be placed above the broad mass. For Burke, it is argued, such a group already exists, whereas for some of the later figures, it is an ideal to be brought about.

The third current that Williams identifies expresses more left-wing responses and arguments. The figures of importance here begin with Cobbett, who, interestingly, is considered alongside Burke.[34] Wiliams perceives quite marked similarities in the responses from these figures, who are normally thought to be very different. This is illustrated by Cobbett's early anti-Jacobinism and his attachment to an idealised, past England. The leftist current is traced by Williams through the works of Robert Owen, William Morris, Shaw and the Fabians to Orwell and some of the Marxist writers of the 1930s.[35]

There are many problems with Williams' approach, notably his neglect of the class base of many of the authors he discusses, the utilisation of a concept of industrialism rather then industrial capitalism, the simple focus on the author and the text and his concentration on England. However, it is possible to see how, with further consideration, his analysis could be adapted to the categories I have described above. Thus, it is possible to see how particular authors are expressing beliefs and sets of ideas which relate to their social location and hence to class, gender and racial cleavages, and that the response to a particular set of events is conditioned by these positions, ultimately relating to the movements of capitalism and patriarchy. These groups address the situations of other groups and the beliefs associated with other social actors. These groups are related in struggle. Different forms of belief and knowledge are associated with particular groups.

In this section, I have stressed the significance of Mannheim's approach for the discussion of the social in the contemporary sociology of knowledge. I have shown how it can be developed along particular lines to provide a fuller analysis. Such a perspective can aid the further development of the sociology of knowledge. However, it is only one part of such a sociology and I now wish to move on to consider the next important area, that of knowledge.

KNOWLEDGE

I have demonstrated in the earlier part of this book how Mannheim distinguishes between what I have called the specific and general levels of knowledge. I have shown in particular how he utilises these levels of knowledge in his seminal study of conservative thought. This distinction and its utilisation by Mannheim was a great innovation in the sociology of knowledge and contemporary work must develop it. Such an operation will help overcome some of the difficulties with Mannheim's own account. Three main issues should be considered: first, how can the specific categories that Mannheim formulated be extended?; second, how can the 'underlying' or 'general' category be theorised?; and, finally, what is the relationship between the different levels?

Specific categories

Mannheim's focus falls on various different concepts at this level. As I have argued, this is at least partly due to his reservations, despite his use of it, about the concept of ideology, this being linked to Mann-heim's suspicions of Marxism. Such reservations about ideology and Marxism are pertinent to today's debates. However, despite its many critics I feel that the concept of ideology should be retained, but that in a Mannheimian fashion it needs to be complemented by other categories. Going beyond Mannheim, the sociology of knowledge has to specify the nature of the relationships between ideology and other specific categories of knowledge to be used in research. Hence, I suggest that the concepts to be used at this level are ideology and discourse.

Ideology

One common definition of ideology is to use it to refer to any relatively coherent set of ideas, especially those in the political realm. This sort of use often crops up even in the work of writers who are also using ideology in a more specific sense, as is the case where Mannheim uses the term in distinction from utopia as well as in a much less specialised way. A typical definition of ideology along these lines would be:

> An ideology, unlike an attitude, requires a self-conscious attempt to provide an explicit and coherent theory of man, society and the world.[36]

Such usages have very little analytical purchase and will not be adopted here. The concept of ideology has been most profitably developed by Marxist and Marxist-influenced writers.[37] The two most prominent trends in this development I will term class-related/restricted and structural/expanded.

The first strand stresses the centrality of ideology in class struggle and vice versa. Ideologies are class-related and class weapons. As McCarney says, for example,

> For Marx, ideological forms of consciousness are distinguished by their tendentiousness in the class struggle.[38]

Furthermore, many of these sorts of approach relate ideology to the interests of the dominant class in class struggle; as Larrain notes,

> the function of ideology is not defined by class origin but by the objective concealment of contradictions which inevitably work in favour of the dominant class.[39]

In many ways this parallels the use that Mannheim made of the concept.

Another important aspect of this position is the restriction of the scope of ideology. Ideology does not refer to the whole of consciousness, but is restricted to certain sets of ideas and practices in particular contexts. In addition, ideology is normally distinguished from science. Larrain, for example, has expressed doubts about the usefulness of the expansion of the concept of ideology to make it equivalent to that of the ideological superstructure. For Larrain confusion stems from the fact that Marx had two basic theories of ideology; first, that the base determines the superstructure and, second, that social being determines consciousness.[40]

Three main aspects of this approach are of particular contemporary relevance. First, ideology is related to class; second, ideology is connected to the dominant class and third, ideology is restricted in scope and does not refer to all forms of knowledge in society.

Most of the writers in the second trend began by following Althusser. They attempted to broaden Marx's positions by adding ideas from other disciplines. Such work has focused on the structural interpretation of Marx's work. Hence, from this perspective, ideology is not a form of consciousness related to social being, but is a material structure in its own right. Ideology is central to the reproduction of the capitalist system as a whole, but is not directly related to the class struggle. Ideology, rather has a functional role:

> The operation of ideology in human life basically involves the constitution and patterning of how human beings live their lives as conscious reflecting initiations of acts in a structured meaningful world. Ideology operates as discourse, addressing or as Althusser puts it, interpellating human beings as subject.[41]

In this approach ideology is given a broad meaning and is understood in structural-functional terms. Ideology is often still distinguished from science, but it has much wider connotations than in the previous perspective.

The class-related and restricted view of ideology is convincing. Ideology should be confined to refer to forms of thought which conceal exploitative social relations and which therefore operates in favour of dominant groups. If such a position is not adopted the category of ideology becomes impossibly broad. In this way, by adopting such a view of ideology, Mannheim's own analysis of ideology (from his work in *Ideology and Utopia*) can be connected to contemporary debate.

One particularly important point to note here is that while an ideology *may* be effective in concealing exploitative relationships, it also may not be. The judgement of whether a form of knowledge can be said to be an ideology rests on an examination of its form, content and relationship to the social groups and structures identified in the last section. Hence, it can be recognised again that Mannheim's analysis of this area introduced important issues and approaches, which can be very fruitful when placed in the context of current debates.

It is important to stress that the theory of ideology is one part of the sociology of knowledge. As Mannheim showed, ideology should be restricted to one area of meaning. Consequently, ideology should not be used as a general category to refer to any system of ideas. Approaches which restrict the scope of ideology are, therefore, powerful. However, precisely because of this restriction they are relatively unhelpful in the consideration of how other forms of thought (that are not ideological) may be considered sociologically. If the concept of ideology is to have restricted use, it is necessary to discuss how other forms of knowledge can be studied. The concept that I wish to introduce to serve this purpose is discourse.

Discourse

My major source for the concept of discourse is Michel Foucault, whose work can be roughly divided into three phases, the earliest being more substantive, the middle more epistemological and structuralist, with the last being centred in studies of power and genealogy.[42] During the middle period Foucault devotes much of his energy to the theorisation of the concept of discourse. For example, he attempts to specify the rules of formation of discourse, defining the concept as follows:

> We shall call discourse a group of statements in so far as they belong to the same discursive formation; it does not form a rhetorical or formal unity, endlessly repeatable whose appearance or use in history might be indicated (and, if necessary explained); it is made up of a limited number of statements for which a group of conditions of existence can be defined.[43]

In his later work Foucault pays much more attention to the meshing of power with discourse.[44] In modern societies power is integral to discourses and operates through them. For example, for Foucault, the mushrooming of discourses on sex is a component of the operation of power rather than an index of liberation from repression.[45] Such views are a form of the sociology of knowledge and Foucault's discussion and definition of discourse can be adopted and adapted in further theoretical and empirical work. It should not be thought that Foucault's work is free from difficulties,[46] and it may be argued that he essentialises power and confuses the relation between text and practice, for example; however, it is very important in the current context.

From my point of view discourses are relatively coherent bodies of knowledge, which are intimately related to relatively formalised practices and strategies of particular social actors and groups. I do not follow Foucault in simply relating discourse to power as such. Rather, I stress the perspective elaborated, on the basis of Mannheim's pioneering work in the earlier part of this chapter. Discourses are generated by, and used in, the struggles between social groups divided along class, gender and racial lines. For example, different groups (like the rugby club referred to above) will develop and utilise ideas formed into discourses, in attempts to carry through aims and strategies related to their social situations.

The categories of ideology and discourse are the most important constituents of the specific level of knowledge. The question of how to separate one *form* of ideology or one *form* of discourse from another form still has to be considered and the consideration of this issue leads directly to a discussion of the nature of the underlying category of knowledge.

The underlying or general category

I have shown how Mannheim separates the specific from the underlying or general category of knowledge. I have shown how this underlying category is often called a *Weltanschauung* (world-view) or style of thought by Mannheim and how his analysis in 'On the Interpretation of *Weltanschauug*' influences the structure of argument in his later, more sociological, works. Other approaches have adopted a similar sort of structure. For example, in *The Order of Things* Foucault shows how particular sciences and discourses are related to an underlying episteme. He discusses three particular fields of knowledge, 'biology', 'language' and 'economics' in three historical periods—the pre-classical, classical and modern.[47] The differences between the approaches lie, amongst other things, in Foucault's stress on language. However, the similarities in hermeneutic approach should be noted.[48]

These sorts of approach are very important and can be adapted in the current period. It is clear, as I have stressed many times already, that Mannheim anticipates many important contemporary writers and that his general scheme is useful today. However, in common with the discussion of specific categories it is important to recognise that a new label for the underlying category is needed and that such a re-labelling also involves the development of the concept. I wish to use the category of conceptual structure to refer to the underlying level.

In some respects the underlying, conceptual structure level, consists of groupings of statements similar to Weber's ideal types. As is well known, Weber defines an ideal type as follows:

> An ideal type is formed by the one-sided accentuation of one or more points of view and by the synthesis of a great many difuse, discrete, more or less present and occasionally absent concrete individual phenomena, which are arranged according to those one-sidedly emphasized viewpoints into a unified analytical construct. In its conceptual purity, this mental construct cannot be found anywhere in reality. It is utopia.[49]

For the present discussion the important elements here are those of construction and synthesis. Conceptual structures are formed from the analysis of designated texts and statements which have been defined as belonging to the form of thought for which the conceptual structure is being constructed. A problem with Weber's view in this respect is his stress on one-sided accentuation. This must be rejected, as there is no need for any aspect of the conceptual structure to be accentuated unless it is proved necessary by the nature of the conceptual structure itself. Another difficulty with Weber's view is his separation of the mental from the real, in order to argue that his ideal type will not be found in reality. It is not clear why such a strong divide should be accepted. If conceptual structures are seen as partly existing in a textual form then such distinctions are well on the way to being blurred. Furthermore, there are no reasons why a conceptual structure should not be found in its pure state.

The construction of a conceptual structure is the outcome of a process like that involved in the hermeneutic circle or spiral described above. Parts are related into a whole in successive operations. However, the main object in formulating a conceptual structure is not the gaining of understanding *per se*, but rather to provide an analysis on the structural plane which will aid explanation at the more specific level. Of course, in a number of respects the separation of explanation from understanding is artificial, relying on caricatured views.

It must be stressed, in accord with such themes, that the construction of conceptual structures is an interpretive act. The texts and statements that are used as raw material for the construction of the conceptual structure are neither completely closed nor open to the analyst. They contain social 'preferred readings' which are drawn out by the analyst/reader.[50] Thus it should be clear that conceptual structures are not idealist categories, constructed merely as methodological tools, but structures which exist within texts and forms of knowledge such as discourses and ideologies. The fact that they can only be drawn out and recognised through a process of work does not mean that they are pure constructions.

The conceptual structures of forms of thought consist of different levels which contain sets of related statements. This is not to say that conceptual structures do not contain contradictions, as themes may be recognised as belonging to the same conceptual structure, whilst being in structural contradiction. However, it is much more likely that the conceptual structure will be relatively contradiction free, with struggle between sets of ideas existing at the discourse and ideology levels.

Following Mannheim, especially his analysis of 'Conservative Thought', it is important to recognise that the first task of the sociologist of knowledge is the analysis of texts and statements to produce a conceptual structure of the form of thought which is under analysis. This is the procedure followed by Mannheim and elucidated above. I will perform a similar exercise in the brief discussion of more contemporary conservatism in the conclusion to this book. It is only on the conceptual structure level that the complete separation of different forms of thought can be carried out. This provides the basis for the relative separation of different discourses on the more specific level.

An example can be mentioned. It is possible to see how, in the realm of ideas of imprisonment, there are a finite number of conceptual structures of imprisonment. Briefly, these are punishment, rehabilitation, normalisation and containment. These conceptual structures are derived from contemporary debates about the purposes and philosophy of the prison. Discourses of imprisonment use themes from them, but do not necessarily manifest their features in a pure form. So one may expect that discourses such as 'humane containment',[51] 'training and treatment'[52] and 'positive custody'[53] will have varied features even if they are close to a particular conceptual structure. The number of discourses that are current in a particular discursive struggle may be infinite; it is very likely that the number of conceptual structures will not be.[54]

To take another example, it is easily seen how within the political arena there are three main conceptual structures: conservatism, liberalism and socialism. The natures of these structures can be derived from the texts of the particular writers within the traditions. At any one point in history or society there will be, of course, competing conservative, liberal and socialist ideologies and discourses. These will all manifest characteristics of the conceptual structures to which they relate. These different discourses and ideologies are often formed by the joining of different sets of ideas together. For example, Marxism is a particular type of socialist discourse, built upon the essentials of the socialist conceptual structure. It is formed, as Lenin saw, from the confluence of German idealist philosophy, British economics and French Socialism. Different discourses influenced and produced Marx's variant of the socialist conceptual structure. Of course, this development itself is the result of both material and discursive struggle. Marx had to struggle to produce his ideas and this process has often been neglected, though it has been discussed in a stimulating way by Alvin Gouldner.[55] Indeed, the importance of struggle must be stressed again and I will consider it further in the next subsection. It should be stressed here that a conceptual structure is not, however, simply a construct of the sociology of knowledge. It also acts as a resource for social actors to draw upon in discursive struggle.

The relationship between levels: the importance of struggle and the conceptual structure as a resource

Groups engaging in struggle utilise conceptual structures and discourses to formulate the sets of ideas that they use in such struggles.

This follows Mannheim's emphasis on how world-views or styles of thought act in this manner for groups formulating particular types of thought. The levels of analysis (the specifics of discourse and ideology and the generalities of conceptual structure) are thus related along two dimensions, which follow those used by Mannheim (though he expressed them in very different terminology) in his study of conservatism. It will be remembered that I showed above how Mannheim used an explanatory/interpretive circle in this work (see Figure 2.4).

This is a general model that must be followed in future research and analysis. I have already spent some time in the previous section examining the interpretive aspect, showing how conceptual structures are derived from the study of particular texts and statements. Again, Mannheim's study of conservatism is paradigmatic. In addition, I showed how such an approach would be applicable to other areas. It is also important to consider further, however, how this conceptual structure acts as a resource for groups in struggle. This is the other aspect pointed up by Mannheim. Hence, it is possible to delimit the following general model of the relationship between discourses and ideologies on the one hand and conceptual structures on the other:[56]

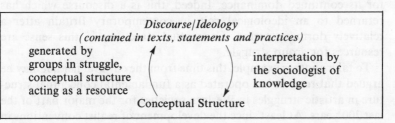

FIGURE 4.1   *The Relationship between the Specific and General Levels*

An important discussion of individualism has deployed a similar framework.[57] Abercrombie, Hill and Turner argue that the process they term the 'Discovery of the Individual' acts as a base for the more specific discourses of individualism that they describe. As they say:

> Our argument will be that the specific discourses develop out of the general Discovery of the Individual, which is therefore a sort of primitive discourse that provides the historical ground for the development. Specific discourses are, in turn, appropriated by social groups, engaged not only in social struggle but also in ideological struggle, one of whose components is a debate over the proper role of individuals. One of the paradoxies of ideological

struggle is that the parties to that struggle have to have some common ground in order to debate. There has to be a set of common moral, social and political categories in the same way that there is a common language. In our view, it is the Discovery of the Individual that provides the basic categories of the general import- ance of the individual, and the ideological debates between the proponents of specific discussions are attempts to use those cate- gories for different ends.[58]

In my terms the 'Discovery of the Individual' is the conceptual structure from which the more specific discourses of the individual are developed. These specific discourses can become ideologies at certain times depending on the relationships between social groups, deter- mined by capitalist and patriarchal structures. Such is the argument advanced by Abercrombie, Hill and Turner, when they note how discourses of individualism articulate with capitalism in different ways at particular historical moments. For example, in Victorian England it can be argued that the dominant capitalist class relied mainly on a discourse of individualism to provide ideological support for its continued dominance. Indeed, this is a discourse which has returned to an ideological role in contemporary Britain after a relatively dormant period. Conceptual structures in this sense are resources for group struggle.

To take another example, this time from the cultural field, it may be argued that realism has operated as a fundamental conceptual struc- ture in artistic struggles in Western societies for the major part of the last 200 years. At least since the development of realist conventions in the novel, as traced by Watt[59] and in oil painting as considered by Berger,[60] realism has formed a bedrock for disputes about artistic validity and merit as well as political and moral value. Successive champions of new types of art have adopted the slogan of realism in criticising previously dominant forms. This is true of both popular and high culture. Groups often criticise previous cultural forms for being out of touch with current conditions. Their realism or lack of it is criticised.

One particular episode of this type occurred in mid-1970s British pop music where great stress was placed on the 'realism' of their music by punks. It was seen to address the contemporary situation of young people in Britain, in a way that previously dominant forms were failing to do. The basic conceptual structure of realism was used as a resource from which to develop a particular specific discourse of realism which had particular features relating to the struggles of the groups who articulated it in their music and statements. Of course, this does not mean that the actual music created by the punks actually depicted reality any better than previous forms. What is important is that realism was used as an articulating device and base for cultural and social struggle. The claim to be real or more real is powerful and has a good chance of mobilising support from onlookers to the struggle. Hence, many of the political left mobilised behind punk, precisely because of this appeal to the real and its depiction of social conditions in mid-to-late 1970s Britain. Such supporters were often disappointed when the 'revolution' was not carried through.[61] Various 'folk music' revivals have operated in a similar fashion, drawing on the realist conceptual structure often in combination with ideas of authenticity, to attempt to criticise the unreal and inauthentic glossiness of pop or rock music. These are seen as incorporated in the system of dominant values or social structure in a way in which the folk music which articulates *real* themes and authentic ideas of the self is not.

It can be seen from these examples that the basic conceptual structure of realism can be joined with other discourses to produce the particular discourse mobilised at a particular time. Punks often used a proto-socialist or anarchic orientation to produce their specific discourse of the real, whereas folk musicians have often drawn upon a much more 'organised' political consciousness deriving from their allegiances to revolutionary leftist parties, as well as a discourse of personal individual authenticity to articulate their specific form of realist discourse, relevant to the circumstances of their own struggle.

The examples of the mobilisation of a realist conceptual structure could be multiplied endlessly and I will restrict myself to one more. This is the very clear case of debate around the realist conceptual structure identified by Lovell.[62] Lovell maintains that 'all realists share, then, firstly the claim that the business of art is to show things as they really are, and secondly, some theory of the nature of the reality to be shown and the methods which must be used to show it'.[63]

Lukács produced the best known development of a theory of Marxist realism in culture. For Lukács, art must depict the real. As he says:

The goal of all great art is to provide a picture of reality, in which the contradiction between appearance and reality, the particular and the general, the immediate and the conceptual, etc., is so resolved that the two converge into a spontaneous integrity . . .

For Lukács, realism achieves its effects through typicality.

Lukács' views were extensively criticised by Brecht[65] but it is important to note, as Lovell has so clearly pointed out, that Brecht's criticisms were made in the name of realism.[66] Whilst Brecht's method was a modernist one, centred in the attempt to break down the previous conventions of artistic realism, his aims were realist and he mobilised realist ideas in defence of his art.[67] As Lovell maintains:

> Brecht's critique was mounted from within an epistemological realism which he shared with Lukács . . . his point of departure from Lukács was the latter's belief that the conventions of realism developed in the nineteenth-century novel were adequate to the task of exposing the nature of society and history in art.[68]

Here the conceptual structure of realism is related to one theory of the nature of the cultural text and its relation to the audience in Brecht and another one in Lukács. Different realist discourses are produced by drawing on the realist conceptual structure and articulating it with another form of discourse. In the case of Brecht this could be said to be a modernist artistic sensibility and in the case of Lukács a more conventional stress on narrative and typicality. Nonetheless, realism acts as the basic conceptual structure organising the production of discourses in struggle.

I will now summarise briefly the set of categories which I have derived from an analysis of Mannheim's Sociology of Knowledge and extended by drawing selectively on some recent literature. I have retained the concept of ideology, restricting its meaning to those forms of thought which conceal exploitative social relations. For example, in contemporary Britain ideologies conceal exploitative social relations and operate in favour of dominant groups. It should be noted that this does not mean that ideology is always successful or that it operates through the incorporation of dominated groups. It may be, as Abercrombie, Hill and Turner have argued, 'that the dominant ideology operates to ensure the cohesion of the ruling class rather than to incorporate the ruled'.[69] Within such a scheme, then, ideology has a restricted role, corresponding to the uses that Marx made of it, to which McCarney and Larrain draw attention, and to the views that Manheim developed at particular points in his work.

Ideology is an important concept but one which does not refer to the whole realm of ideas in society.

Discourse is used to refer to the wider specific level of structured ideas in society. I derived this concept partly from Foucault. Ideologies may be fashioned from discourses and, of course, it is quite possible for ideological ideas to become discourses. An example of this is the changing role of conservative thought as, following Mannheim, it can be seen how conservative ideas functioned as an ideology in the pre-capitalist period; however, with the rise to dominance of capitalism, these became discourses—relatively coherent sets of ideas which are used for political aims.[70]

Discourses are related to groups and institutions structured along gender, class and ethnic lines. Within the category of discourse itself there is a hierarchy of levels and types, which can only be drawn out after further study. Discourses are used strategically by groups in struggle in the context of the relationship between capitalism and patriarchy. In shorthand it may be said that these are struggles over power and domination. However, it is important to remember that power is not an abstracted quality but relates to structures.

I have said little about the broader level of ideas, where knowledge exists in a related unsystematised state. In a conventional formulation this might be called the 'commonsense' level. The ideas that exist here can be formed into discourses and ideologies and can also result from these forms, though there is no necessity for this to be the case. They can always spring in a relatively direct way from everyday practice.

The most basic analytical tool in the perspective that I have been developing from Mannheim in this chapter is that of the conceptual structure. This is used to distinguish one body of thought from another and is derived from the analysis of texts and statements. In addition, conceptual structures act as resources for groups formulating ideologies and discourses in the course of social and discursive struggle. There is also struggle within the tenets of ideology and discourse. For example, different ideologies may compete for the role of the dominant ideology. Furthermore, the realm of discourse is fissured by struggle and competition, with a plurality of sets of ideas being mobilised.

In this section, therefore, I have developed a set of categories of forms of knowledge to be used in the sociology of knowledge. From the general framework associated with Mannheim these are ideologies, discourses and conceptual structures. I have shown how these relate to each other. I now wish to move on to consider the relationships between knowledge and the social.

DETERMINATION

So far I have distinguished a set of categories and relationships within the social and knowledge. I have based these in Mannheim's Sociology of Knowledge, but have attempted to develop his perspective utilising some more recent sociology. In this section I will continue this elaboration of Mannheim's work by maintaining that, again, the approach that he took to the area of determination was correct in its essentials, even though it does require modernisation to take account of recent debates and approaches.

In the earlier chapters of this book I maintained that two distinct approaches to the relationship between knowledge and social structure could be found in Mannheim's work. On one hand, Mannheim criticised Marxist-influenced interest accounts in arguing for the idea of 'commitment' and, on the other, retained a 'correspondence' or 'functional' account of the relationship between knowledge and social structure. In this section I will develop these themes. I will argue that Mannheim was correct to focus on the area of commitment and interests, and that it would certainly be possible to maintain that orthodox Marxist accounts of class interests and economic determination are too narrow to cope with the diversity of contemporary social life and the nature of the relationships between knowledge and social structure. There has been much contemporary debate about this concept and its continuing use in the recent sociology of knowledge. My view, based on analysis of such discussion, is that the term can be retained. Hence it will be maintained that Mannheim developed the correct approach in stressing the diversity of interests in contemporary society. I will consider some of the contemporary debates in what follows. In addition I will maintain that 'correspondence' accounts can have a valid place in the contemporary sociology of knowledge. provided that it is made clear that such accounts will be supplanted eventually by causal explanations in terms of interests once further empirical work has been carried out. Such a 'functional' focus on Mannheim's part can be related to contemporary work in anthropology, which has influenced much recent sociology of knowledge. The work of Mary Douglas and in particular her grid/group scheme has been particularly important in this respect.[71] However, it will be stressed that such work can only be utilised as a shorthand due to its explanatory deficiencies. I begin by examining the area of interest.

Interests

The identification and explanation of social interests has been a major area of debate in social science. In Marxism, for example, class interests have been identified and actions evaluated in terms of their appropriateness to the interests of a particular class. In other ways the concept of interest has been used to provide an explanation of *why* a class formulates or utilises a particular kind of knowledge or belief.[72] More recent accounts in the sociology of knowledge have used the concept in a generalised fashion to refer to different types of interest, relating these to different groups in particular contexts.[73]

In the course of my discussion of the concept of interest I wish to consider three issues. First, it is important to ask how interests are identified by the analyst; second, to consider what the most important interests are; and, finally, to scrutinise how interests are worked through in practice. My argument is that it is essential that the sociology of knowledge retain a concept of interest and that this be linked with strategies and group struggle. In a particular situation, dependent on the structural articulation of capitalism and patriarchy, groups will (or attempt to) formulate and utilise ideologies and discourses in accord with their interests. I believe that this is an unexceptional type of assumption made by social scientists at many points in their work, even though this is not always acknowledged.

In recent years writers associated with the 'strong programme' in the sociology of knowledge have utilised the concept of interest. Bloor details the tenets of the 'strong programme' as being 'causality', 'impartiality'. 'symmetry' and 'reflexivity'.[74] maintaining that the sociology of scientific knowledge 'would be causal, that is, concerned with the conditions which bring about belief or states of knowledge', 'would be impartial with respect to truth and falsity, rationality or irrationality, success or failure', 'would be symmetrical in its style of explanation. The same types of cause would explain, say, true and false beliefs'. Further, Bloor argues that such a sociology 'would be reflexive. In principle its patterns of explanation would have to be applicable to sociology itself'.[75]

For the strong programme, knowledge is a product of actors with social interests. As Barnes states, 'All knowledge is actively produced by men with particular technical interests in particular contexts'.[76] Two particularly important aspects of the use of interests in the strong programme should be noted. First, the focus of research is often on a particular controversy, where parties are in explicit disagreement.[77] Second, interests are considered at two levels: the instrumental interests involved in the more 'technical' aspects of the dispute between scientists and the more general social interests to which these relate. As Barnes and Mackenzie state:

> What we wish to show is that opposed paradigms and hence opposed evaluations may be sustained, and probably are in general sustained, by divergent sets of instrumental interests usually related to divergent social interests.[78]

These principles have been worked through in several important and stimulating studies. One of the most detailed of these is Mackenzie's discussion of debates in statistics in the late 19th and early 20th centuries in Britain.[79] Mackenzie provides much fine detail in his study in the course of arguing that the debates and controversies in these areas of science can be related to the interests of the actors involved. So, for example, Mackenzie states, typically, that

> the detailed technical judgements made by the two sides reflect at least in part the social interests of groups of scientific practitioners with differing skills.[80]

It can be seen how Mackenzie's account, and those produced by writers adopting similar views, relate to the themes I have been developing from Mannheim in this chapter. I have argued that attention must be paid to how groups in struggle develop or adapt forms of knowledge to further their aims, that is, how groups develop beliefs in accord with their interests. At the most fundamental level these interests relate to the two dominant structures of contemporary society as well as the most prominent social cleavages. For example, following Mackenzie, it can be argued that professional groups in universities develop interests that relate to this particular context, but these, in turn, are related to a wider context, for example, class interests, which themselves relate to the dominant forms of exploitation.[81] Hence, not every interest is directly a class one, but interests must be seen in a class context (among others) which itself is contextualised.

The concept of interest is the subject of continuing debate. Yearley, for example, has made some penetrating points raising significant issues which continue to stimulate debate.[82] In an important contribution, Yearley raises two issues of particular importance. First, he notes how interests are often defined rather widely in much of the work using the concept. Second, and more importantly, he contends that often there is no discussion of the possibility of a hierarchy of interests, so that when the analysis comes to consider specific cases it is always possible for a particular interest to be selected as important.[83]

Yearley's work leads him in an ethnomethodological direction (see below) but his criticisms can be adopted in part, without following this road. His views can prompt other criticisms of the strong programme, similar to those developed from Mannheim earlier. In effect, the strong programme neglects to provide a theory of social structure, which could be used to rank those social interests generated in particular social settings. In Mannheim the failing related to his stress on the essentially competitive nature of human social life; for the strong programme the problem is the culturalisation of social structure.

This can be seen very clearly in Barnes' work. For him, 'representations' result from 'human activity'.[84] In itself this is basically uncontentious, but it does lead to a stress on concepts such as 'community' and 'way of life', the use of the first being, in part, a result of Barnes' adoption of a modified Kuhnian position. As Barnes states:

> In the last analysis a community evaluates all its cognitive authorities in relation to its overall way of life, not by reference to a specific set of verbal standards.[85]

Writers associated with the strong programme concentrate, on one level, on activity and interactions of human beings, and on another, on overly integrated communities and ways of life. Consequently, it is difficult for them to evaluate (or even to address) the effects and determinations of political and economic factors. Their use of an anthropological concept of culture means that it is difficult for them to abstract different aspects of the social structure as being of particular importance. Following Yearley, it is possible to see that the strong programme cannot rank interests; the reason for this, however, is that it has an underdeveloped theory of the social structure. Its proponents' approach can lead to an overly integrated, rather 'harmonious' view of society, as consisting of well-bounded communities, sub-cultures and ways of life. Often this does not square very well with the concentration on the conflict involved in scientific disputes.

These brief comments should not be taken as implying that the strong programme is inherently flawed, either in its aims or analyses. It does mean, rather, that these and its attention to interests must be integrated into a clearer sociological account of the social structure. Once this is realised and completed, it can be shown how the interests expressed, mobilised and constructed in discourse relate to a hierarchy of determinations. Interests structure disputes and discursive struggle.

In another useful and well documented study, Yearley has addressed further the issue of the nature and role of interests.[86] He argues that the conventional mode of ascribing interests to particular social actors has been increasingly subject to criticism as it 'tends to imply that both social interests and knowledge claims are fixed and specifiable entities'.[87] However, such a process is, paradoxically, Yearley maintains, common in the everyday world. His solution to the interests problem follows suggestions by Callon and Law to the effect that 'people's interests are postulated or constructed in the course of appeals to those interests'.[88] Hence, texts seek to 'enrol' people's interests. Interests are not fixed, but are mobilised and constructed in appeals to them. Yearley applies such a perspective to an examination of a text by the 18th century geologist, Hutton.

Hindess formulates a similar view in different sociological realm. He stresses action and the social construction of interests, maintaining that

> interests have consequences only in so far as they provide some actor or actors with reasons for acting, that they must be formulated or find expression in reasons for action that are formulated; and that actors may find reasons for action in interests they ascribe to themselves and in interests they ascribe to others.[89]

For Hindess 'There are definite connections between actors' social locations and the interests they acknowledge and act upon, but there is no simple correspondence between the two'.[90]

Such approaches are valuable, but there is a danger of overstating the critique of the structural location and identification of interests. Therefore, it is correct to follow Yearley and Hindess in arguing against oversimplifying interests in, for example, an economist Marxist fashion. However, this does not mean that interests are simply to be seen as discursively constructed. Social locations predispose social actors to mobilise or recognise particular interests or have certain interests constructed. Readers' responses to texts do not simply depend on the text alone, or the interests that the text appeals to, but partly on the social location of the reader. Interests may be structured, detailed or expressed in textual appeals, often produced by popularisers or professional writers. This latter, is a point well recognised by Mannheim in his writings in the intellectuals, where he argued that these writers often expressed a group's beliefs or knowledge in a clearer way than they could express it themselves.

Although it is important to take the arguments of such as Yearley and Hindess seriously, this does not mean that previous approaches need be rejected. The sociology of knowledge should move towards an interpretation of the relationship between knowledge and social structure as interactive. An example of this sort of approach can be found in the work of Abercrombie, Hill and Turner,[91] who argue that capitalism and individualism connect at various points and times, without one necessarily determining the other. They interact and interpenetrate in complicated ways. Despite this, however, it is important I feel, to retain the analytic primacy of social structure. In the final analysis discourses are determined by the social. This, of course, does not mean that discourses and ideologies are not powerful or important; indeed the opposite is the case. Interests are not unchanging or always well bounded; they may conflict and be structured discursively, but in the end they relate to social location and social struggles.

This discussion of interests may be concluded by considering the three issues with which I began the section. Social scientists and commentators have spent much time and energy considering the issue of imputation—whether it is legitimate to impute or ascribe certain interests to particular social groups.[92] Essentially this can be solved empirically once the correct theoretical framework has been adopted. I have argued that the social is structured in a certain fashion. Thus, the interests imputed to certain groups in distinct situations are to be related to this social structure. Once this is realised, the decision as to whether the imputation of an interest to a group in a certain situation is coherent or not is a matter for debate. Evidence can be offered in support of the interpretation, but, as with many other areas of social science, it is unlikely that any final or complete explanation or account will be reached. In effect, the interpretation of interests is a matter of reading and interpretation on the part of the analyst. This does not mean that this is necessarily problematic; rather that sociological explanation and accounting is open to debate and revision. In this respect imputation is not a problem. Of course, this does not mean that the sociologist is free to make imputations on any basis he/she likes. Such analyses must always be grounded in a coherent theory of the social structure and empirical research into the case and dispute under study. The sociology of knowledge should be attempting to follow the strengths of Mannheim's study of conservative thought, while avoiding its pitfalls. From the account of this work given above, it can be seen that Mannheim imputes particular interests to those groups opposed to the spread of capitalistic rationalism and attempts to explain forms of knowledge by reference to this account. It is possible to criticise Mannheim's theory of the social structure as well as his lack of specification of the relationship between forms of knowledge; however, his general method stands as an outline paradigm for the sociology of knowledge.

On the second issue, the specification of the most important interests, I have stressed at several points how the theory of the social developed from Mannheim's work in the earlier part of this chapter provides the basis of a method for ranking interests. I have shown, following Yearley in part, how such a method and theory is absent from the strong programme in the sociology of knowledge. At base, the relationship between capitalist and patriarchal structures sets up relationships between groups along class, gender and ethnic lines. Hence it is possible to see how these cleavages will be more important ultimately than interests relating to other aspects of social life and other social struggles. As in Mackenzie's work, technical interests must be related to wider social interests in a historical fashion. However, such social interests must be theorised: an adequate theory of social structure is absolutely essential.

Third, it is important to consider how interests are worked through in practice. It is the case that, in addition to showing what interests are operating in a particular struggle or case, the sociology of knowledge must show how these are structured, mobilised and expressed in particular texts and statements. Here, Yearley's work is a significant resource. This can be used to show how interests are mobilised by the appeals of particular texts. Interests do not exist independently of the social structure and knowledge claims themselves. Again this brings the analysis back to the need for theoretically based empirical investigation of interests.

In conclusion, there are two general points to be made about the concept of interest. First, it is to be used in the context of causal analysis of the relationship of knowledge to social structure. Groups formulate or adopt particular discourses because of their interests. Second, whilst a group may express or possess several (or indeed many) interests, the most fundamental are those which relate to capitalist and patriarchial structures. For example, the fundamental interests of any group of men are the defence of their class and patriarchal interests against other groups of men and women.

These comments show how necessary the concept of interest is to the contemporary study of discourse and ideology; however, in a Mannheimian sense, it should be used sceptically. Interest is a structural concept related to capitalism and patriarchy. It is important that the concept be used in the analysis of particular cases to aid the understanding of why groups act in particular ways and to provide a base for the understanding and explanation of strategy and practice.

In this latter respect it is partly posible to follow Child in his discussion of Lukács.[93] Child maintains that the concept of interest is only useful in the consideration of relatively small-scale cases where there are well-defined social groups. He argues that Lukács' broad historical sweep militates against the successful utilisation of class interests.[94] It is possible to agree with Child in stressing the detailed analysis of particular cases. However, these only become illuminating and important when they are placed in a wider social, historical and theoretical context. This opens the way for further explanatin of why groups and classes act in the ways they do.

Consequently, in general, it can be seen how Mannheim's ideas can be recast and developed, through drawing on contemporary work, to provide the basis for a general concept of interest to be utilised in the causal analysis of the relationship between knowledge and social structure. As I have stressed throughout, it is possible and fruitful to develop Mannheim's pathbreaking sociology of knowledge. In addition to promoting a causal, interest-based sociology of knowledge, Mannheim also, at times, as I have indicated above, relied on a more general account of the relationship of knowledge to social structure. He argues, for example, that forms of belief correspond to certain social locations, social structures or societies. It is such a perspective that Mannheim carries through to his later work on democracy, planning and education. Again, it is posible to see how such an approach relates to contemporary research.

Correspondence

Assertions that forms of belief correspond to society or social structure are common, often being associated with writers who would not necessarily see themselves as sociologists of knowledge in the strict sense. Correspondence theories, as I shall call them, utilise a variety of concepts to express the nature of correspondence examples being 'structural homology' or 'elective affinity'. In general, a body of knowledge and society are shown to have themes in common or parallel. The explanation of these correspondences tends to be ignored (as in some classical variants of the sociology of knowledge), ascribed to an entity such as the essence of social life or the nature of the human mind, or assumed to be transparent. For example, in his study of children's comic books and literature, Dorfman argues that the structures of knowledge contained in these forms correspond to stages in the development of capitalism.[95] He provides little explanation of how these changes and correspondences occur or why specific structures of knowledge are formulated.

The contemporary sociology of knowledge which draws on cultural or social anthropological literature tends to produce a similar type of approach. The influence of this sort of literature on the 'strong programme' has already been noted in the course of the discussion above, where failure to provide a method for ranking interests was related to the culturisation of society and the utilisation of holistic concepts of social organisation.

In many correspondence theories patterns of belief or action are related to the whole of society. Analysts influenced by Mary Douglas' grid/group scheme have adopted such a view.[96] Such approaches are often stimulating due to the provision of detail, whilst being rather lacking in explanation of the social relationships and causal mechanisms involved. It should be noted, however, that not all uses of the grid/group scheme are subject to this failing, and one study which does avoid some of the pitfalls is that of the International Socialists by Steven Rayner.[97]

It is important to note how Rayner defines grid/group. For Rayner 'the group variable represents the degree of social incorporation of the individual in a social unit'.[98] 'Grid' is defined as a measure of the constraining rules that bear upon members of any social grouping.[99] Rayner shows how the organisational structure of International Socialism moved through the grid/group quadrants from low grid/low group to high grid/high group.[100] Rayner's account is important, as he stresses the change in organisation, the dynamic nature of the relationship between grid and group and because he 'portrays routinisation as a conscious strategy, instigated by leaders wishing to formalise a voluntary association into a complex organisation'.[101] Hence, it can be seen how the development of particular forms of thought in International Socialism relate to internal and external struggles, and the changing pattern of grid/group organisation. However, the causal relationships are less well explained. It would be interesting to ask, for example, how those organisational changes relate to wider social processes.

Functional accounts can be seen as another category of correspondence theory. Functional accounts or statements should be distinguished from functional explanations. This follows G. A. Cohen, who states:

> Explanations which possess the distinction we seek have been called 'functional explanations', and there is a large literature on the meaning of the statement form, 'The function of x is to 0'. It is widely assumed that such statements are, by virtue of their meaning, functional explanations, but we shall not make that assumption: we shall not identify attributing a function with providing a functional explanation.[102]

Cohen argues that Marxist explanations should be functional ones, making strong claims for the centrality of functional explanation.[103] The problem with functional explanation is that, in common with correspondence accounts, it lacks analysis of how the functional relationship between social structure and knowledge operates. This is clear in one of the examples of functional explanation given by Cohen. He states:

> If a Marxist says that the bourgeois media report industrial conflicts in a style which favours the capitalist class *because* that style of reportage has the asserted tendency, he may be able to justify his explanatory claim even when he cannot yet display *how*

the fact that reportage in the given style favours the capitalist class explains the fact that industrial conflicts are reported in that way.[104]

Cohen relies on the accumulation of knowledge to provide an explanation of how this relationship operates. However, such a view neglects the possibility that this form of approach may *block* the development of explanation as in many cases the functional or correspondence description is held to be sufficient. Therefore, for a contemporary sociology of knowledge, the attribution of a function or a correspondence account may stand as an adequate description of the relationship between a form of knowledge and a part of the social structure. However, in itself this is not an explanation (as Cohen stresses). The description of a relationship may show that the knowledge form operates to support the aims of a particular group, for example, but this does not explain how it came to stand in this relation. This can only be done by examining a chain of casual mechanisms as the move towards functional explanation will often block effective explanation.

It is possible therefore to identify three main failings of correspondence accounts. First, they tend to be static; forms of knowledge are related to a form of society at a particular moment. Furthermore, if social change is considered, the account tends to be presented in a rather chronological fashion. Different forms of knowledge follow on from others paralleling changes in society. Knowledge and society are treated as a succession of stages. Often the details of, and reasons for, social change are neglected in the generalising sweep.

Second, perhaps because of their roots in anthropology, some correspondence theories have an overly cultural view of society, which is seen as structured into a well bounded 'way of life' or 'ways of life'. As I have noted above, in considering the 'strong programme', such accounts neglect social structure, its cleavages and divisions. Indeed 'culturisation' may have the further effect of reducing the social to language. Social structure must be stressed in the sociology of knowledge and overly cultural theories rejected.[105]

The final problem with correspondence accounts which relates to those already identified, is that the static, often cultural approach often leads to a downplaying of social *struggle* in the production and utilisation of discourses and ideologies. Again, this is something that I have stressed at many places in this chapter so far.

However, these problems do not mean that correspondence accounts and Mannheim's use of a general account of the relationship between knowledge and social structure are to be rejected out of hand. Whilst such accounts must always be superseded by detailed considerations of interests, social struggles and structural social location, they can be used as a very useful form of shorthand to provide an initial characterisation of the nature of the form of knowledge which relates to a particular society or region of social structure. As descriptions correspondence accounts are very useful.

To conclude this section I wish to reiterate the point that the relationship between the social and knowledge must be examined in terms of the interests which relate to the social locations of particular social actors and are mobilised in certain texts and statements. Interests may be seen as structural (but changing and hence not reified) and textual. It is possible to argue, for example, that rationalist thought developed because it was in the interests of the bourgeois class. However, once it exists it can have many effects and make many appeals. For example, it may serve to unify the bourgeois class,[106] structuring the interests of the class and systematising the otherwise incoherent appeals and claims expressed by members of the different sections of the class. Rationalist thought might have other effects, which, in the language of functionalism, would be dysfunctional for the bourgeoisie. As Mannheim argued, forms of thought and struggle may develop in opposition to rationalism.[107] Once a form of thought has been brought into existence, it can be used as a resource by groups in struggle. New forms of thought will be developed by social groups, but they relate to other types and the conceptual structures which underlie them.

I have followed Mannheim's structure of argument. He produced two main views; a stress on commitments and interests, and a correspondence theory. I have maintained that commitment theory can be related to contemporary interest accounts. Further, I stressed the descriptive utility of correspondence accounts. However, these are not explanations, and the sociology of knowledge must concern itself primarily with the explanation of the relation between knowledge and social structure.

CONCLUSION

Throughout this chapter I have stressed how Mannheim provided a framework for the contemporary sociology of knowledge. Mannheim is not just of significance historically, or important because of his attention to the place of intellectuals and sociology in the modern world. He was the main founder of one of the most important subdisciplines of contemporary sociological inquiry. The current upsurge of interest in the sociology of knowledge is stimulating and much theoretical and empirical work has been forthcoming. Such developments are continuing at a great pace and are to be welcomed enthusiastically. However, they have tended to occur in disparate spheres and to be theoretically and empirically unintegrated. Of course, because of the competing paradigms mobilised in such research, any wished for systematisation may be a chimera. Nevertheless, I believe that Mannheim's fundamental framework and the elaborations signposted in this chapter can perform such a role. Others have attempted briefly to do this,[108] though there has been little work in this general direction.

In addition, the discussion of Mannheim has tended to be 'scholarly' and exegetical. Commentators have contended themselves, in the main, with interpretations of his work, neglecting, or only briefly commenting on, the stimulating possibilities for further development from it. This is not to criticise such work in itself. Indeed, I have, at many points, drawn on the scholarly and pathbreaking accounts by such as Kettler, Stehr and Meja, Simonds, Loader and Woldring.[109] Those beginning an analysis of Mannheim now can thank such writers for opening up the discussion of his work and eliminating many of the widespread stereotypes of it. It should by now be clear that Mannheim was not a foolish relativist who accepted intellectual domination.

Mannheim's thought is valuable and thought-provoking on many issues, some of which are now being elaborated.[110] His central place in sociology is increasingly recognised, which is welcome. I have maintained that one part of Mannheim's work is of particular importance, stressing the value of his detailed sociology of knowledge. In the earlier part of this book I have, of necessity, provided an intrepretation of Mannheim's work. It would be impossible to argue for Mannheim's importance without this. However, as will be remembered, the main aim of this book is not to interpret Mannheim, but to use him. Hence in chapter 3 I have engaged with critics and criticism of him, producing my own critique. This led to the present chapter, where I have sought to develop Mannheim's views on the social, knowledge and determination, by drawing on some of the most important recent literature in the sociology of knowledge and the theory of ideology. Of course, this has been selective.

I have recast Mannheim's stress on competitive style into a focus on structurally contextualised social struggles. I have identified important social groups and how they relate along particular lines of social cleavage. I demonstrated the value of the concept of discourse, how discourses are built up from conceptual structures, and the relationship between ideology and discourse. Conceptual structures are concepts formulated analytically by sociologists and are resources for groups in struggle. In this respect, as others, I have drawn heavily upon the structure of argument of Mannheim's analysis of conservatism. Mannheim's discussion of commitment and interest has also been developed using contemporary research on interests. Further, I have maintained that correspondence accounts have descriptive value in the contemporary sociology of knowledge. In the overall conclusion to this book I provide a brief illustration of how such an analysis could be used in the study of contemporary conservatism. Before I conclude with this example, however, I wish to outline briefly those areas to be developed and considered in further research.

I have structured the discussion in this chapter around three main issues. First, I have been concerned with the explanation of social struggles within the context of a general theory of the social. Second, I have addressed the relationship between categories of knowledge. Third, I considered the form of the relationship between knowledge and social structure. Each of these areas can, and should, be developed further in the sociology of knowledge.

I have provided a context for the description and explanation of those social struggles which generate and express discourses and ideologies. In the future research should, for example, concern itself with the exact relationship between hierarchies of groups as well as the precise linkages and contradictions between different social cleavages. The relations between class, race and gender need to be explored further. In this context, as in many others, the sociology of knowledge should pay attention to general debates in sociology as well as to those taking place within other specialisms in the discipline. For example, much consideration has been given to the relationship between class and gender in work on employment and occupational segregation, as well as in much contemporary feminist writing where the contradiction between gender and race has also been a focus of attention.[111] Any tendency to isolationism on the part of the sociology of knowledge should be resisted.

Any total reliance on an anthropological account of society must be ended. I have stressed the dangers of a culturisation of society which is to be resisted in both its anthropological and literary forms. The sociology of knowledge should be open to sociological influences, as a proper structural theory is constructed. Anthropological and ethnomethodological accounts have their uses but ultimately they are flawed.

Similarly the relationships between different categories and forms of knowledge must be explored further. The distinctions between conceptual structures, discourses and ideologies need to be elaborated in the course of further theoretical and empirical work. For example, I have not so far discussed the different levels of discourse and it may be possible to separate more from less structured forms of discourse, more from less coherent.

In addition I have said very little about 'commonsensical' or 'everyday' forms of knowledge. Of course, such a level would relate to other levels and may provide the building bricks of discourse. Ultimately the sociology of knowledge must also be concerned with issues of language structure and use. Important studies have considered language and power[112] and the insights produced must be incorporated into the overall scheme.

The analysis of the nature of the relationship between knowledge and social structure must also be further detailed. The mechanisms that I have introduced and argued for in this chapter must be considered further. The relationship between a structural account of interest and a 'discursively formed' view must be explored. I have attempted to begin to develop an approach which incorporates the best aspects of both these approaches. Many rejections of structural accounts seem to rest on a stereotyped view of these. However, the sociology of knowledge must be open to further developments in this region.

The consideration of determination must lead to a further examination of the nature of explanation in the sociology of knowledge. I favour a causal approach, but this does not preclude interpretation in the sociology of knowledge. Indeed, following Mannheim (and Weber) it must be recognised that the sociology of knowledge, like all sociology, must be causal and interpretive.

All of these areas will need further examination and discussion. However, I have shown how a framework for the sociology of knowledge can be developed from Mannheim's work. I feel that this is something that Mannheim would have appreciated, as he always stressed the exploratory and programmatic nature of his work. I have tried to take him at his word and elaborate on his work in a creative fashion.

5 Conclusion: Conservative Thought

In this book I have derived a framework for the contemporary sociology of knowledge from an analysis of Karl Mannheim. I have argued that Mannheim's work is of central relevance to the study of knowledge in contemporary society. Such an approach differs from other recent accounts of Mannheim which have tended to remain on a relatively exegetical level or argue for his relevance in rather general philosophical or political terms.[1] These studies are important and Mannheim scholars will realise my debt to them, but I maintain that, in the final analysis, it is Mannheim's relevance as an empirical and theoretical sociologist or knowledge that must be stressed.

In the final chapter I have developed Mannheim's work, taking into account those criticisms made of him by other analysts as well as my own views. I have maintained that the articulation of capitalism and patriarchy structures relationships between social groups, who produce and utilise discourses and ideologies from conceptual structures in the course of social struggles. Further, I have argued that discourses and ideologies stem from the interests of groups.

In this conclusion I will elaborate briefly on how this framework can be applied to the analysis of conservative thought. I have shown in chapter 4 how important the conceptual structure level of knowledge is, both as a resource for groups in struggle and as an analytical tool for the sociologist of knowledge. Hence, I begin this conclusion by setting out the conceptual structure of conservative thought, before moving on to consider briefly its social base, analysing both structural and group levels. This leads to a discussion of the importance of interests and struggle and a brief glance at the nature of contemporary conservatism. I would stress that this analysis only provides the barest of outlines but it does, hope, show the potential of the framework I have elaborated from Mannheim.[2]

THE CONCEPTUAL STRUCTURE OF CONSERVATISM

In beginning to elucidate the conceptual structure of conservative thought attention must first be paid to the definitions produced by

136

earlier analysts. One difficulty which has obsessed analysts of conservative thought (and some conservatives themselves) is the supposed conservative distrust of general statements of philosophy.[3] Encountering this problem has led some writers to adopt different strategies for defining conservatism. Robert Eccleshall, for example, defines conservatism as the 'ideology' of the dominant group in society, functioning 'to obscure the nature of power relationships by presenting them as permanent and desirable features of human life. It is this mystifying theme which provides conservatism with its distinctive coloration'.[4]

Eccleshall argues that there are three distinctive elements to the 'conservative case'. First, conservatives stress the inevitability of social differences and class rule; second, they think this is a desirable state of affairs and that the elite maintains the national interest; and third, that dominated groups are excluded from rule because they are deficient in political judgement.[5]

This is unhelpful as it is possible to think of a range of ideas which might fit into such a definition. Eccleshall compounds this problem when he states that conservatism is 'one manifestation of bourgeois ideology',[6] which confuses conservative with 'bourgeois thought', a distinction clearly made by Mannheim.[7] Of course, in itself, bourgeois thought is by no means an unproblematic category.

Other discussions of conservative thought also encounter the problem of specificity. For example, Lipset and Raab, who see conservatism as the set of ideas attached to disaffected groups in American society,[8] tend to describe how particular groups use particular discourses in certain situations. Such an analysis may be useful empirically, but it does not advance the theoretical specification of conservatism.

It may be, as Bennett has suggested, that conservatives and commentators make too much of the issue of the conservatives' supposed dislike of the articulation of general theory. As he comments on Greenleaf's analysis of conservatism:

> Greenleaf is correct in stressing that there is no monolithic unity to conservatism and, in the most obvious sense, it cannot be reduced to one single pattern. But this is true of all the main ideologies such as communism, socialism and liberalism. They all have internal variations.[9]

If this is the case, it is possible to begin to build a meaningful conceptual structure. Various authors can be consulted. For Bennett conservatism consists of four main elements: 'a particular attitude towards political and social change'; 'a dislike of abstract rationalism'; 'a qualified pessimism as regards human nature'; and, finally, 'the view that government is a limited and primarily remedial, institution'.[10] For Bennett, King and Nugent there are three main principles which define the nature of 'the Right': nationalism and patriotism; a desire for hierarchy and elite rule; and a belief in a fixed human nature.[11]

O'Sullivan argues that there are two main aspects to conservatism; it is based on a limited style of politics and emphasises human imperfection. Huntington identifies the following as major components: a stress on the importance of religion, an organic view of society, reliance on instinct and emotion, the placing of community above the individual, emphasis on human inequality and the belief that attempts to rectify evil often lead to a greater evil.[12] Buck describes four aspects: 'stress on the organic, rejection of violent social change (whilst permitting controlled social change), concern with the welfare of the community as a whole and desire for a strong leader'.[13]

Abercrombie argues that

for conservatives, society, or more particularly, capitalist society, has a number of closely connected defects. Chief among these is the anarchy and disorder of social relations. Secondly, there is the conception of society as a mass-society where people are like atoms. This in turn has the effect that the relations between people are not meaningful or organic but are merely instrumental. One additional feature of people-as-atoms is that the mass is relatively undifferentiated and there is little scope for the pursuit of individual talents.[14]

Robert Nisbet notes the following important components of conservative thought, 'which have most clearly affected the development of sociology'[15]: 'the priority of the social', 'the functional interdependence of social elements', 'the necessity of the sacred', 'intermediate association', 'hierarchy', 'the specter of social disorganization' and 'historicism'.[16] It would be possible to carry on listing different specifications of conservatism. However, the conservative 'dogmatist' Roger Scruton has produced an elegant statement which reaches deep into the conservative conceptual structure and I will spend some time in looking at this.[17]

Views that human beings are naturally imperfect and unequal socially lie at the heart of Scruton's analysis.[18] These have effects on several levels. For example, these unequal beings need to be ordered, necessitating institutions which ensure the individual's allegiance to the state. This can occur in several ways. For Scruton the family is important in socialising individuals into their place in society, as well as providing an exemplar of authority in society as a whole. For Scruton the father's power is homologous to that of the state and the sovereign.[19] Scruton also maintains that the family arises out of the 'natural necessity' of human beings 'to love, need and depend upon one another',[20] but his main focus is on authority and legitimation. The family transmits state power to everyday life.

Generally, conservatism aims at maintaining what exists. Scruton wishes to conserve the structures which represent the essence of English social tradition. He stresses the importance of institutions such as the House of Lords and the judiciary which, being non-elected can, for Scruton, safeguard the traditions of the broad framework of 'English society', by counteracting the reforming thrust to the House of Commons.[21] For Scruton wishes to preserve the basic structure of a society cemented by allegiance to the Nation State. This is clear from his discussion of the role of change in the constitution:

> It may change and develop in accordance with its own inner logic— the logic of precedent, practice and judicial abstraction. The conservative instinct is not to prevent that change—since it is the vital motion of the state—but to guard the essence which survives it, and which enables us to say that its various stages are stages in the life of one state or nation. And the constitutional essence guards in its turn the social essence. Here, then, is the conservative case in politics.[23]

The stress that Scruton places on the institutions of private property leads him to a limited defence of capitalism, which upholds private property in a general sense even if it is not the true conservative form which involves rights and obligations. In Scruton's view the upholding of capitalism is 'forced upon us'.[23] Here, it is again possible to see the direct relevance of Mannheim's arguments in 'Conservative

Thought' and *Conservatism*. In many ways Scruton opposes bourgeois liberalism and capitalist aims. However, ultimately, he is forced
into a pragmatic defence of capitalism.

In parallel with the German Romantics Scruton stresses the collective dimensions of social life. This is especially manifested in his
emphasis on the collective authority of the state. Scruton is also anti-
individualist. What matters to him is the defence of the state and
nation as ideals, institutions and social essence.[24] This involves a
particular concept of the individual, which is again brought out by
Mannheim in his contrast between the universal abstract individual of
bourgeois thought and the conservative 'concrete' individual.[25] In
these respects and in many others Scruton's thoughts manifest some
of the core conservative themes identified by Mannheim. He stresses
the state and the nation over reason and individuals and sees the
social whole as an organic hierarchy.

It is now possible after considering these various accounts and
analyses to construct the conceptual structure of conservative
thought. At the centre of conservative thought lies a particular view of
human nature, which is pessimistic about human potential and argues
that people are by nature unequal. Consequently, structural forms of
differentiation are inevitable: people are unequal, therefore societies
contain inequality. Any attempt to overcome such inequalities is
doomed to fail, but must still be fought, because of its potentially
pernicious effects. Conservatives recognise that inequalities may
cause social conflict; however, this can be averted if society is
correctly ordered, and ideas of organism or ordered social hierarchy
are important in this respect. The conservative stress on the community, the power of the state and the importance of the nation are all
tied together, as Roger Scruton recognises. On a different level the
family binds society together. 'Voluntary' organisations are also
important, as is religion. This may either be formal, organised religion
or a generalised spirituality that will integrate the differentiated and
warring factions of a mass society.[26] The limited role of the *government* (as opposed to the widespread symbolic power of the state) is
due to human nature, which restricts its scope for action. Social
change is permitted, as quite radical measures may be needed to
conserve the state from attacks. The aspect of social change and the
responses to it are not that important in the definition of conservatism. It is not so much change itself that is important, but what is
perceived to be changing.

This is the conceptual structure of conservative thought. At the moment this characterisation remains rather descriptive and I have only completed the first stage of the analysis. I now wish to consider the definition and constitution of conservative discourse in struggle.

THE SOCIAL BASE OF CONSERVATISM

In accord with the analysis developed from Mannheim earlier I will divide my analysis here into two stages. I begin by examining the relationship of conservative thought to the structural social level, before moving on to consider the nature of its group bases.

As Mannheim argues, conservative thought opposes rationalism. At the deepest level historically, therefore, conservatism is opposed to bourgeois discourse and capitalism. Conservative thought rejects the individualist, rationalistic anarchy associated with capitalism, preferring 'traditional' forms of behaviour. However, monopolist developments in capitalism facilitated the articulation of conservative themes with capitalist practice. One particular example of this is the role of the state. Conservatism's political statism contradicts liberal capitalist arguments for minimal state intervention, and as such makes conservatism particularly appropriate to capitalism's monopoly phase.[27]

Relating conservatism to the development and nature of capitalism is not sufficient, however, to explain the content and persistence of conservative thought itself. Conservative principles can only be fully explained through the additional utilisation of the category of patriarchy.

The two aspects of patriarchy noted by Barrett are useful in the study of conservative thought. She argues that

The term 'patriarchy' was taken by the sociologist, Max Weber, to describe a particular form of household organization in which the father dominated other members of an extended kinship network and controlled the economic production of the household. Its resonance for feminism, however, rests on the theory put forward by early radical feminism and in particular by American writers such as Kate Millett of patriarchy as an over-arching category of male dominance.[28]

With reference to the first aspect, the central role played by the patriarchal family in conservative thought is immediately apparent.[29]

As Scruton argues, the family and the relations of authority it inculcates represent the form of order that is necessary for society more widely. The acceptance of the rule of the father underpins the acceptance of the legitimate power of the sovereign and the state.[30] The religious aspect that often figures in conservative discussions can be expressed in terms of the symbolic role of the notion of 'God the Father', which itself has effects on the acceptance of legitimate modes of authority.[31] These sorts of position have also been prevalent in 'intellectual' debates.[32] For example, Rosalind Coward has noted Bachofen's argument that

> The real triumph of humanity is when love can be based on intellectual appreciation, embodied in the love a father can have for his child. This is the prototype for the altruism at the basis of civilization. It is the form of love which defines allegiance to the family, to the state and to the nation.[33]

Coward shows how one position formed in 19th-century anthropological debates stressed 'coherence between the forms of authority exercised by the state over its subjects and those exercised by the patriarchs over their families which allowed the hypothesis to be formed of the homogeneity between the family, the state and the nation'.[34]

Coward also provides pointers to the understanding of the conservative ideas of property, when she notes the extent to which the 'organisation of patriarchal familial relations . . . is related to ownership or property'.[35] However, she mistakenly links this to a *bourgeois* rather than a *conservative* sense of property, in the 'capacity to calculate and dispose of the labour power of others.[36] The organisation of patriarchal family relations should be related to the conservative idea of the rights and *duties* of the property owner in an ordered system of production.

The late 19th-century struggle between liberal and conservative ideas can also be illustrated by examining the growth of the feminist movements of the period. Evans, for example, argues that feminism was advocated mainly by bourgeois women,[37] whose arguments were mainly of a liberal, individualistic nature. They wished to apply the liberal idea of the rights of the individual to women as well as men. In this respect they desired individual rather than patriarchal treatment, demonstrating the relatively non-patriarchal (in the narrow sense) nature of the liberal conceptual structure within which these ideas were articulated, and the distinction of bourgeois-liberalism from patriarchal-conservatism.[38]

On the wider level, conservative thought has continued to exist partly because of its usefulness as a discursive weapon for men to use in their attempts to defend their power over women. For example, if the rationalising thrust of competitive capitalism is taken seriously, then there is no reason to believe that there would not be equal competition between men and women in labour markets. Conservative discourses reject this, stressing the importance of women's place within the patriarchal family. Therefore, the forms of reformism adopted by the Conservative Party in the 19th century flow logically from conservatism.

Conservative thought can be related to capitalism and patriarchy therefore. Conservatism is at base anti-capitalist, arguing against the social relations associated with this social form. However, its form and content, as well as the nature of its opposition to capitalism, are also patriarchal. In the narrower patriarchal sense, conservatism argues for the subordination of women to the father. Furthermore, conservative ideas justify women's wider subordination as it is not just women in families who are oppressed patriarchally. So far, I have related the conceptual structure of conservative thought to capitalism and patriarchy. I now wish to look more specifically at the relationship between conservative thought and particular social groups.

One of the most obvious ways of relating conservative thought to a particular social base is to see it as residing in a conservative party, which might then represent a coalition. This strategy is often adopted by political scientists, such as Norton and Aughey.[39] After characterising British conservatism in terms of five principles, these authors assume that the Conservative Party expresses them, despite their later characterisation of splits within the Conservative Party, centred on the distinction between Toryism and Whiggery.[40] Linking conservative thought to this particular base is problematic, as the Conservative Party may not always espouse these themes straightforwardly. Indeed, it may be argued that the discourses associated with the British Conservative Party result from a struggle which draws on the conceptual structures of liberalism and conservatism. Hence, it never expresses a 'pure' conservatism.

Another way of 'grounding' a discourse is to link it to a particular event. For example, in much of the writing on the initial stirrings of conservatism it is seen as a response to the French Revolution,[41] the effects of which were felt in particular ways in different countries. It is important to realise that a focus on an event (or events) may be useful, but that, in addition, the causes of an event (or events) need to be examined in detail.

It may be that, following Mannheim, conservatism is best seen as a discourse propagated or articulated by disaffected or marginalised groups in society. In this respect the study by Lipset and Raab already mentioned can provide important empirical information.[42] In addition, also following Mannheim, as well as Raymond Williams,[43] conservative themes are often expressed by disaffected intellectual groups. Sometimes these are groups which have previously been characterised as socialist. Abercrombie has noted how artistic groups of the 1930s which have often been classed as socialist, were in fact conservative.[44] Furthermore, previously socialist groups or individuals often become spokespersons for right-wing ideas. In general, therefore, it is important to recognise the role of disaffected intellectuals in formulating and propagating conservative ideas. However, in any full analysis, it would be necessary to examine in detail why such groups accept and disseminate such a discourse. It may be particularly relevant that conservatism stresses hierarchy and traditional authority.

It is important to consider another group whose conservatism has recently been studied in both the United States and Britain. Dworkin and Campbell[45] have both pointed to the exposition of conservative themes by groups of women. At first sight this is paradoxical given the conservative defence of patriarchy. However, it is precisely this aspect that is stressed by Dworkin. The disruption attendant upon capitalist development is seen to produce real and potential danger for women in contemporary societies, and one form of protection and refuge can (ideally) be sought in the patriarchal family and its associated forms of authority and discipline.[46] Campbell has pointed to conservative women's recognition of many of the problems that confront women in contemporary Britain; however, not surprisingly, their solutions differ from those expressed by Campbell. Such a confluence of recognition can be recognised in the moralistic/family-centred critique of pornography expressed by such as Mary Whitehouse, and the political/feminist opposition to such degrading forms articulated by groups such as *Women against Violence against Women*. Of course, again, the proposed (or implicit solutions) are very different.

In conclusion to this section it can be seen that the starting point for the analysis of conservative thought is its relationship to capitalist and patriarchal structures. It is not possible to identify one social group or institution which is *the* social base of conservatism. Conservative ideas will often be expressed and developed by disaffected or marginalised social groups, but the exact relationship of these groups to deeper social processes will repay further investigation. It is also necessary to consider why these groups adopt these particular conservative discourses as obviously there is no necessary reason why they should do so.[47] I now briefly wish to consider the relationship between social structure and discourse with reference to conservative thought.

DETERMINATION, INTERESTS AND STRUGGLE

I have derived the core themes of the conservative conceptual structure from various analysts and conservative thinkers. This conceptual structure is used as a resource by particular social groups engaging in social struggles and, for example, it is one of the discursive resources for the Conservative Party in contemporary Britain. It may be argued that conservative thought is developed and utilised by men in attempts to ensure patriarchal dominance, as this is threatened by the development of a competitive capitalism entailing concepts of individual right.

The development and utilisation of particular conservative discourses out of conservative conceptual structure, at particular times, relates to the interests of the groups which are engaged in particular practices and struggles at that moment. It can also be argued that conservative discourse attempts to structure the individual's consciousness in particular ways.[48] One very important site of this structuring is the family, where people are interpellated, as gendered subjects, into relationships of dominance and submission.[49] While liberal discourses, in the present form, hail the individual, conservative discourses construct the subject as a part of a gendered hierarchy.

In a shorthand form the conservative conceptual structure can be said to correspond to a particular moment in the movements of the relations between capitalist and patriarchal structures. This is only a shorthand, however, and once analysis is developed it can be seen that conservative discourses relate to struggles between classes and gendered groups over power, which are themselves in the long run determined by capitalism and patriarchy. Discourses are formulated in the course of interest-situated social struggles. One way in which this operates is through the patterning of human subjectivity. These relationships can be represented diagrammatically:

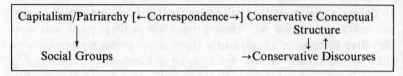

FIGURE 5.1   *Conservative Thought and the Sociology of Knowledge*

CONTEMPORARY BRITAIN

In this conclusion I have suggested that it is possible to define a conservative conceptual structure. I have also maintained, in accord with the perspective developed from Mannheim, that such a structure is used as a resource for groups in struggle over power and dominance, which are ultimately structured by the relationship between capitalism and patriarchy. This does not mean that such a view can be applied mechanically to the study of any particular society at a particular moment. To illustrate these points further it is possible to look briefly at contemporary Britain.

In Britain, over the past 10–15 years it is clear that there has been a shift to the right in politics.[50] Political developments and proposals that would have seemed unthinkable in the early 1970s have become reality. A reforming (or indeed revolutionary) conservative government under Margaret Thatcher has won three successive elections, ensuring a significant period of time during which to implement one of the most thought-out and clearly articulated political programmes to have appeared in recent times. This has led many commentators to examine the nature of contemporary conservatism and Thatcherism.[51]

'Thatcherism' (for want of an alternative formulation) is a hybrid of discourses developed by groups in struggle, inside and outside the Conservative Party. The politics of the contemporary Conservative Party combine arguments for the nation state, the centralisation of political and national power, which are clearly anti-individualist or anti-local, with anti-state rhetoric in the economic sphere. The privatisation strategy seeks to return industries to 'the people', in the form of widespread share holding. Such a perspective is also manifested in the sale of council housing. It *appears* that these measures are expressed in terms of individual choice.

In many ways these policies express central conservative themes. The trappings of the strong state are central; however, this state must exist in a proper relation to the people (not necessarily to individuals) who should own property and live in families. It is the sale of family homes that is important rather than, for example, of flats for independent (and possibly essentially rootless) individuals. Individuals must be slotted into hierarchical social relationships. Male conservative Ministers may have affairs, but in the end they can survive politically if they do the 'right thing' and return to their families.

While, of course, a political discourse such as that expressed by the dominant Thatcher Wing of the Conservative Party will never express the conservative conceptual structure in a full sense, it is clear that the prior elucidation of such a structure enables analysis to proceed from a firm base. A full study of contemporary political struggle based on sociology of knowledge principles needs to be undertaken as a matter of urgency. The sociology of knowledge, especially in the form derived from Mannheim in this book can, I think, shed special light on the nature of contemporary discursive struggle. Perhaps it is time that the sociology of knowledge addressed itself to politics again and moved away from the focus on natural science, which it has acquired in recent years. A fuller analysis would need to show how political discourses are related to conceptual structures, which groups are expressing and formulating such discourses and how they relate to social struggle. In this conclusion I have only been able to provide a few, I hope suggestive, pointers to the direction that should be taken.

CONCLUSION

The dominant theme of this book, which I hope is clear, is that Mannheim was a very important sociologist whose ideas can be developed by drawing on recent work in the sociology of knowledge. In many respects, in this book, I have begun to formulate a post-Mannheimian sociology of knowledge. This sociology of knowledge can be used in the analysis of contemporary discursive phenomena, and in this conclusion I have provided some pointers to analysis of contemporary conservative thought. In other work I hope to use the perspective adopted here to inform studies of contemporary popular culture and decision-making in the Scottish Prison system.

This book has interpreted Mannheim, but for a purpose. The scholarly attention that has been paid to his work is of fundamental importance and without it much of this book would have been less rich in detail. However, my main aim has not been to provide another interpretation of Mannheim, though this has been necessary to provide a base for my main aim. I hope that this is an interpretation that makes sense to other Mannheim scholars. However, Mannheim's work is too important to be left to the experts. It should be developed and used in contemporary social analysis.

Notes

Introduction

1. See, for example, recently, Michel Foucault, *The History of Sexuality, Vol. 2: The Use of Pleasure* (Harmondsworth: Penguin, 1987); Pierre Bourdieu, *Distinction: A Social Critique of the Judgement of Taste* (London: Routledge & Kegan Paul, 1984) and '*Theory, Culture and Society*' in Special Issue, *Norbert Elias and Figurational Sociology*, Vol. 4 (June 1987) Nos. 2–3.

2. For useful introductions to the contemporary sociology of science see John Law and Peter Lodge, *Science for Social Scientists* (London: Macmillan, 1984) and Karin Knorr-Cetina and Michael Mulkay (eds), *Science Observed: Perspectives on the Social Study of Science* (London: Sage, 1983).

3. A survey of recent developments in literary studies can be found in Terry Eagleton, *Literary Theory* (Oxford: Blackwell, 1983).

4. As in the study of popular culture, see, for example, Iain Chambers, *Popular Culture: The Metropolitan Experience* (London: Methuen, 1986), Colin MacCabe (ed.), *High Theory/Low Culture: Analysing Popular Television and Film* (Manchester University Press, 1986) and Tony Bennett *et al.* (eds), *Popular Culture and Social Relations* (Milton Keynes: Open University Press, 1986). This is not meant to be an exhaustive list of the contents of the sociology of knowledge.

5. See, for example, Greg Myers, 'Texts as Knowledge Claims: The Social Construction of two Biology articles', *Social Studies of Science*, Vol. 15 (November 1985) No. 4, pp. 593–630.

6. See A. P. Simonds, *Karl Mannheim's Sociology of Knowledge* (Oxford: Clarendon, 1978), David Kettler, Volker Meja and Nico Stehr, *Karl Mannheim* (Chichester and London: Ellis Horwood and Tavistock, 1984), Colin Loader, *The Intellectual Development of Karl Mannheim: Culture, Politics and Planning* (Cambridge: Cambridge University Press, 1985) and Henk E. S. Wolding, *Karl Mannheim: The Development of his Thought: Philosophy, Sociology and Social Ethics with a Detailed Biography* (Assen/Maastrict, The Netherlands: Van Gorcum, 1986).

7. Susan Hekman suggests that this error was made in Nicholas Abercrombie and Brian Longhurst, 'Interpreting Mannheim', in *Theory, Culture and Society*, Vol. 2 (1983) No. 1, pp. 5–15, see S. Hekman, 'Re-Interpreting Mannheim', *Theory, Culture and Society*, Vol. 3 (1986) No. 1, pp. 137–42. I have clarified the position in Brian Longhurst, 'On Interpretation: A Note', *Theory, Culture and Society*, Vol. 5 (1988) No. 1.

1   Text and Context

1. This summary, while catching the main movement in Mannheim's work is, of course, a drastic oversimplification, as are all periodisations

149

of this kind. Gunter W. Remmling's *The Sociology of Karl Mannheim* (London: Routledge & Kegan Paul, 1975) exhibits the worst aspects of the overutilisation of this device, a point also recognised by David Frisby in *The Alienated Mind: The Sociology of Knowledge in Germany 1918–33* (London: Heinemann, 1983), pp. 107–8, though not developed in any detail.

2. The Hungarian period of Mannheim's life is usefully treated in Eva Gabor, 'Mannheim in Hungary and in Weimar Germany', *The Newsletter of the International Society for the Sociology of Knowledge*, Vol. 9 (August 1983) Nos. 1 and 2, pp. 7–14. However, the most important source of information here is David Kettler, 'Culture and Revolution: Lukács in the Hungarian Revolution of 1918/19', *Telos* (Winter 1971) No. 10, pp. 35–92. See also David Kettler, Volker Meja and Nico Stehr, *Karl Mannheim* (Chichester and London: Ellis Horwood/Tavistock, 1984), pp. 18–21 and Lee Congdon, 'Karl Mannheim as Philosopher', *Journal of European Studies*, Vol. 7, Pt. 1 (March 1977) No. 25, pp. 1–18. The character of Hungarian Marxism is discussed in Joseph Gabel, 'Hungarian Marxism', *Telos* (Autumn 1975) No. 25, pp. 185–91.

3. Karl Mannheim, 'Letters to Lukács, 1910–1916', *The New Hungarian Quarterly*, Vol. XVI (Spring 1975) No. 57, pp. 93–105, p. 95.

4. D. Kettler, op.cit.

5. See A. P. Simonds, *Karl Mannheim's Sociology of Knowledge* (Oxford: Clarendon Press, 1978), pp. 2–3. Simond's book is one of the most interesting commentaries on Mannheim. However, despite this, I disagree with the emphasis he places on Mannheim's hermeneutic work. A shorter version of his position can be found in A. P. Simonds, 'Mannheim's Sociology of Knowledge as a Hermeneutic Method', *Cultural Hermeneutics*, Vol. 3 (1975), pp. 81–104.

6. Unfortunately this has not been translated into English. It has, however, been published in German as 'Seele und Kultur' in Kurt H. Wolff (ed. and intro.) *Wissenssoziologie: Auswahl aus dem Werk* (Berlin and Neuwied: Herman Luchterhand Verlag, 1964), pp. 64–84.

7. All of Mannheim's later works contain this theme, but see especially Karl Mannheim, *Diagnosis of Our Time: Wartime Essays of a Sociologist* (London: Kegan Paul, Trench, Trubner, 1943) (henceforth cited as DT).

8. Writers that Mannheim studied include the Hungarian poet Endre Ady, Dostoyevsky and Kant, see E. Gabor, op.cit., pp. 7 and 12, and K. Mannheim, 'Letters to Lukács 1910–1916'.

9. Kettler, op.cit., pp. 68–70.

10. The nature of Mannheim's exile from Hungary, that is, whether he was 'kept out' or chose to remain an exile, is debated in Mannheim scholarship. Earlier commentaries emphasise the former, whereas the latter is more stressed by David Kettler, Volker Meja and Nico Stehr, 'Karl Mannheim and Conservatism: The Ancestry of Historical Thinking', *American Sociological Review*, Vol. 49 (February 1984) No. 1, pp. 71–6. The latter view carries more weight.

11. Ibid., pp. 75–6.

12. Examples of Mannheim's discussions of Nazi Germany can be found in his *Systematic Sociology* (London: Routledge & Kegan Paul, 1957) (henceforth cited as SS), p. 88 and in DT, pp. 95–9.

13. Karl Mannheim, 'Structural Analysis of Epistemology' in Karl Mannheim, *Essays on Sociology and Social Psychology*, pp. 15–73 (henceforth cited as SAE).

14. On Mannheim's early period in Germany, see Gabor, op.cit., pp. 9–10, David Kettler, Volker Meja and Nico Stehr, 'Karl Mannheim and Conservatism', *The Newsletter of the International Society for the Sociology of Knowledge*, Vol. 9 (August 1983) Nos. 1 and 2, pp. 3–6, especially p. 4; David Kettler, Volker Meja and Nico Stehr, 'Karl Mannheim and Conservatism: The Ancestry of Historical Thinking', pp. 75–6 and David Kettler, Volker Meja and Nico Stehr, 'Introduction: the Design of Conservatism' in Karl Mannheim, *Conservatism: A Contribution to the Sociology of Knowledge* (London: Routledge & Kegan Paul, 1986).

15. SAE, p. 48.

16. Ibid., p. 17.

17. Ibid., pp. 20–1, 34–5.

18. Ibid., p. 21.

19. On science see, for example, Karl Mannheim, 'Historicism' in his *Essays on the Sociology of Knowledge* (London: Routledge & Kegan Paul, 1952), pp. 84–133 (henceforth cited as H), p. 117. On art see, for example, Karl Mannheim, 'On the Interpretation of *Weltanschauung*' in his *Essays on the Sociology of Knowledge*, pp. 33–83 (henceforth cited as OIW), p. 36, and Karl Mannheim, 'The Sociology of Knowledge' in his *Ideology and Utopia: An Introduction to the Sociology of Knowledge* (London: Routledge & Kegan Paul, 1936) p. 276. In this book I treat *Ideology and Utopia* as a book of essays and consequently will cite the chapters as separate essays. *Ideology and Utopia* is henceforth cited as *I & U*, and 'The Sociology of Knowledge' as 'SK'.

20. SAE, p. 37.

21. OIW.

22. George Eliot, *The Mill on the Floss* (Harmondsworth: Penguin, 1979).

23. There are now many studies in feminist literary analysis, see, for example, Elizabeth Abel, *Writing and Sexual Difference* (Brighton: Harvester, 1982); Mary Eagleton (ed.), *Feminist Literary Theory: A Reader* (Oxford: Blackwell, 1986); Gayle Greene and Coppélia Kahn (eds), *Making a Difference: Feminist Literary Criticism* (London: Methuen, 1985); Toril Moi, *Sexual/textual politics: feminist literary theory* (London: Methuen, 1985); Judith Newton and Deborah Rosenfelt (eds), *Feminist Criticism and Social Change: Sex, Class and Race in Literature and Culture* (New York and London: Methuen, 1985); Elaine Showalter (ed.), *The New Feminist Criticism: Essays on Women, Literature and Theory* (London: Virago, 1986).

24. On the concepts of the hermeneutic circle and hermeneutic spiral see Zygmunt Bauman, *Hermeneutics and Social Science: Approaches to Understanding* (London: Hutchinson, 1978), p. 28.

25. David Kettler, 'Sociology of Knowledge and Moral Philosophy: The
     Place of Traditional Problems in the Formation of Mannheim's
     Thought', *Political Science Quarterly*, Vol. LXXXII (1967) No. 3,
     pp. 399–426, has argued that G. Lukács, *History and Class Conscious-
     ness: Studies in Marxist Dialectics* (London: Merlin, 1971) was particu-
     larly significant to this development in Mannheim's thought. See below
     for a discussion of the degree of influence of Lukács on Mannheim's
     work.
26. These are 'The distinctive character of cultural sociological knowledge'
     and 'A sociological theory of culture and its knowability (conjunctive
     and communicative thinking)' in Karl Mannheim, *Structures of Think-
     ing* (London: Routledge & Kegan Paul, 1982), pp. 31–139 and 141–288.
27. 'The distinctive character of cultural sociological knowledge', for
     instance, pp. 91–4.
28. H.
29. See G. Lukács, *History and Class Consciousness*, for instance, pp. 46–
     82.
30. H, p. 84.
31. Ibid.
32. Ibid., for example, pp. 85–6.
33. The differences can be seen by contrasting OIW with 'The Problem of a
     Sociology of Knowledge' in *Essays on the Sociology of Knowledge*,
     pp. 134–90 (henceforth cited as PSK).
34. H, p. 122.
35. An error repeated by Gabor, op.cit., pp. 9–10.
36. See N. Abercrombie and B. Longhurst, 'Interpreting Mannheim',
     Theory, Culture and Society, Vol. 2 (1983) No. 1, pp. 5–15, especially
     pp. 8–13.
37. Gabor, op.cit., p. 10.
38. Karl Mannheim, 'Conservative Thought' in his *Essays on Sociology
     and Social Psychology*, pp. 74–164, especially p. 126 (henceforth cited
     as CT). The full manuscript of Mannheim's study of conservatism has
     now been published in English, Karl Mannheim, *Conservatism: A
     Contribution to the Sociology of Knowledge* (London: Routledge &
     Kegan Paul, 1986), edited by David Kettler, Volker Meja and Nico
     Stehr. I continue to cite from the early edition for consistency;
     however, I also give the page reference to the new edition. In this case
     p. 118. (*Conservatism* henceforth cited as C). For the best discussion of
     Mannheim's views on the intellectuals see John Heeren, 'Karl Mann-
     heim and Intellectual Elite', *British Journal of Sociology*, Vol. 22
     (March 1971) No. 1, pp. 1–15.
39. Colin Loader has shown convincingly that Lukács' influence on
     Mannheim has been overstated. See Colin Loader, *The Intellectual
     Development of Karl Mannheim: Culture, Politics and Planning* (Cam-
     bridge University Press, 1985), p. 65.
40. PSK.

41. Karl Mannheim, 'The Ideological and the Sociological Interpretation of Intellectual Phenomena' in Kurt H. Wolff (ed.), *From Karl Mannheim* (New York: Oxford University Press, 1971) (henceforth cited as ISIIP).

42. Karl Mannheim, 'The Problem of Generations' in his *Essays on the Sociology of Knowledge*, pp. 276–320 (henceforth cited as PG).

43. CT and C.

44. Karl Mannheim, 'Competition as a Cultural Phenomenon' in his *Essays on the Sociology of Knowledge*, pp. 191–299 (henceforth cited as CCP).

45. For a discussion of German work in the sociology of knowledge prior to Mannheim's contribution, see D. Frisby, op.cit., pp. 26–206. For Max Weber see Colin Loader, op.cit., for example, pp. 121–4.

46. PSK, p. 186.

47. Ibid., p. 184.

48. Ibid., p. 186.

49. ISIIP, p. 121.

50. Ibid., p. 125.

51. CT, p. 126, C, p. 118.

52. CCP, p. 191.

53. Ibid., p. 211.

54. Kettler *et al.*, *Karl Mannheim*, pp. 107–18, discuss the nature of the changes in *I & U* from the original German version.

55. Karl Mannheim, 'Ideology and Utopia', in *I & U*, pp. 49–96 (henceforth cited as Id & Ut).

56. K. Mannheim, 'Preliminary Approach to the Problem' in *I & U*, pp. 1–48 (henceforth cited as PAP), p. 36.

57. K. Mannheim, 'The Utopian Mentality' in *I & U*, pp. 173–236 (henceforth cited as UM), p. 183.

58. CCP, p. 198.

59. Theodor W. Adorno, 'The Sociology of Knowledge and its Consciousness' in his *Prisms* (London: Spearman, 1967), pp. 37–49. See also Theodor W. Adorno, *Negative Dialectics* (London: Routledge & Kegan Paul, 1973), pp. 197–8. For a discussion of the Frankfurt School's general criticisms of Mannheim see Martin Jay, 'The Frankfurt School's Critique of Karl Mannheim and the Sociology of Knowledge', *Telos* (1974) No. 20, pp. 72–89. Jay's views have been criticised by James Schmidt in his 'Critical Theory and the Sociology of Knowledge', *Telos* (1974–75) No. 21, pp. 168–80. Jay has responded to this in 'Crutches v Stilts: An Answer to James Schmidt on the Frankfurt School', *Telos* (Winter 1974–75) No. 22, pp. 106–17.

60. T. W. Adorno, 'The Sociology of Knowledge and its Consciousness', p. 37.

61. Ibid., p. 41.

62. Ibid., p. 48.

63. Hannah Tillich, *From Time to Time* (New York: Stein and Day, 1973), especially the section on Frankfurt.

64. A. P. Simonds, *Karl Mannheim's Sociology of Knowledge*, p. 5. For Adorno's loyalty to Mannheim, see S. Buck-Morss, *The Origins of Negative Dialectics* (Hassocks: Harvester, 1977) fn. 76, p. 226.

65. See, for example, Karl Mannheim, 'On the Nature of Economic Ambition and its Significance for the Social Education of Man' in his *Essays on the Sociology of Knowledge*, pp. 230–75 (henceforth cited as ONEA), especially pp. 230–5.

66. Ibid., p. 275.

67. Ibid.

68. Ibid., p. 233.

69. Mannheim scholarship debates the role and importance of his Jewishness. I would especially like to thank Henk Woldring for our discussions of this topic.

70. On the mechanics of this and Mannheim's subsequent difficulties at the LSE, see Kettler *et al.*, *Karl Mannheim*, pp. 118–24.

71. See, for example, Karl Mannheim, 'American Sociology' in his *Essays on Sociology and Social Psychology*, pp. 185–95.

72. Themes of planning and social reconstruction were, of course, intellectually and practically central in Britain at that time, attracting attention from all sides. For an interesting Conservative expression of some of the themes involved, see Harold Macmillan, *The Middle Way: A Study of the Problem of Economic and Social Progress in a Free and Democratic Society* (London: Macmillan, 1938). The similarities between the views expressed in this book and some of Mannheim's later statements are striking. There are some interesting discussions of the 1930s in J. Clarke *et al.* (eds), *Culture and Crisis in Britain in the '30s* (London: Lawrence & Wishart, 1979).

73. Karl Mannheim, *Man and Society in an Age of Reconstruction* (London: Kegan Paul, Trench, Trubner, 1940) (henceforth cited as *M & S*). This is another book with a complicated publishing history, as it is based on the shorter, German-language edition first published in Holland in 1935.

74. Discussions of 'mass society' theory can be found in Salvador Giner, *Mass Society* (London: Martin Robertson, 1976) and William Kornhauser, *The Politics of Mass Society* (London: Routledge & Kegan Paul, 1960). The application of the theory to culture is discussed and criticised in Alan Swingewood, *The Myth of Mass Culture* (London: Macmillan, 1977).

75. *M & S*, pp. 79–107.

76. Ibid., p. 73. This is the sort of position that so infuriates Karl Popper; see his *The Poverty of Historicism* (London: Routledge & Kegan Paul, 1961), especially pp. 78–81, 99–102, which criticises *M & S*, characterising it as 'historicist' in Popper's terms.

77. *M & S*, Part I, pp. 344 and 356–9.

78. Ibid., pp. 86–96. This combines the two strands in mass society theory analytically separated by Kornhauser, op.cit.

79. Ibid., pp. 159–62.

80. Ibid., p. 250.

81. Ibid., pp. 79–107.

82. Themes that are being increasingly analysed in recent Mannheim scholarship.

83. DT.

84. Ibid, pp. 69–70.

85. It is, of course, a theme in George Orwell's *Nineteen Eighty-Four* (Harmondsworth: Penguin, 1954).

86. DT passim.

87. Ibid., CVII.

88. On the difficulties that Mannheim had in finding a sociological audience for his work in Britain, see D. Kettler *et al.*, *Karl Mannheim*, pp. 118–24. For one view of Mannheim's role in the 'Moot', see H. A. Hodge, 'Lukács on Irrationalism' in George H. R. Parkinson (ed.) *Georg Lukács: The Man, his work and his ideas* (London: Weidenfeld & Nicolson, 1970), pp. 86–108. To my mind Hodge is incorrect to see Mannheim in the 'hired expert' role, as the 'Moot's' concerns were very close to his own.

89. Karl Mannheim and W. A. C. Stewart, *An Introduction to the Sociology of Education* (London: Routledge & Kegan Paul, 1962). Stewart discusses Mannheim's views on education in his *Karl Mannheim on Education and Social Thought* (London: Harrap, 1967).

90. Karl Mannheim, *Freedom, Power and Democratic Planning* (London: Routledge & Kegan Paul, 1951) (henceforth cited as *FPDP*).

91. Ibid., p. 7.

92. Ibid., p. 98.

93. Ibid., pp. 105, 119 and 124.

94. Ibid., pp. 134–5.

95. Ibid., p. 153.

96. Ibid., pp. 136–7.

97. SS.

98. Ibid., p. 76.

99. Karl Mannheim, *Essays on the Sociology of Culture* (London: Routledge & Kegan Paul, 1956).

100. It can be hypothesised that the editors at times had a major effect on Mannheim's texts, seeking to present him in particular ways, though, of course, Mannheim also revised his own work for an English audience; see Kettler *et al.*, *Karl Mannheim*, pp. 107–118.

101. As discussed by Loader, op.cit., pp. 180–3.

102. Kettler *et al.*, *Karl Mannheim*, pp. 118–24.

103. Montgomery Belgion, 'The Germanization of Britain', *New English Weekly*, Vol. 26, Pt. 18 (15 February 1945), pp. 137–8.

104. Karl Mannheim, 'The Function of the Refuge: A Rejoinder', *New English Weekly*, Vol. 27, Pt. 1 (19 April 1945), pp. 5–6.

2 Mannheim's Sociology of Knowledge

1. Robert K. Merton, 'The Sociology of Knowledge' in his *Social Theory and Social Structure* (New York: Free Press, 1968), pp. 510–42.

2. The use of the term 'determination' here does not imply a positivist conception of the linkages between knowledge and social structure.
3. As a Marxist would argue.
4. See, apart from PG, for example, DT, chapter 3.
5. PG, pp. 286–7.
6. Ibid., pp. 276–86.
7. Ibid., p. 290.
8. Ibid.
9. Ibid., p. 303.
10. Ibid.
11. Ibid., p. 302.
12. Ibid., p. 303.
13. Ibid., p. 304.
14. Ibid., p. 291.
15. For a discussion of commentators who see Mannheim as a Marxist, see N. Abercrombie and B. Longhurst, *op.cit.*, pp. 5–6. For a critique of this view see pp. 8–13. See also below, chapter 3.
16. CCP.
17. The essay was originally presented as a lecture at the sixth Congress of German Sociologists, Zurich, 17–19 September 1928, CCP, fn. 1, p. 191.
18. CCP, p. 191.
19. Ibid., p. 195.
20. Ibid., pp. 196–7.
21. Ibid., p. 198.
22. Ibid., p. 199.
23. Ibid., p. 198.
24. Ibid.
25. Ibid.
26. Ibid.
27. Ibid., p. 203.
28. Ibid., p. 207.
29. Ibid.
30. The most important manifestation of a theory of human nature in Mannheim's sociology of knowledge comes in his discussion of traditionalism in CT, pp. 94–8; C, pp. 83–6.
31. CCP, p. 211.
32. SS, pp. 76, 88.
33. Ibid., p. 88.
34. CCP, p. 198.
35. OIW.
36. In much of *I & U*, for example.
37. OIW, p. 35.
38. A position that occurs at many points in Mannheim's work, for example; OIW, p. 36, and SK, p. 276.
39. For a discussion of the different meanings of culture, see Raymond Williams, *Keywords: A Vocabulary of Culture and Society* (London: Fontana, 1983) pp. 87–93.
40. OIW, pp. 43–4.

41. Ibid., p. 45.
42. Ibid., p. 46.
43. Ibid.
44. Ibid., p. 47.
45. Ibid.
46. Roland Barthes, *Mythologies* (St. Albans, Herts.: Granada, 1976), p. 116; see also p. 118.
47. ISIIP, p. 121.
48. OIW, pp. 38–9.
49. ISIIP, fn. 4, p. 121.
50. Ibid., pp. 116–7.
51. Ibid., p. 119.
52. A distinction that is also revealed in Marxist theories of ideology.
53. Id and Ut, pp. 49–53. Mannheim often relies on examples discussing an 'individual' rather than 'social' situations. On Mannheim's use of individualistic examples, see T. W. Adorno, 'The Sociology of Knowledge and its Consciousness', pp. 41, 46.
54. Despite Mannheim's own use of 'psychological' terms here. Id & Ut, pp. 50–1.
55. Ibid., pp. 57–8.
56. Ibid., p. 68.
57. Ibid., pp. 68–9.
58. Ibid., p. 69.
59. Ibid., p. 75.
60. Ibid., p. 77.
61. Ibid., p. 93.
62. Ibid., p. 86.
63. See, for example, Karl Mannheim, 'Towards the Sociology of the Mind', in his *Essays on the Sociology of Culture* (London: Routledge & Kegan Paul, 1956), pp. 15–89.
64. PSK, p. 171.
65. Ibid.
66. SK, p. 239.
67. CT, p. 74.
68. CT, p. 75.
69. CT, p. 75.
70. SK, p. 276.
71. Ibid., p. 277.
72. On this distinction see Kettler *et al.*, *Karl Mannheim*, pp. 42–4. For a more complex set of distinctions, see Henk E. S. Woldring, *Karl Mannheim: The Development of his Thought: Philosophy, Sociology and Social Ethics with a Detailed Biography*, pp. 160–1.
73. This distinction is, therefore, not as clear as Kettler *et al.* and Woldring contend.
74. For an introduction to the relationship between the sociology of knowledge and the study of science, see Michael Mulkay, *Science and the Sociology of Knowledge* (London: Allen & Unwin, 1979).
75. On the $2 \times 2 = 4$ example, see, for instance, SK, p. 263. Mannheim's positions on the social study of mathematics are discussed in David

Bloor, 'Wittgenstein and Mannheim on the Sociology of Mathematics', *Studies in History and Philosophy of Science*, Vol. 4 (1973) No. 2, pp. 173–91. See also David Bloor, *Knowledge and Social Imagery*.

76. H, p. 117.
77. Ibid., fn. 1, p. 117.
78. The sociological study of scientific knowledge is the biggest 'growth area' in the sociology of knowledge. For a useful introduction to some of the perspectives used here, see Karin Knorr-Cetina and Michael Mulkay (eds), *Science Observed: Perspectives on the Social Study of Science* (London: Sage, 1983).
79. CT, p. 95; C, p. 73.
80. CT, p. 95; C, p. 73.
81. Robert K. Merton, 'Karl Mannheim and the Sociology of Knowledge', in his *Social Theory and Social Structure* (New York: Free Press, 1968) pp. 543–62, especially p. 552.
82. H, p. 96.
83. Id & Ut, p. 54.
84. PSK, p. 134.
85. Ibid., p. 144.
86. ISIIP, p. 119.
87. Id & Ut, p. 55.
88. PSK, p. 186.
89. Id & Ut, p. 51.
90. SK, p. 241.
91. PSK, p. 184.
92. Ibid.
93. Ibid., p. 183.
94. SK, p. 239.
95. Ibid., fn., p. 239.
96. For Merton's critique of Mannheim, see 'Karl Mannheim and the Sociology of Knowledge'.
97. See especially H and 'A Sociological theory of culture and its knowability (conjunctive and communicative thinking)', in *Structures of Thinking*, pp. 141–271.
98. In this respect, see A. P. Simonds, *Karl Mannheim's Sociology of Knowledge*.
99. See Bauman, *Hermeneutics and Social Science*, pp. 28–31. Bauman's book is probably the best introduction to hermeneutic social science. See also Joseph Bleicher, *Contemporary Hermeneutics: Hermeneutics as Method, Philosophy and Critique* (London: Routledge & Kegan Paul, 1980), Hans-Georg Gadamer, *Truth and Method* (London: Sheed & Ward, 1975), Anthony Giddens, *Central Problems in Social Theory: Action, Structure and Contradiction in Social Analysis* (London: Macmillan, 1979), William Outhwaite, *Understanding Social Life: The Method Called Verstehen* (London: Allen & Unwin, 1975), Paul Ricoeur, *The Conflict of Interpretations: Essays in Hermeneutics* (Evanston: North Western University Press, 1974), John B. Thompson, *Critical Hermeneutics: A Study in the Thought of Paul Ricoeur and Jurgen Habermas* (Cambridge University Press, 1981) and Janet Wolff,

Hermeneutic Philosophy and the Sociology of Art: An approach to some of the epistemological problems of the sociology of knowledge and the sociology of art and literature (London: Routledge & Kegan Paul, 1975).

100. OIW, p. 74.
101. Ibid., p. 80.
102. Ibid., p. 81.
103. Ibid.
104. CCP, p. 221.
105. Ibid.
106. On this in the German context see Peter Gay, *Weimar Culture: the outsider as insider* (London: Secker, 1969) and John Willett, *The New Sobriety: art and politics in the Weimar period* (London: Thames & Hudson, 1978).
107. On Mannheim and Marxism see N. Abercrombie and B. Longhurst, 'Interpreting Mannheim' and below, chapter 3.
108. D. Kettler, 'Culture and Revolution', and E. Gabor, op.cit.
109. Mannheim's most important account of the rise of the Nazis, which sees it as an outcrop of competition, comes in SS, for instance, p. 88.
110. Themes linked in the idea of the need for a regeneration of culture, see T. S. Eliot, *The Idea of a Christian Society* (London: Faber & Faber, 1939), and T. S. Eliot, *Notes Toward the Definition of Culture* (New York: Harcourt, Brace and Co., 1949). For *Scrutiny's* discussion of these themes, see the analysis in Francis Mulhern, *The Moment of 'Scrutiny'* (London: New Left Books, 1979).
111. FPDP, p. 216.
112. CT, C.
113. The full-length version of the study of conservative thinking, C, contains much more discussion of these writers.
114. CT, p. 74.
115. Ibid., p. 75.
116. Ibid., p. 78.
117. Ibid.
118. OIW.
119. For instance, PSK, pp. 184–6.
120. CT, pp. 80, 135–8; C, pp. 45, 125–9.
121. Ibid., p. 85, C, p. 60.
122. Ibid., p. 87, C, p. 63.
123. Ibid., pp. 79–80, C, pp. 44–5.
124. Ibid., p. 101, C, p. 86.
125. Ibid., p. 102, C, p. 87.
126. Ibid., p. 102–4, C, pp. 88–9.
127. Ibid., pp. 104–5, C, pp. 89–90.
128. Ibid., pp. 107–8, C, pp. 92–3.
129. Ibid., p. 114, C, p. 100.
130. Ibid., p. 117, C, pp. 107–8.
131. Ibid., p. 126, C, p. 118.

3   Problems in Mannheim's Work

1.   Michael Mulkay, *Science and the Sociology of Knowledge* (London: Allen & Unwin, 1979), p. 11.
2.   Gunter W. Remmling, *The Sociology of Karl Mannheim* (London: Routledge & Kegan Paul, 1975), p. 43.
3.   Helmut R. Wagner, 'Mannheim's Historicism', *Social Research*, Vol. 19 (1952) No. 3, pp. 300–21, p. 309.
4.   Mulkay, op.cit., p. 11.
5.   Remmling, op.cit., pp. 9–10.
6.   Lewis A. Coser, *Masters of Sociological Thought*, 2nd ed. (New York: Harcourt Brace Jovanovich, 1977), p. 431.
7.   Frank E. Hartung, 'Problems of the Sociology of Knowledge' in James E. Curtis and John W. Petras (eds), *The Sociology of Knowledge* (London: Duckworth, 1970), pp. 686–705, p. 694, and Wagner, op.cit., p. 310.
8.   David Kettler, 'The Sociology of Knowledge and Moral Philosophy: The Place of Traditional Problems in the Formation of Mannheim's Thought', *Political Science Quarterly*, Vol. LXXXII (1967) No. 3, pp. 399–426. For an alternative account of Mannheim's relation to Lukács, see C. Loader, op.cit., pp. 96–124.
9.   Ibid., p. 419.
10. An example of this is Martin Jay, 'The Frankfurt School's Critique of Karl Mannheim and the Sociology of Knowledge', *Telos* (1974) No. 20, pp. 72–89, especially p. 76.
11. For a consideration of the different ways in which Mannheim links knowledge and social structure see Robert K. Merton, 'Karl Mannheim and the Sociology of Knowledge' in his *Social Theory and Social Structure* (New York: Free Press, 1968), pp. 543–62, especially pp. 552–6.
12. SK, p. 278.
13. Ibid., pp. 278–80. Of course, the different sources of the sociology of knowledge have been recognised by many writers, see, for example, G. W. Remmling, op.cit. For a discussion of Mannheim's Weberian 'intellectual debt' see Peter Hamilton, *Knowledge and Social Structure: An introduction to the classical argument in the sociology of knowledge* (London: Routledge & Kegan Paul, 1974), pp. 121–2. Rex places Mannheim in a Weberian tradition, see John Rex, *Key Problems of Sociological Theory* (London: Routledge & Kegan Paul, 1961) p. 87. More recently, Colin Loader has stressed Mannheim's links to Weber, op.cit., pp. 96–124.
14. SK, p. 241.
15. There are many commentaries on Marx's theory of ideology. See, for example, N. Abercrombie, *Class, Structure and Knowledge* (Oxford: Blackwell, 1980), pp. 11–32; Jorge Larrain, *The Concept of Ideology* (London: Hutchinson, 1979), pp. 35–67; Jorge Larrain, *Marxism and Ideology* (London: Macmillan, 1983); Bhikhu Parekh, *Marx's Theory of Ideology* (London: Croom Helm, 1982); and Martin Seliger, *The Marxist Conception of Ideology* (Cambridge University Press, 1977).

16. One example of this can be found in SK, p. 278.
17. See, for example, David Kettler, 'Culture and Revolution: Lukács in the Hungarian Revolutions of 1918/19', *Telos* (Winter 1971) No. 10, pp. 35–92, especially pp. 66–7.
18. The most important works here are Theodore W. Adorno, 'The Sociology of Knowledge and its Consciousness' in his *Prisms* (London: Spearman, 1967); Georg Lukács, *The Destruction of Reason* (London: Merlin, 1980), pp. 632–41. For a commentary on the Frankfurt School see Martin Jay, 'The Frankfurt School's Critique of Karl Mannheim and the Sociology of Knowledge', *Telos* (1974) No. 20, pp. 72–89. This has been criticised by James Schmidt, see 'Critical Theory and the Sociology of Knowledge', *Telos* (1974/75) No. 21, pp. 168–80. For Jay's reply see 'Crutches v Stilts: An Answer to James Schmidt on the Frankfurt School', *Telos* (Winter 1974/75) No. 22, pp. 106–17.
19. Lukács, op.cit., p. 633.
20. Ibid.
21. Adorno, op.cit., p. 41.
22. Ibid.
23. M. Jay, 'The Frankfurt School's Critique of Karl Mannheim and the Sociology of Knowledge', pp. 81–2.
24. Adorno, op.cit., p. 44.
25. Ibid.
26. Ibid., p. 46.
27. Ibid.
28. M. Jay, op.cit., pp. 80–1.
29. Lukács, op.cit., p. 635.
30. Adorno, op.cit., p. 48.
31. Ibid.
32. Ibid.
33. Ibid., p. 49.
34. There are many discussions of the nature of sociology. For a discussion of sociology's lack of disciplinary specificity see John Urry, 'Sociology as Parasite: some vices and virtues', in Philip Abrams *et al.* (eds), *Practice and Progress: British Sociology 1950–1980* (London: Allen & Unwin, 1981), pp. 25–38.
35. The more hermeneutic aspects of Mannheim's method have been borrowed by Garfinkel, who adopts Mannheim's concept of 'documentary meaning'. See Harold Garfinkel, *Studies in Ethnomethodology* (Englewood Cliffs, New Jersey: Prentice Hall, 1967), pp. 77–9. Reprinted, Cambridge: Polity, 1984).
36. Zygmunt Bauman, *Hermeneutics and Social Science: Approaches to Understanding* (London: Hutchinson, 1978), pp. 89–110.
37. A. P. Simonds, *Karl Mannheim's Sociology of Knowledge* (Oxford: Clarendon, 1978), p. 20.
38. Ibid., p. 37.
39. Especially in CT and C.
40. See, for example, Anthony Giddens, *Central Problems in Social Theory: Action, Structure and Contradiction in Social Analysis* (London: Macmillan, 1979).

41. N. Abercrombie, *Class, Structure and Knowledge*, p. 47.

42. As I have argued above, chapter 2, p. 39–43.

43. Barry Barnes and David Bloor, 'Relativism, Rationalism and the Sociology of Knowledge' in Martin Hollis and Steven Lukes (eds), *Rationality and Relativism* (Oxford: Blackwell, 1982), pp. 21–47, p. 26.

44. N. Abercrombie, op.cit., pp. 45–7.

45. Ibid., p. 46.

46. A. P. Simonds, op.cit., p. 31.

47. M. Hollis and S. Lukes, 'Introduction' to Hollis and Lukes, op.cit., pp. 1–20.

48. A frequently quoted study of this is by Ralph Bulmer, 'Why is the cassowary not a bird? A problem of zoological taxonomy among the Karam of the New Guinea Highlands', *Man*, new series, Vol. 2 (March 1967) No. 1, pp. 5–25.

49. Hollis and Lukes, 'Introduction', p. 7.

50. Ibid., p. 9.

51. Ibid., p. 10.

52. Ibid., pp. 11–12.

53. Ibid., p. 11.

54. Barnes and Bloor, op.cit., p. 21.

55. Ibid., pp. 22–3.

56. See, for example, Harry Collins, 'Stages in the Empirical Programme of Relativism', *Social Studies of Science*, Vol. 11 (February 1981) No. 1, pp. 3–10. Much of Collins most important work can be found in *Changing Order* (London: Sage, 1985).

57. Steven Yearley, *Science and Sociological Practice* (Milton Keynes: Open University, 1984), p. 63.

58. Ibid., p. 66.

59. As has been argued by John Law and Peter Lodge, *Science for Social Scientists* (London: Macmillan, 1984), pp. 255–62.

60. Here I use culturalist to signify the understanding of the social structure as a culture. Such an approach neglects the importance of economic and political dimensions or subsumes them within an all-embracing category, such as a 'way of life'. The use of this is adopted from Richard Johnson. See, for example, 'Three Problematics: elements of a theory of working-class culture' in John Clarke, Chas Critcher and Richard Johnson (eds), *Working Class Culture: Studies in history and theory* (London: Hutchinson, 1979), pp. 201–37 and 'Histories of Culture/Theories of Ideology: Notes on an Impasse', in Michele Barrett *et al.* (eds), *Ideology and Cultural Production* (London: Croom Helm, 1979), pp. 49–77.

61. Alexander von Schelting, 'Review of *Ideologie and Utopie*', 2nd ed., *American Sociological Review*, Vol. 1 (August 1936) No. 4, pp. 664–74, p. 673.

62. John Heeren, 'Karl Mannheim and the Intellectual Elite', *British Journal of Sociology*, Vol. 22 (March 1971) No. 1, pp. 1–15, p. 1.

63. As is pointed out by Abercrombie; see *Class, Structure and Knowledge*, p. 32.

64. See Simonds, op.cit., p. 129, fn. 36 and 'The Prospects of Scientific Politics' in *I & U*, pp. 97–171, especially pp. 140–2.
65. Heeren, op.cit., p. 1.
66. Abercrombie, op.cit., p. 127.
67. Mannheim, 'The Prospects of Scientific Politics', p. 137.
68. Raymond Williams, *Culture* (Glasgow: Fontana/Collins, 1981).
69. Ibid., p. 214.
70. Ibid., p. 218.
71. Here the reference is, of course, to Alfred Weber.
72. Williams, *Culture*, p.. 223.
73. Abercrombie, *Class, Structure and Knowledge*, p. 127.
74. Ibid.
75. See, for example, PSK, pp. 171–9.
76. See, for example, SK, p. 266.
77. This is an exercise that Mannheim carries out in many places, for example, 'The distinctive character of cultural sociological knowledge' in his *Structures of Thinking* and in SS.
78. See, for example, *M & S*, pp. 217–20 and all through Mannheim's later work.
79. See Karl Mannheim, UM, pp. 173–236.
80. On the dangers of this type of concept of history see, for example, Louis Althusser and Etienne Balibar, *Reading Capital* (London: New Left Books, 1970), pp. 119–44.
81. See J. Urry, op.cit.
82. This is also the case in some Marxist scholarship, for example, Joe McCarney, *The Real World of Ideology* (Brighton: Harvester, 1980).
83. For a penetrating discussion of Marx's theory of modes of production see G. A. Cohen, *Karl Marx's Theory of History: A Defence* (Oxford: Clarendon, 1978).
84. On the distinction between 'class-theoretical' and 'mode-theoretical' see N. Abercrombie, *Class, Structure and Knowledge*, p. 110.
85. See ibid., p. 50.
86. Christine Delphy, 'Women in Stratification Studies', in Helen Roberts (ed.), *Doing Feminist Research* (London: Routledge & Kegan Paul, 1981), pp. 114–28, p. 125. See also C. Delphy, *Close to Home: a materialist analysis of women's oppression* (London: Hutchinson, 1984).
87. Delphy, 'Women in Stratification Studies', p. 127.
88. For a critique see Michele Barrett and Mary McIntosh, 'Christine Delphy: Towards a Materialist Feminism?' *Feminist Review* (1979) No. 1, pp. 95–106.
89. This is a much debated area; for contributions see, for example, Diana Adlam, 'The Case against Capitalist Patriarchy', *m/f* (1979) No. 3, pp. 83–102; Michele Barrett, *Women's Oppression Today: Problems in Marxist Feminist Analysis* (London: Verso and New Left Books, 1980); Veronica Beechey, 'On Patriarchy', *Feminist Review* (1979), No. 3, pp. 66–82; Zillah R. Eisenstein, 'Developing a Theory of Capitalist Patriarchy and Socialist Feminism' and 'Some Notes on the Relations of Capitalist Patriarchy' in Zillah R. Eisenstein (ed.), *Capitalist Patriarchy and the Case for Socialist Feminism* (New York: Monthly

Review, 1979), pp. 5–40 and 41–55; Heidi I. Hartmann, 'The Unhappy
Marriage of Marxism and Feminism: towards a more progressive
union', *Capital and Class* (Summer 1979) No. 8, pp. 1–33; this paper is
reprinted in Lydia Sargent (ed.), *Women and Revolution: a discussion of
the Unhappy Marriage of Marxism and Feminism* (London: Pluto,
1981), pp. 1–41; Heidi I. Hartmann, 'Capitalism, Patriarchy, and Job
Segregation by Sex' in Eisenstein, *Capitalist Patriarchy*, pp. 206–47;
Juliet Mitchell, *Psycholanalysis and Feminism* (Harmondsworth: Penguin, 1975). For a clear discussion of the relations between capitalism
and patriarchy see Sylvia Walby, *Patriarchy at Work* (Cambridge:
Polity, 1986).

90. On housing, see, for example, Peter Saunders, 'Beyond Housing
classes: the sociological significance of private property rights in means
of consumption', *International Journal of Urban and Regional Research*, Vol. 8 (1984) No. 2, pp. 202–27. For a critique of this see
Michael Harloe, 'Sector and Class: a critical comment', *International
Journal of Urban and Regional Research*, Vol. 8 (1984) No. 2, pp. 228–
37.

91. For a much contested analysis of Rastafari, see Ernest Cashmore,
Rastaman: the Rastafarian Movement in England (London: Allen &
Unwin, 1979). For criticisms of Cashmore, see, for example, Errol
Lawrence, 'In the abundance of water the fool is thirsty: sociology and
black "pathology"' in Centre for Contemporary Cultural Studies, *The
Empire Strikes Back: Race and racism in 70s Britain* (London: Hutchin-
son, 1982), pp. 95–142, particularly pp. 118 and 124–5; and Paul
Gilroy, 'Steppin' out of Babylon—race, class and autonomy', ibid.,
pp. 276–314, especially p. 291. For an introduction to Rastafari in
Jamaica, see Joseph Owens, *Dread: the Rastafarians of Jamaica* (London: Heinemann, 1979).

92. See Centre for Contemporary Cultural Studies, op.cit., and S. Hall *et
al.*, *Policing the Crisis: mugging, the state and law and order (London:
Macmillan, 1978)*.

93. See, for example, Noel O'Sullivan, *Conservatism* (London: Dent,
1976), p. 9.

94. SS, p. 2. This is only one example of this in Mannheim's work.

95. Again, the analysis in SS is one of the best examples of this.

96. This is especially true in the later works.

97. This is now happening more widely; see, for example, John Law (ed.)
Power, Action and Belief: A New Sociology of Knowledge? (London:
Routledge & Kegan Paul, 1986).

98. The study of 'texts' and of science are both growth areas in contemporary social analysis. For an introduction to the contemporary social
study of science, see Karin Knorr-Cetina and Michael Mulkay (eds),
Science Observed: Perspectives on the Social Study of Science (London:
Sage, 1983). For introduction to new modes of literary criticism see, for
example, Jonathan Culler, *Structuralist Poetics: Structuralism,
Linguistics and the Study of Literature* (London: Routledge & Kegan
Paul, 1975); Jonathan Culler, *On Deconstruction: Theory and Criticism
after Structuralism* (London: Routledge & Kegan Paul, 1983), Terry

Eagleton, *Marxism and Literary Criticism* (London: Methuen, 1977) and T. Eagleton, *Literary Theory* (Oxford: Blackwell, 1983). Some different perspectives on literary criticism, practice and English can be found in Catherine Belsey, *Critical Practice* (London: Methuen, 1980) and Peter Widdowson (ed.), *Re-Reading English* (London: Methuen, 1982).

99.   Terry Lovell, *Pictures of Reality: Aesthetics, Politics, Pleasure* (London: BFI, 1980), p. 51. The concern to refocus analysis on belief is also contained in Nicholas Abercrombie *et al.*, *The Dominant Ideology Thesis* (London: Allen & Unwin, 1980).

100.   Mannheim's comments on Max Weber are scattered throughout his work. For G. H. Mead, see especially *FPDP*, pp. 238–41.

101.   As in the 'structuralism' versus 'culturalism' debate in Britain in the late 1970s, see on the 'structuralism' side: Richard Johnson, 'Thompson, Genovese, and Socialist Humanist History', *History Workshop* (Autumn 1978) No. 6, pp. 79–100; Richard Johnson, 'Three Problematics: elements of a theory of working-class culture' in John Clarke, Chas Critcher and Richard Johnson (eds), *Working-Class Culture* (London: Hutchinson, 1979), pp. 201–37; Richard Johnson, 'Histories of Culture/Theories of Ideology: Notes on an Impasse' in M. Barrett *et al.* (eds), *Ideology and Cultural Production*, pp. 49–77. For 'Culturalism' see E. P. Thompson, 'The Poverty of Theory: or an Orrery of Errors' in his *The Poverty of Theory and Other Essays* (London: Merlin, 1978), pp. 193–397. Johnson's 'Thompson, Genovese and Socialist Humanist History' provoked a debate in the pages of *History Workshop*; the most important contributions to this are Keith McClelland, 'Some Comments on Richard Johnson, "Edward Thompson, Eugene Genovese, and Socialist-Humanist History"', *History Workshop* (Spring 1979) No. 7, pp. 101–15; Gavin Williams, 'In Defence of History', *History Workshop* (Spring 1979) No. 7, pp. 116–24; Simon Clarke, 'Socialist Humanism and the Critique of Economism', *History Workshop* (Autumn 1979) No. 8, pp. 138–56; Gregor McLennan, 'Richard Johnson and his Critics: Towards a Constructive Debate', *History Workshop* (Autumn 1979) No. 8, pp. 157–66. The 'debate' reached a polemical height in the exchanges reprinted in Raphael Samuel (ed.), *People's History and Socialist Theory* (London: Routledge & Kegan Paul, 1981). These are Stuart Hall, 'In Defence of Theory', pp. 378–85; Richard Johnson, 'Against Absolutism', pp. 386–96 and E. P. Thompson, 'The Politics of Theory', pp. 397–408. The best overall assessment of Thompson's work is in Perry Anderson's *Arguments within English Marxism* (London: New Left Books and Verso, 1980). See also the essays in Centre for Contemporary Cultural Studies, *Making Histories: Studies in history-writing and politics* (London: Hutchinson, 1982) and Keith Neild and John Seed, 'Theoretical poverty or the poverty of theory: British Marxist historiography and the Althusserians', *Economy and Society*, Vol. 8 (November 1979) No. 4, pp. 381–416, as well as Paul Hirst's 'The necessity of theory', *Economy and Society*, Vol. 8 (November 1979) No. 4, pp. 417–45.

102. Both of which can be seen in CT and C.

4 Mannheim and the Sociology of Knowledge Today

1. R. K. Merton, 'The Sociology of Knowledge', op.cit.
2. OIW.
3. For a useful summary of work in the sociology of science see Michael Mulkay, 'Sociology of Science in the West' Part 1 of the Trend Report, 'The Sociology of Science in East and West', *Current Sociology*, Vol. 28 (Winter 1980) No. 3, pp. 1–184.
4. An example of this would be David Bloor's work on Mathematics; see D. Bloor, 'Wittgenstein and Mannheim on the Sociology of Mathematics', *Studies in History and Philosophy of Science*, Vol. 4 (1973) No. 2, pp. 173–91. *Knowledge and Social Imagery*, pp. 74–140.
5. Hence I disagree with Simonds' hermeneutic interpretation.
6. For further detail see my *Towards the Developed Sociology of Knowledge*, Ph.D. Thesis, University of Lancaster, 1984.
7. In the results of current collaborative research on decision-making in the Scottish Prison System with Michael Adler and on popular culture with Nicholas Abercrombie and Scott Lash.
8. See below for discussion of conventional meanings of ideology.
9. A very useful summary of such studies is contained in Steven Shapin, 'History of Science and Sociological Reconstructions', *History of Science*, Vol. 20 (1982), pp. 157–211.
10. See Brian Longhurst, 'The Attribution of Credit in a Scientific Community', Report on a research project, *mimeo*, Department of Sociology, University of Lancaster, 1985.
11. N. Abercrombie, S. Hill and B. Turner, *Sovereign Individuals of Capitalism* (London: Allen & Unwin, 1986).
12. Ibid.
13. For analysis of disorganised capitalism see Scott Lash and John Urry, *The End of Organized Capitalism* (Cambridge: Polity, 1987) and Claus Offe, *Disorganised Capitalism* (Cambridge: Polity, 1985).
14. See above.
15. R. Coward, *Patriarchal Precedents*, op.cit.
16. In lecture notes in the Mannheim Archive at the University of Keele.
17. For a useful discussion of the development of feminist theory and the concept of patriarchy see Hester Eisenstein, *Contemporary Feminist Thought* (London: Unwin Paperbacks, 1984).
18. Heidi Hartman, 'The Unhappy Marriage of Marxism and Feminism', op.cit., p. 11.
19. See H. Hartman, 'The Unhappy Marriage of Marxism and Feminism' and 'Capitalism, Patriarchy and Job Segregation by Sex' op.cit.; also S. Walby, op.cit.
20. Joe McCarney, *The Real World of Ideology*, p. 113.
21. Ibid., p. 39.
22. See the works cited in note 23, chapter 1.

23. See Angela McRobbie and Jenny Garber, 'Girls and Subcultures' in Hall and Jefferson (eds), *Resistance through Rituals*, pp. 209–22; Angela McRobbie, 'Working Class Girls and the Culture of Feminity' in Women's Studies Group Centre for Contemporary Cultural Studies, *Women Take Issue: Aspects of Women's Subordination* (London: Hutchinson, 1978), pp. 96–108; Angela McRobbie, 'Settling Accounts with Subcultures: A Feminist Critique', *Screen Education* (1980) No. 34, pp. 37–49; Simon Frith and Angela McRobbie, 'Rock and Sexuality', *Screen Education* (1978/79) No. 29, pp. 3–19. For a critique of this last paper see Jenny Taylor and Dave Laing, 'Disco-Pleasure-Discourse: On "Rock and Sexuality"', *Screen Education* (Summer 1979) No. 31, pp. 43–8. Simon Frith's work draws on many of McRobbie's insights; see, for example, *Sound Effects: Youth, Leisure and the Politics of Rock 'n' Roll* (London: Constable, 1983).

24. See, for example, C. Delphy, 'Women in Stratification Studies'.

25. See, for example, the papers given at the Segregation in Employment Symposium, University of Lancaster, 10–12 July 1985.

26. For a useful introduction to these distinctions see Centre for Contemporary Cultural Studies, *The Empire Strikes Back: Race and Racism in 70s Britain* (London: Hutchinson, 1982).

27. Cynthia Cockburn's work, for example, illustrates this process—see *Brothers: male dominance and technological change* (London: Pluto, 1983) and *Machinery of Dominance: women, men and technical know-how* (London: Pluto, 1985)—as does Heidi Hartman in the papers already cited.

28. On sport, see, for example, Jenifer Hargreaves (ed.) *Sport, Culture and Ideology* (London: Routledge & Kegan Paul, 1982); John Carroll, 'Sport: Virtue and Grace', *Theory, Culture and Society*, Vol. 3 (1986) No. 1, pp. 91–8; David Whitson, 'Structure, Agency and the Sociology of Sport Debates', *Theory, Culture and Society*, Vol. 3 (1986) No. 1, pp. 99–107; Jenifer Hargreaves, 'Where's the Virtue? Where's the Grace? A Discussion of the Social Production of Gender Through Sport', *Theory, Culture and Society*, Vol. 3 (1986) No. 1, pp. 109–21; John Hargreaves, *Sport, Power and Culture* (Cambridge: Polity, 1986).

29. Raymond Williams, *Culture and Society 1780–1950* (Harmondsworth: Penguin, 1963).

30. Ibid., pp. 23–39, 65–98, 120–36, 224–38, 246–56.

31. Ibid., pp. 65–84, 137–61, 182–7.

32. Ibid., pp. 99–119.

33. Ibid., pp. 115–117. For a further discussion of this theme, see R. Williams, 'A Hundred Years of Culture and Anarchy' in *Problems in Materialism and Culture* (London: Verso/NLB, 1980), pp. 3–8.

34. Ibid., pp. 23–39. For a longer analysis of Cobbett, see R. Williams, *Cobbett* (Oxford University Press, 1983).

35. R. Williams, *Culture and Society*, op.cit., pp. 43–7, 153–61, 182–7, 258–84.

36. N. O'Sullivan, *Conservatism*, p. 9.

37. There are, of course, others which I do not discuss here. The most notable omission is the work of Habermas.

38. J. McCarney, op.cit., p. 13.

39. Jorge Larrain, 'On the Character of Ideology: Marx and the Present Debate in Britain', *Theory, Culture and Society*, Vol. 1 (Spring 1982) No. 1, pp. 5–22, p. 15.

40. See J. Larrain, *The Concept of Ideology* (London: Hutchinson, 1979), pp. 64–5. Also N. Abercrombie, S. Hill and B. S. Turner, *The Dominant Ideology Thesis*, p. 8.

41. Goran Therborn, *The Ideology of Power and the Power of Ideology* (London: New Left Books and Verso, 1980), p. 5. For a critique of Therborn, see N. Abercrombie, S. Hill and B. S. Turner, 'Determinacy and Indeterminacy in the Theory of Ideology', *New Left Review*, No. 142 (November/December 1983), pp. 55–66. Therborn has replied, criticising Abercrombie *et al.*'s work in 'The New Questions of Subjectivity', *New Left Review*, (January–February 1984), pp. 97–107.

42. The main works of the early period are *Madness and Civilization: A History of Insanity in the Age of Reason* (London: Tavistock, 1967) and *The Birth of the Clinic: An Archaeology of Medical Perception* (London: Tavistock, 1973). The middle period is represented by *The Order of Things: An Archaeology of the Human Sciences* (London: Tavistock, 1970) and *The Archaelogy of Knowledge* (London: Tavistock, 1972) and the later by *Discipline and Punish: The Birth of the Prison* (Harmondsworth: Penguin, 1979) and *The History of Sexuality: Volume One. An Introduction* (Harmondsworth: Penguin, 1981). There is now a growing secondary literature on Foucault. See, for example, Alan Sheridan, *Michel Foucault: The Will to Truth* (London: Tavistock, 1980), Hubert L. Dreyfus and Paul Rabinow, *Michel Foucault: Beyond Structuralism and Hermeneutics* (Brighton: Harvester, 1982), Barry Smart, *Foucault, Marxism and Critique* (London: Routledge & Kegan Paul, 1983), Pamela Major-Poetzl, *Michel Foucault's Archaeology of Western Culture: Towards a New Science of History* (Brighton: Harvester, 1983), Mark Cousins and Athar Hussain, *Michel Foucault* (London: Macmillan, 1984), Mark Poster, *Foucault, Marxism and History: Mode of Production versus Mode of Information* (Cambridge: Polity in association with Oxford: Blackwell, 1984), Martin O'Brien, 'Foucism, Marxory and Histault: A Critical Appraisal of Poster's *Foucault, Marxism and History*', *Theory, Culture and Society*, Vol. 3 (1986) No. 2, pp. 115–23.

43. M. Foucault, *The Archaeology of Knowledge*, p. 117.

44. See, for example, *The History of Sexuality*, Vol. 1, pp. 100–102.

45. Ibid.

46. As is brought out in the secondary literature cited above, note 42.

47. These fields are not seen as developing 'essences', however.

48. See Dreyfus and Rabinow, op.cit.

49. Max Weber, *The Methodology of the Social Sciences* (New York: The Free Press, 1949), p. 90.

50. The concept of 'preferred reading' is deployed in, for example, D. Morley, *The 'Nationwide' Audience: Structure and Decoding*, London:

British Film Institute, 1980 and criticised in D. Morley, 'The *"Nation-wide" Audience*—A critical postcript', *Screen Education* (Summer 1981) No. 39, pp. 3–14.

51. Roy King and Rod Morgan, with J. P. Martin and J. E. Thomas, *The Future of the Prison System* (Farnborough: Gower, 1980).
52. As discussed in the 'May' Report, *Committee of Inquiry into the United Kingdom Prison Services, 1979* (London: HMSO, 1979), Cmnd. 7673, especially pp. 61–73, paras 4.1–4.48.
53. As recommended by the May Report, ibid., pp. 67–73, paras 4.25–4.48.
54. These ideas are being developed in the course of research at the University of Edinburgh. I would like to thank Michael Adler, Sheila Henderson and Roy Sainsbury for useful discussions of this area.
55. Alvin Gouldner, *Against Fragmentation: The Origins of Marxism and the Sociology of the Intellectuals* (New York: Oxford University Press, 1985).
56. The relationship between discourse and ideology is not considered for the moment.
57. N. Abercrombie, S. Hill and B. Turner, *Sovereign Individuals of Capitalism*.
58. Ibid., pp. 72–3.
59. Ian Watt, *The Rise of the Novel: Studies in Defoe, Richardson and Fielding* (Harmondsworth: Penguin, 1963).
60. John Berger, *Ways of Seeing* (London: British Broadcasting Corporation and Harmondsworth: Penguin, 1972).
61. On Punk see, for example, Simon Frith, 'Post-punk blues', *Marxism Today*, Vol. 27 (1983) No. 3, pp. 18–21; David Widgery, *Beating Time: Riot 'n' Race 'n' Rock 'n' Roll* (London: Chatto, 1986); Dave Laing, 'Interpreting Punk Rock', *Marxism Today*, Vol. 22 (March 1978) No. 4, pp. 123–8; Dave Laing, *One-Chord Wonders* (Milton Keynes: Open University Press, 1985).
62. T. Lovell, *Pictures of Reality*.
63. Ibid., p. 65.
64. G. Lukács, *Writer and Critic* (London: Merlin Press, 1970), p. 34 quoted in Lovell, op.cit., p. 71.
65. Lovell, op.cit., pp. 76–8 and E. Bloch *et al.*, *Aesthetics and Politics* (London: New Left Books, 1977).
66. See also Raymond Williams, *Politics and Letters: Interviews with New Left Review* (London: New Left Books, 1979), pp. 214–29.
67. The relationship between modernism, post-modernism and realism is of great interest; see, for example, *Theory, Culture and Society*, Special Issue on the Future of Modernity, Vol. 2 (1985) No. 3.
68. Lovell, op.cit., p. 76.
69. N. Abercrombie *et al.*, *The Dominant Ideology Thesis*, op.cit.
70. CT and C. See also the discussion of individualism in Abercrombie *et al.*, *Sovereign Individuals of Capitalism*.
71. See, for example, M. Douglas, *Cultural Bias* (London: Royal Anthropological Society, 1978) and M. Douglas (ed.) *Essays in the Sociology of Perception* (London: Routledge & Kegan Paul, 1982).
72. N. Abercrombie, *Class, Structure and Knowledge*, for example, p. 55.

73. See J. Law and P. Lodge, *Science for Social Scientists*, pp. 125–54.

74. D. Bloor, *Knowledge and Social Imagery*, p. 5.

75. Ibid., pp. 4–5.

76. B. Barnes, *Interests and the Growth of Knowledge* (London: Routledge & Kegan Paul, 1977), p. 19.

77. See, for example, D. Bloor, *Knowledge and Social Imagery*, pp. 48–73 and Donald Mackenzie, *Statistics in Britain, 1865–1930: The Social Construction of Scientific Knowledge* (Edinburgh University Press, 1981).

78. M. B. Barnes and D. Mackenzie, 'On the Role of Interests in Scientific Change', in R. Wallis (ed.) *On the Margins of Science: The Social Construction of Rejected Knowledge*, Sociological Review Monograph, 27 (University of Keele, 1979) pp. 49–66, p. 54.

79. D. Mackenzie, op.cit.

80. Ibid., p. 31.

81. Ibid., p. 129.

82. Steven Yearley, 'Interactive-orientation and argumentation in scientific texts' in J. Law (ed.) *Power, Action and Belief: A New Sociology of Knowledge?* pp. 132–57.

83. S. Yearley, 'The Relationship between Epistemological and Sociological Cognitive Interests: Some Ambiguities Underlying the use of Interest Theory in the Study of Scientific Knowledge', *Studies in History and Philosophy of Science*, Vol. 13 (December 1982) No. 4, pp. 353–88, pp. 374–5.

84. B. Barnes, *Interests and the Growth of Knowledge*, p. 9.

85. B. Barnes, *T. S. Kuhn and Social Science* (London: Macmillan, 1982) p. 93.

86. S. Yearley, 'Interactive-orientation and argumentation in scientific texts', op.cit.

87. Ibid., p. 132.

88. Ibid., p. 133.

89. Barry Hindess, '"Interests" in political analysis' in J. Law (ed.) op.cit., pp. 112–31, p. 128.

90. Ibid., p. 129.

91. N. Abercrombie *et al.*, *Sovereign Individuals of Capitalism*, op.cit.

92. See Arthur Child, 'The Problem of Imputation in the Sociology of Knowledge', *Ethics*, Vol. 51 (January 1941) No. 2, pp. 200–19 and 'The Problem of Imputation Resolved' in J. Curtis and J. Petras (eds), *The Sociology of Knowledge* (London: Duckworth, 1970) pp. 96–109.

93. A. Child, 'The Problem of Imputation in the Sociology of Knowledge', pp. 213–8.

94. Ibid., p. 218.

95. Ariel Dorfman, *The Empire's Old Clothes: What Lone Ranger, Barbar and other innocent heroes do to our minds* (London: Pluto, 1983).

96. M. Douglas, op.cit. One study which uses the grid/group formula in a stimulating fashion is Celia Bloor and David Bloor, 'Twenty Industrial Scientists: A Preliminary Exercise' in M. Douglas (ed.) op.cit., pp. 83–102.

97. Steven Rayner, 'The politics of schism: routinisation and social control in the International Socialists/Socialist Workers' Party', in J. Law (ed.) op.cit., pp. 46–67.
98. Ibid., p. 48.
99. Ibid., p. 48.
100. Ibid., pp. 61.
101. Ibid., p. 65.
102. G. A. Cohen, *Karl Marx's Theory of History*, p. 250. Cohen's work has provoked a large critical response, which is detailed and considered in G. A. Cohen, 'Forces and Relations of Production' in Betty Matthews (ed.) *Marx: A Hundred Years On* (London: Lawrence & Wishart, 1983) pp. 111–34.
103. G. A. Cohen, *Karl Marx's Theory of History*, pp. 249–96, 'Forces and Relations of Production', pp. 115–21.
104. G. A. Cohen, *Karl Marx's Theory of History*, pp. 271–2.
105. Raymond Williams has developed one such cultural theory. For a critique see B. Longhurst, *Towards the Developed Sociology of Knowledge*, pp. 148–64.
106. For example, N. Abercrombie *et al.*, *The Dominant Ideology Thesis*, p. 3.
107. CT and C.
108. John Law, 'Editor's Introduction: Power/Knowledge and the Dissolution of the Sociology of Knowledge', in J. Law (ed.) op.cit., pp. 1–19.
109. David Ketter, Volker Meja and Nico Stehr, *Karl Mannheim*, op.cit.; A. P. Simonds, *Karl Mannheim's Sociology of Knowledge*, op.cit.; Colin Loader, *The Intellectual Development of Karl Mannheim*, op.cit.; Henk Woldring, *Karl Mannheim*, op.cit.
110. See, for example, S. Hekman, *Hermeneutics and the Sociology of Knowledge* (Cambridge: Polity, 1986) and Alan Scott, 'Politics and Method in Mannheim's *Ideology and Utopia*'. *Sociology*, Vol. 21 (February 1987) No. 1, pp. 41–54.
111. As at the ESRC symposium on segregation cited above, *Feminist Review* 17 (Autumn 1984), Special Issue, 'Many Voices, one Chant: Black Feminist Perspectives'.
112. For example, Raymond Williams, *Key Words: A Vocabulary of Culture and Society* (London: Fontana (Flamingo) 1983).

5 Conclusion: Conservative Thought

1. See, for example, Loader, op.cit., and Woldring, op.cit.
2. Having already spent a great deal of time on Mannheim's own study of conservatism I discuss it relatively little in this conclusion.
3. A point made by nearly all discussions of conservatism.
4. Robert Eccleshall, 'English Conservatism as Ideology', *Political Studies*, Vol. XXV, No. 1 (1977), pp. 62–83, p. 67.

5. Ibid., p. 62 and pp. 72–83.
6. Robert Eccleshall, 'Ideology as Commonsense: the case of British Conservatism', *Radical Philosophy*, No. 25 (Summer 1980), pp. 2–8.
7. CT and C.
8. Seymour Martin Lipset and Earl Raab, *The Politics of Unreason: Right-Wing Extremism in America, 1790–1970* (London: Heinemann, 1971).
9. R. J. Bennett, 'The Conservative Tradition of Thought: a right-wing phenomenon' in Neil Nugent and Roger King (eds), *The British Right: Conservative and Right Wing Politics in Britain* (Westmead: Saxon House, 1977), pp. 11–25.
10. Ibid.
11. R. J. Bennett, R. King and N. Nugent, 'Introduction: the concept of "the Right"' in Nugent and King, op.cit., pp. 3–10, pp. 8–9.
12. Samuel P. Huntington, 'Conservatism as an Ideology', *American Political Science Review*, Vol. 51, No. 2 (June 1957), pp. 454–73.
13. P. W. Buck, 'Introduction' to P. W. Buck, *How Conservatives Think* (Harmondsworth: Penguin, 1975).
14. N. Abercrombie, *Class, Structure and Knowledge*, p. 65.
15. Robert Nisbet, 'Conservatism' in T. Bottomore and R. Nisbet (eds), *A History of Sociological Analysis* (London: Heinemann, 1978), pp. 80–117, p. 97. See also, Robert Nisbet, *Conservatism: Dream and Reality* (Milton Keynes: Open University Press, 1986).
16. Ibid., pp. 97–105.
17. Roger Scruton, *The Meaning of Conservatism* (Harmondsworth: Penguin, 1980).
18. Ibid., p. 103. Assumptions about human nature occur all through Scruton's book, for example, p. 21, p. 25, pp. 28–9, p. 31, p. 75, p. 89, p. 102, p. 108.
19. Ibid., pp. 32–3.
20. Ibid., p. 31.
21. Ibid., pp. 56–8.
22. Ibid., pp. 52–3.
23. Ibid., p. 112.
24. Ibid., pp. 46–70.
25. CT, p. 113, C, p. 99.
26. As in Mannheim's later work and, for example, T. S. Eliot's social criticism.
27. The consideration of the relationship of conservatism to different periods and forms of capitalism could be profitably developed further. English conservatism's antipathy to industrial capitalism is discussed in a clear and informative fashion by Martin J. Wiener in his *English Culture and the Decline of the Industrial Spirit, 1850–1980* (Harmondsworth: Penguin, 1985).
28 As recognised by Nisbet, op.cit., p. 95.
29. Foucault's analysis in the first half of *Discipline and Punish* describes
30. the nature of power centred around the sovereign.

31. For a discussion of this general area see Mary Daly, *Gyn-Ecology: The Metaethics of Radical Feminism* (London: The Women's Press, 1979), especially pp. 37–8 and 73–105.

32. See Mackenzie, op.cit., p. 143; Bloor, *Knowledge and Social Imagery*, pp. 54–7; K. L. Caneva, 'From Galvinism to Electrodynamics: the transformation of German physics and its social context' in *Historical Studies in the Physical Sciences*, Vol. 9 (1978), pp. 63–159; William Coleman, 'Bateson and Chromosomes: Conservative Thought in Science', *Centaurus*, Vol. 15 (1970) Nos. 3–4, pp. 228–314; and Brian Wynne, 'Natural Knowledge and Social Context: Cambridge Physics and the Luminiferous Ether' in Barry Barnes and David Edge (eds), *Science in Context: Readings in the Sociology of Science* (Milton Keynes: Open University Press, 1982) pp. 212–31.

33. R. Coward, *Patriarchal Precedents*, p. 34.

34. Ibid., p. 54.

35. Ibid., p. 66.

36. Ibid., p. 67.

37. Richard Evans, *The Feminists* (London: Croom Helm, 1977).

38. For a rather different characterisation of liberalism, which attempts to demonstrate its changing patriarchal nature, see Zillan R. Eisenstein, *The Radical Future of Liberal Feminism* (New York: Longman, 1981).

39. Philip Norton and Arthur Aughey, *Conservatives and Conservatism* (London: Temple Smith, 1981).

40. Ibid., pp. 53–89.

41. For example, N. O'Sullivan, *Conservatism*, p. 9. See also R. Nisbet, 'Conservatism', op.cit., who in addition relates conservatism to the Industrial Revolution.

42. Lipset and Raab, op.cit.

43. R. Williams, *Culture and Society*.

44. See N. Abercrombie, 'Mass Society and the Planning Mind', unpublished.

45. Andrea Dworkin, *Right-Wing Women: The Politics of Domesticated Females* (London: The Women's Press, 1983) and Beatrix Campbell, *The Iron Ladies: Why do Women Vote Tory?* (London: Virago, 1987).

46. A. Dworkin, op.cit., especially p. 231.

47. As maintained in N. Abercrombie and B. Longhurst, 'Interpreting Mannheim', pp. 10–11. This argument has been criticised by Scott, op.cit., fn. 2, p. 53.

48. Therefore interpellating the subject in a particular fashion. See Louis Althusser, 'Ideology and Ideological State Apparatuses; Notes Towards an Investigation' in his *Lenin and Philosophy and other Essays* (London: New Left Books, 1971), pp. 121–73.

49. As might be derived from a reading of Freud; see, for example, Sigmund Freud, 'Three Essays on the Theory of Sexuality' in *On Sexuality* (Harmondsworth: Penguin, 1977), pp. 39–169 and S. Freud, 'Feminity' in *New Introductory Lectures on Psychoanalysis* (Harmondsworth: Penguin, 1973), pp. 145–69.

50. See Stuart Hall, 'The Great Moving Right Show' in S. Hall and M. Jacques (eds), *The Politics of Thatcherism* (London: Lawrence & Wishart, 1983).
51. For Stuart Hall's analyses see, for example, S. Hall and M. Jacques (eds), op.cit. These are criticised by Bob Jessop *et al.* 'Authoritarian Populism, Two Nations and Thatcherism', *New Left Review* (September/October 1984) No. 147, pp. 32–60. Hall has replied in S. Hall, 'Authoritarian Populism', *New Left Review* (May-June 1985) No. 151, pp. 115–24. This prompted further comment from Jessop *et al.*, 'Thatcherism and the Politics of Hegemony: a reply to Stuart Hall', in *New Left Review* (September-October 1985) No. 153, pp. 87–101. For other recent analyses of the Right, Conservatism and Thatcherism see, for example, Ruth Levitas (ed.), *The Ideology of the New Right* (Cambridge: Polity, 1986) and K. Minogue and R. Biddis *Thatcherism: Personality and Politics* (London: Macmillan, 1987).

Bibliography

Archive Sources

The Mannheim papers at the University of Keele.

Books and Articles

Abel, Elizabeth (ed.), *Writing and Sexual Difference* (Brighton: Harvester, 1982).
Abercrombie, Nicholas, *Class, Structure and Knowledge: Problems in the Sociology of Knowledge* (Oxford: Blackwell, 1980).
——, 'The Sociology of Knowledge as a Discipline', *Transactions of the Annual Conference of the British Sociological Association* held at the University of Lancaster, 8–11 April 1980, Vol. III, pp. 871–81.
——, 'Relativism', unpublished paper.
——, 'Mass Society and the Planning Mind', unpublished paper.
Abercrombie, Nicholas, Hill, Stephen, Turner, Bryan S., *The Dominant Ideology Thesis* (London: Allen & Unwin, 1980).
——, 'Determinacy and Indeterminacy in the Theory of Ideology', *New Left Review*, No. 142 (November-December 1982), pp. 55–66.
——, *Sovereign Individuals of Capitalism* (London: Allen & Unwin, 1986).
Abercrombie, Nicholas and Longhurst, Brian, 'Mannheim's Soul: A Comment on Vallas', *Sociology*, Vol. 15 (August 1981) No. 3, pp. 424–7.
Abercrombie, Nicholas and Longhurst, Brian, 'Interpreting Mannheim', *Theory, Culture and Society*, Vol. 2 (1983) No. 1, pp. 5–15.
Abercrombie, Nicholas and Turner, Bryan S., 'The Dominant Ideology Thesis', *British Journal of Sociology*, Vol. 29 (1978) No. 2, pp. 149–70.
Abercrombie, Nicholas and Urry, John, *Capital, Labour and the Middle Classes* (London: Allen & Unwin, 1983).
Adlam, Diana, 'The Case against Capitalist Patriarchy', *m/f* (1979) No. 3, pp. 83–102.
Adlam, Diana *et al.*, 'Psychology, Ideology and the Human Subject', *Ideology and Consciousness* (May 1977) No. 1, pp. 5–56.
Adorno, T. W., 'The Sociology of Knowledge and its Consciousness' in his *Prisms*, pp. 37–49.
——, *Prisms* (London: Spearman, 1967).
——, *Negative Dialectics* (London: Routledge & Kegan Paul, 1973).
Althusser, Louis, 'Ideology and Ideological State Apparatuses' in his *Lenin and Philosophy and Other Essays*, pp. 121–73.
——, *Lenin and Philosophy and Other Essays* (London: New Left Books, 1971).
——, 'Marxism and Humanism' in his *For Marx*, pp. 221–47.
——, *For Marx* (London: New Left Books, 1977).

Althusser, Louis and Balibar, Etienne, *Reading Capital* (London: New Left Books, 1970).

Anderson, Perry, *Arguments within English Marxism* (London: New Left Books/Verso, 1980).

——, *In the Tracks of Historical Materialism: The Wellek Library Lectures* (London: Verso, 1983).

Ashcraft, Richard, 'Political Theory and Political Action in Karl Mannheim's thought: Reflections upon *Ideology and Utopia* and its critics', *Comparative Studies in Society and History*, Vol. 23 (1981) No. 1, pp. 23–50.

Ascoli, Max, 'On Mannheim's *Ideology and Utopia*', *Social Research*, Vol. 5 (February 1938) No. 1, pp. 101–6.

Bantock, G. H. 'The Cultural Implications of Planning and Popularization', *Scrutiny*, Vol. 14 (1947) No. 3, pp. 171–84.

Barnes, Barry, *Scientific Knowledge and Sociological Theory* (London: Routledge & Kegan Paul, 1974).

——, *Interests and the Growth of Knowledge* (London: Routledge & Kegan Paul, 1977).

——, *T. S. Kuhn and Social Science* (London: Macmillan, 1982).

——, 'On the conventional character of knowledge and cognition', in Knorr-Cetina, Karin and Mulkay, Michael (eds), op.cit., pp. 19–51.

Barnes, Barry and Bloor, David, 'Relativism, Rationalism and the Sociology of Knowledge' in Hollis, Martin and Lukes, Steven (eds), *Rationality and Relativism* (Oxford: Blackwell, 1982) pp. 21–47.

Barnes, Barry and Edge, David (eds), *Science in Context: Readings in the Sociology of Science* (Milton Keynes: The Open University Press, 1982).

Barnes, Barry and Shapin, Steven (eds), *Natural Order: Historical Studies of Scientific Culture* (Beverley Hills/London: Sage, 1979).

Barnes, M. B. and Mackenzie, Donald, 'On the Role of Interests in Scientific Change' in R. Wallis (ed.), *On the Margins of Science: The Social Construction of Rejected Knowledge*, Sociological Review Monograph 27, University of Keele, 1979, pp. 49–66.

Barrett, Michèle, *Women's Oppression Today: Problems in Marxist Feminist Analysis* (London: Verso and New Left Books, 1980).

Barrett, Michèle and McIntosh, Mary, 'Christine Delphy: Towards a Materialist Feminism?', *Feminist Review* (1979) No. 1, pp. 95–106.

Barrett, Michèle *et al.* (eds), *Ideology and Cultural Production* (London: Croom Helm, 1979).

Barthes, Roland, *Mythologies* (St. Albans, Herts.: Granada, 1976).

Baum, Gregory, *Truth Beyond Relativism: Karl Mannheim's Sociology of Knowledge* (Milwaukee: Marquette University Press, 1977).

Bauman, Zygmunt, *Hermeneutics and Social Science: Approaches to Understanding* (London: Hutchinson, 1978).

Beechy, Veronica, 'On Patriarchy', *Feminist Review* (1979) No. 3, pp. 69–82.

Belgion, Montgomery, 'The Germanization of Britain', *New English Weekly*, Vol. 26 (February 15 1945) No. 18, pp. 137–8.

Belsey, Andrew, 'The Real Meaning of Conservatism', *Radical Philosophy* (Summer 1981) No. 28, pp. 1–15.

Belsey, Catherine, *Critical Practice* (London: Methuen, 1980).

Bennett, R. J., 'The Conservative tradition of thought: a right-wing phenomena', in Nugent, Neil and King, Roger (eds), op.cit., pp. 11–25.

Bennett, R. J., King, Roger, and Nugent, Neil, 'Introduction: The concept of "the Right"', in Nugent, Neil and King, Roger (eds), op.cit., pp. 3–10.

Bennett, Tony *et al.* (eds), *Popular Culture and Social Relations* (Milton Keynes: Open University Press, 1986).

Benton, Ted, '"Objective" Interests and the Sociology of Power', *Sociology*, Vol. 15 (1981) No. 2, pp. 161–84.

Berdahl, R. M. 'Prussian Aristocracy and Conservative Ideology: A Methodological Examination', *Social Science Information*, Vol. 15 (1976) Nos. 4 and 5, pp. 583–99.

Berger, John, *Ways of Seeing* (London: British Broadcasting Corporation and Harmondsworth: Penguin, 1972).

Berger, Peter and Luckmann, Thomas, *The Social Construction of Reality* (Harmondworth: Penguin, 1971).

Blake, Robert, *The Conservative Party from Peel to Churchill* (London: Fontana/Collins, 1972).

Bleicher, Josef, *Contemporary Hermeneutics: Hermeneutics as method, philosophy and critique* (London: Routledge & Kegan Paul, 1980).

Bloch, Ernst (ed.), *Aesthetics and Politics* (London: New Left Books, 1977).

Bloor, Celia and Bloor, David, 'Twenty Industrial Scientists: A Preliminary Exercise' in Douglas, Mary (ed.) op.cit., pp. 83–102.

Bloor, David, 'Wittgenstein and Mannheim on the Sociology of Mathematics', *Studies in History and Philosophy of Science*, Vol. 4 (1973) No. 2, pp. 173–91.

——, *Knowledge and Social Imagery* (London: Routledge & Kegan Paul, 1976).

——, 'Durkheim and Mauss Revisited: Classification and the Sociology of Knowledge', *Studies in History and Philosophy of Science*, Vol. 13 (December 1982) No. 4, pp. 267–97.

——, 'Reply to Gerd Buchdahl', *Studies in History and Philosophy of Science*, Vol. 13 (December 1982) No. 4, pp. 305–11.

——, 'Reply to Steven Lukes', *Studies in History and Philosophy of Science*, Vol. 13 (December 1982) No. 4, pp. 319–23.

——, 'Polyhedra and the Abominations of Leviticus: Cognitive Styles in Mathematics' in Douglas, Mary (ed.), op.cit., pp. 191–218.

——, *Wittgenstein: A Social Theory of Knowledge* (London: Macmillan, 1983).

Bogardus, Emory S., 'Mental Processes and Democracy', *Sociology and Social Research*, Vol. 41 (November-December 1956) No. 2, pp. 127–32.

——, 'Mannheim and Systematic Sociology', *Sociology and Social Research*, Vol. 43 (January–February 1959) No. 3, pp. 213–7.

Boskoff, Alvin, 'Karl Mannheim: Theories of Social Manipulation in Transitional Society' in his *Theory in American Sociology: Major Sources and Applications* (New York: Crowell, 1969) pp. 159–81.

Bottomore, Tom B., 'Some Reflections on the Sociology of Knowledge', *British Journal of Sociology*, Vol. 7 (March 1956) No. 1, pp. 52–8.

Bourdieu, Pierre, *Distinction: A Social Critique of the Judgement of Taste* (London: Routledge & Kegan Paul, 1984).

Brake, Mike, *Comparative Youth Culture: The Sociology of Youth Cultures and Youth Subcultures in America, Britain and Canada* (London: Routledge & Kegan Paul, 1985).

Brenner, Johanna and Ramas, Moria, 'Rethinking Women's Oppression', *New Left Review* (March-April 1984) No. 144, pp. 33–71.

Brewster, Ben, 'Fetishism in *Capital* and *Reading Capital*', *Economy and Society*, Vol. 5 (1976) No. 3, pp. 344–51.

Brown, Beverley and Cousins, Mark, 'The Linguistic Fault: The Case of Foucault's Archaeology', *Economy and Society*, Vol. 9 (August 1980) No. 3, pp. 251–78.

Brunsdon, Charlotte and Morley, David, *Everyday Television: 'Nationwide'* (London: British Film Institute, 1978).

Buchdahl, Gerd, 'Editorial Response to David Bloor', *Studies in History and Philosophy of Science*, Vol. 13 (December 1982) No. 4, pp. 299–304.

Buck, Philip W. (ed. and intro.), *How Conservatives Think* (Harmondsworth: Penguin, 1975).

Buck-Morss, Susan, *The Origin of Negative Dialectics* (Hassocks: Harvester, 1977).

Bulmer, Ralph, 'Why is the Cassowary not a Bird? A Problem of Zoological Taxonomy among the Karam of the New Guinea Highlands,' in *Man*, New Series, Vol. 2 (March 1967) No. 1, pp. 5–25.

Campbell, Beatrix, *The Iron Ladies: Why do Women Vote Tory?* (London: Virago, 1987).

Caneva, Kenneth, L., 'From Galvinism to Electrodynamics: the transformation of German Physics and its Social Context', *Historical Studies in the Physical Sciences*, Vol. 9 (1978) pp. 63–159.

Caplan, Jane, 'Conservatism and the Family', *History Workshop* (Autumn 1983) No. 16, pp. 123–8.

Carroll, John, 'Sport: Virtue and Grace', *Theory, Culture and Society*, Vol. 3 (1986) No. 1, pp. 91–8.

Cashmore, Ernest, *Rastaman: the Rastafarian Movement in England* (London: Allen & Unwin, 1979).

Centre for Contemporary Cultural Studies, *Making Histories: Studies in History-Writing and Politics* (London: Hutchinson, 1981).

——, *The Empire Strikes Back: Race and Racism in '70s Britain* (London: Hutchinson, 1982).

Chambers, Iain, *Popular Culture: The Metropolitan Experience* (London: Methuen, 1986).

Chambers, Iain *et al.*, 'Marxism and Culture', *Screen*, Vol. 18 (Winter 1977/78) No. 4, pp. 109–19.

Child, Arthur, 'The Problem of Imputation in the Sociology of Knowledge', *Ethics*, Vol. 51 (January 1941) No. 2, pp. 200–19.

——, 'The Existential Determination of Thought', *Ethics*, Vol. 52 (January 1942) No. 1, pp. 153–85.

——, 'On the Theory of the Categories', *Philosophy and Phenomenological Research*, Vol. 7 (December 1946) pp. 316–35.

——, 'The Problem of Truth in the Sociology of Knowledge', *Ethics*, Vol. 58 (October 1947) No. 1, pp. 18–34.

——, 'The Problem of Imputation Resolved' in Curtis, J. E. and Petras, J. W. (eds), op.cit., pp. 668–85.

Childe, Vere G., *Society and Knowledge* (New York: Harper & Brothers, 1956).

Clarke, J. *et al.* (eds), *Culture and Crisis in Britain in the '30s* (London: Lawrence & Wishart, 1979).

Clarke, John, Critcher, Chas, and Johnson, Richard (eds), *Working-Class Culture: Studies in history and theory* (London: Hutchinson, 1979).

Clarke, John *et al.*, 'Subcultures, Cultures and Class', in Hall and Jefferson (eds), op.cit., pp. 7–74.

Clarke, Simon, 'Socialist Humanism and the Critique of Economism', *History Workshop* (Autumn 1979) No. 8, pp. 138–56.

Clarke, Simon *et al.*, *One-Dimensional Marxism: Althusser and the Politics of Culture* (London: Allison & Busby, 1980).

Cockburn, Cynthia, *Brothers: Male Dominance and Technological Change* (London: Pluto, 1983).

——, *Machinery of Dominance: Women, Men and Technical Knowhow* (London: Pluto, 1985).

Cohen, G. A., *Karl Marx's Theory of History: A Defence* (Oxford: Clarendon Press, 1978).

——, 'Forces and Relations of Production', in Matthews, B. (ed.), op.cit., pp. 111–34.

Coleman, William, 'Bateson and Chromosomes: Conservative thought in Science', *Centaurus*, Vol. 15 (1970) Nos. 3–4, pp. 228–314.

Collins, Harry, 'Stages in the Empirical Programme of Relativism', *Social Studies of Science*, Vol. 11 (Feburary 1981) No. 1, pp. 3–10.

——, *Changing Order* (London: Sage, 1985).

Committee of Inquiry into the United Kingdom Prison Services, 1979 Cmnd. 7673 (The 'May' Report) (London: HMSO, 1979).

Congdon, L., 'Karl Mannheim as Philosopher', *Journal of European Studies*, Vol. 7 (March 1977) No. 1, pp. 1–18.

Coombs, Robert H. 'Karl Mannheim, Epistemology and the Sociology of Knowledge', *Sociological Quarterly*, Vol. 7 (Spring 1966) No. 2, pp. 229–33.

Coser, Lewis A., 'Karl Mannheim 1893–1947' in Coser, L., *Masters of Sociological Thought: Ideas in Historical and Social Context* (New York: Harcourt Brace Jovanovich, 1977) pp. 429–63.

Cousins, Mark and Hussain, Athar, *Michel Foucault* (London: Macmillan, 1984).

Coward, Rosalind, 'Class, "Culture" and the Social Formation', *Screen*, Vol. 18 (Spring 1977) No. 1, pp. 75–105.

——, '"This novel changes lives"; Are Women's novels Feminist Novels?' *Feminist Review* (1980) No. 5, pp. 53–64.

——, *Patriarchal Precedents: Sexuality and Social Relations* (London: Routledge & Kegan Paul, 1983).

Cowling, Maurice (ed.), *Conservative Essays* (London: Cassell, 1978).

Craib, Ian, 'Lukács and the Marxist critique of sociology', *Radical Philosophy* (Summer 1977) No. 17, pp. 26–37.

Culler, Jonathan, *Structuralist Poetics: Structuralism, Linguistics and the Study of Literature* (London: Routledge & Kegan Paul, 1975).

——, *The Pursuit of Signs: Semiotics, Literature, Deconstruction* (London: Routledge & Kegan Paul, 1981).

——, *On Deconstruction: Theory and Criticism after Structuralism* (London: Routledge & Kegan Paul, 1983).

Curtis, James E. and Petras, John W. (eds), *The Sociology of Knowledge* (London: Duckworth, 1970).

Dahlke, H. Otto, 'The Sociology of Knowledge' in Barnes, H. E., Becker, H. and Becker, F. B. (eds), *Contemporary Social Theory* (New York: Russell & Russell, 1971) pp. 64–89.

Daly, Mary, *Gyn/Ecology: The Metaethics of Radical Feminism* (London: The Women's Press, 1979).

Davis, Howard H., *Beyond Class Images: Explorations in the Structure of Social Consciousness* (London: Croom Helm, 1979).

Davis, Mike, 'The New Right's Road to Power', *New Left Review* (July-August 1981) No. 128, pp. 28–49.

Delphy, Christine, *The Main Enemy: A Materialist Analysis of Women's Oppression* (London: Women's Resources and Research Centre, 1977).

——, 'Women in Stratification Studies' in Roberts, H. (ed.), op.cit., pp. 114–28.

——, *Close to Home: A Materialist Analysis of Women's Oppression* (London: Hutchinson, 1984).

Dews, Peter, 'The Nouvelle Philosophie and Foucault', *Economy and Society*, Vol. 8 (May 1979) No. 2, pp. 127–71.

Dixon, Keith, *The Sociology of Belief: Fallacy and Foundation* (London: Routledge & Kegan Paul, 1980).

Donzelot, Jacques, 'The Poverty of Political Culture', *Ideology and Consciousness* (Spring 1979) No. 5, pp. 73–86.

——, *The Policing of Families: Welfare versus the State* (London: Hutchinson, 1980).

——, 'Pleasure in Work', *Ideology and Consciousness* (Winter) 1981/82) No. 9, pp. 3–28.

Dorfman, Ariel, *The Empire's Old Clothes: What the Lone Ranger, Barbar, and other innocent heroes do to our minds* (London: Pluto, 1983).

Douglas, Mary, *Implicit Meanings: Essays in Anthropology* (London: Routledge & Kegan Paul, 1975).

——, *Cultural Bias* (London: Royal Anthropology Society, 1978).

Douglas, Mary (ed.), *Essays in the Sociology of Perception* (London: Routledge & Kegan Paul, 1982).

Dreyfus, Hubert L. and Rabinow, Paul, *Michel Foucault: Beyond Structuralism and Hermeneutics* (Brighton: Harvester, 1982).

Drucker, H., 'Marx's Concept of Ideology', *Philosophy*, Vol. 47 (1972) pp. 152–61.

Dworkin, Andrea, *Right-Wing Women: The Politics of Domesticated Females* (London: The Women's Press, 1983).

Eagleton, Mary (ed.), *Feminist Literary Theory: A Reader* (Oxford: Blackwell, 1986).

Eagleton, Terry, *Marxism and Literary Criticism* (London: Methuen, 1977).

——, 'Text, Ideology, Realism', in Said, Edward W. (ed.), *Literature and Society* (Baltimore: John Hopkins, 1980) pp. 149–73.

——, *Literary Theory* (Oxford: Blackwell, 1983).

Eccleshall, Robert, 'English Conservatism as Ideology', *Political Studies*, Vol. XXV (1977) No. 1, pp. 52–83.

——, 'Ideology as Commonsense: The Case of British Conservatism', *Radical Philosphy* (Summer 1980) No. 25, pp. 2–8.

Editorial Collective, 'Author's Response', *Ideology and Consciousness* (Spring 1978) No. 3, pp. 122–7.

Eisenstein, Hester, *Contemporary Feminist Thought* (London: Unwin, 1984).

Eisenstein, Zillah R., 'Developing a Theory of Capitalist Patriarchy and Socialist Feminism' in Eisenstein (ed.), op.cit., pp. 5–40.

——, 'Some Notes on the Relations of Capitalist Patriarchy' in Eisenstein (ed.), op.cit., pp. 41–55.

——, *The Radical Future of Liberal Feminism* (New York: Longman, 1981).

——, 'The Sexual Politics of the New Right: Understanding the "Crisis of Liberalism" for the 1980s', *Signs*, Vol. 7 (Spring 1982) No. 3, pp. 567–88.

Eisenstein, Zillah R. (ed.), *Capitalist Patriarchy and the Case for Socialist Feminism* (New York: Monthly Review, 1979).

Eliot, George, *The Mill on the Floss* (Harmondworth: Penguin, 1979).

Eliot, T. S., *The Idea of a Christian Society* (London: Faber, 1939).

——, *Notes toward the Definition of Culture* (New York: Harcourt Brace & Co., 1949).

Epstein, Klaus, *The Genesis of German Conservatism* (Princeton: Princeton University Press, 1966).

Evans, Richard J., *The Feminists* (London: Croom Helm, 1977).

Feminist Review, Special Issue, 'Many Voices, One Chant: Black Feminist Perspectives' (Autumn 1984) No. 17.

Fine, Ben, 'Struggles against Discipline: The Theory and Politics of Michel Foucault', *Capital and Class* (Autumn 1979) No. 9, pp. 75–96.

Firestone, Shulamith, *The Dialectic of Sex* (London: The Women's Press, 1979).

Fleming, Donald and Bailyn, Bernard (eds), *The Intellectual Migration: Europe and America, 1930–1960* (Cambridge, Mass.: Harvard University Press, 1969).

Floud, Jean, 'Karl Mannheim' in Raison, Timothy (ed.) op.cit., pp. 272–83.

Foucault, Michel, *Madness and Civilization* (London: Tavistock, 1967).

——, *The Order of Things* (London: Tavistock, 1970).

——, *The Archaeology of Knowledge* (London: Tavistock, 1972).

——, *The Birth of the Clinic* (London: Tavistock, 1973).

——, *Language, Counter-Memory, Practice* (Oxford: Blackwell, 1977).

——, 'Politics and the Study of Discourse', *Ideology and Consciousness* (Spring 1978) No. 3, pp. 7–26.

——, 'On Governmentality', *Ideology and Consciousness* (Autumn 1979) No. 6, pp. 5–21.

——, *Discipline and Punish* (Harmondsworth: Penguin, 1979).

——, *Power/Knowledge: Selected Interviews and Other Writings 1972–1977* (Brighton: Harvester, 1980).

——, 'The Order of Discourse' in Young, R. (ed.), op.cit., pp. 48–78.

——, *The History of Sexuality: Volume 1* (Harmondworth: Penguin, 1981).

——, *The History of Sexuality: Volume 2: The Use of Pleasure* (Harmondsworth: Penguin, 1987).

Freud, Sigmund, 'Feminity' in Freud, S., *New Introductory Lectures on Psychoanalysis*, pp. 145–69.

——, *New Introductory Lectures on Psychoanalysis* (Harmondsworth: Penguin, 1973).

——, 'Three Essays on the Theory of Sexuality' in Freud, S., *On Sexuality*, pp. 39–181.

——, *On Sexuality* (Harmondsworth: Penguin, 1977).

Freudenthal, Gad, 'How Strong is Dr Bloor's "Strong Programme"?' *Studies in History of Science*, Vol. 10 (1979) No. 1, pp. 67–83.

Frisby, David, *The Alienated Mind: The Sociology of Knowledge in Germany 1918–33* (London: Heinemann, 1983).

Frith, Simon, *Sound Effects: Youth, Leisure and the Politics of Rock 'n' Roll* (London: Constable, 1983).

——, 'Post-Punk Blues', *Marxism Today*, Vol. 27 (1983) No. 3, pp. 18–21.

Frith, Simon and McRobbie, Angela, 'Rock and Sexuality', *Screen Education* (Winter 1978/79) No. 29, pp. 3–19.

Fuse, Toyomasa, 'Sociology of Knowledge Revisited: Some Remaining Problems and Prospects', *Sociological Inquiry*, Vol. 37 (Spring 1967) No. 2, pp. 241–53.

Gabel, Joseph, 'Hungarian Marxism', *Telos* (Autumn 1975), No. 25, pp. 185–91.

——, 'The "Mannheim Problem" in France', *The Newsletter of the International Society for the Sociology of Knowledge*, Vol. 9 (August 1983) Nos. 1 and 2, pp. 15–18.

Gabor, Eva, 'Mannheim in Hungary and in Weimar Germany', *The Newsletter of the International Society for the Sociology of Knowledge*, Vol. 9 (August 1983) Nos. 1 and 2, pp. 7–14.

Gadamer, Hans-Georg, *Truth and Method* (London: Sheed & Ward, 1975).

Gamble, Andrew, *The Conservative Nation* (London: Routledge & Kegan Paul, 1974).

——, 'The Decline of the Conservative Party', *Marxism Today*, Vol. 23 (November 1979) No. 11, pp. 6–11.

Garfinkel, Harold, *Studies in Ethnomethodology* (Englewood Cliffs: Prentice-Hall, 1967. Reprinted Cambridge: Polity, 1984).

Garnsey, Elizabeth, 'Women's Work and Theories of Class Stratification', *Sociology*, Vol. 12 (1978) No. 2, pp. 223–43.

Gay, Peter, *Weimar Culture: The Outsider as Insider* (London: Secker & Warburg, 1969).

Gellatly, Angus, 'Logical Necessity and the Strong Programme for the Sociology of Knowledge', *Studies in History and Philosophy of Science* Vol. 11 (1980) No. 4, pp. 325–39.

Geuss, Raymond, *The Idea of a Critical Theory: Habermas and the Frankfurt School* (Cambridge: Cambridge University Press, 1981).

Giddens, Anthony, *Studies in Social and Political Theory* (London: Hutchinson, 1977).

——, *Central Problems in Social Theory* (London: Macmillan, 1979).

——, *A Contemporary Critique of Historical Materialism* (London: Macmillan, 1981).

Giddens, Anthony and Held, David (eds), *Classes, Power and Conflict* (London: Macmillan, 1982).

Gilroy, Paul, 'Steppin' out of Babylon—Race, Class and Autonomy' in Centre for Contemporary Cultural Studies, *The Empire Strikes Back*, op.cit., pp. 276–314.

Giner, Salvador, *Mass Society* (London: Martin Robertson, 1976).

Gluck, Samuel E., 'The Epistemology of Mannheim's Sociology of Knowledge', *Methodos*, Vol. 6 (1954) No. 23, pp. 225–34.

Goldthorpe, John H., 'Women and Class Analysis: In defence of the conventional view', *Sociology*, Vol. 17 (November, 1983) No. 4, pp. 465–88.

Gordon, Joy, 'On Structures of Thinking', *The Newsletter of the International Society for the Sociology of Knowledge*, Vol. 9 (August 1983) Nos. 1 and 2, pp. 19–22.

Gordon, Linda and Hunter, Allen, 'Sex, Family and the New Left: Anti-Feminism as a Political Force', *Radical America*, joint issue, vols. 11 and 12 (November 1977–February 1978), nos. 6 and 1, pp. 9–25.

Gouldner, Alvin, *Against Fragmentation: The Origins of Marxism and the Sociology of the Intellectuals* (New York: Oxford University Press, 1985).

Greene, Gayle and Kahn, Coppelia (eds), *Making a Difference: Feminist Literary Criticism* (London: Methuen, 1985).

Greenleaf, W. H., *Oakeshott's Philosophical Politics* (London: Longmans, 1966).

——, 'The Character of Modern British Conservatism' in Benewick, Robert, Berki, R. N. and Parekh, Bhikhu (eds), *Knowledge and Belief in Politics* (London: Allen & Unwin, 1973) pp. 177–212.

Gurvitch, Georges, *The Social Framework of Knowledge* (Oxford: Blackwell, 1971).

Hall, Stuart, 'Some problems with the Ideology/Subject couplet' *Ideology and Consciousness* (Spring 1978) No. 3, pp. 113–21.

——, 'The Great Moving Right Show' in S. Hall and M. Jacques (eds), op.cit.

——, 'Recent developments in theories of language and ideology: a critical note' in Hall, S. *et al.* (eds), *Culture, Media, Language*, pp. 157–62.

——, 'In Defence of Theory' in Samuel, R. (ed.), op.cit., pp. 378–85.

——, 'The Problem of Ideology: Marxism without Guarantees' in Matthews, B. (ed.), op.cit., pp. 57–85.

——, 'Authoritarian Populism', *New Left Review* (May/June 1985) No. 151, pp. 115–24.

Hall, Stuart and Jacques, Martin (eds), *The Politics of Thatcherism* (London: Lawrence & Wishart, 1983).

Hall, Stuart and Jefferson, Tony (eds), *Resistance through Rituals: Youth subcultures in post-war Britain* (London: Hutchinson, 1976).

Hall, Stuart *et al.*, *Policing the Crisis: Mugging, The State and Law and Order* (London: Macmillan, 1978).

Hall, Stuart *et al.* (eds), *Culture, Media, Language* (London: Hutchinson, 1980).

Hamilton, Peter, *Knowledge and Social Structure: An Introduction to the classical argument in the sociology of knowledge* (London: Routledge & Kegan Paul, 1974).

Hargreaves, Jenifer (ed.), *Sport, Culture and Ideology* (London: Routledge & Kegan Paul, 1982).

Hargreaves, Jenifer, 'Where's the Virtue? Where's the Grace? A Discussion of the Social Production of Gender through Sport', *Theory, Culture and Society*, Vol. 3 (1986) No. 1, pp. 109–21.

Hargreaves, John, *Sport, Power and Culture* (Cambridge: Polity, 1986).

Harloe, Michael, 'Sector and Class: A Critical Comment', *International Journal of Urban and Regional Research*, Vol. 8 (1984) No. 2, pp. 228–37.

Harris, Nigel, *Beliefs in Society* (Harmondsworth: Penguin, 1971).

Hartman, Heidi, 'Capitalism, Patriarchy and Job Segregation by Sex' in Eisenstein, Z. R. (ed.), op.cit., pp. 206–47.

——, 'The Unhappy Marriage or Marxism and Feminism: Towards a More Progressive Union' in Sargent, L. (ed.), op.cit., pp. 1–41, originally published in *Capital and Class* (Summer 1979) No. 8, pp. 1–33.

——, 'Summary and Response: Continuing the Discussion' in Sargent, L. (ed.), op.cit., pp. 363–73.

Hartung, Frank E., 'Problems of the Sociology of Knowledge' in Curtis, James E. and Petras, John W. (eds), *The Sociology of Knowledge* (London: Duckworth, 1970) pp. 686–705.

Harvey, Lee, 'The Use and Abuse of Kuhnian Paradigms in the Sociology of Knowledge', *Sociology*, Vol. 16 (February 1982) No. 1, pp. 85–101.

Heeren, John, 'Karl Mannheim and the Intellectual Elite', *British Journal of Sociology*, Vol. 22 (March 1971) No. 1, pp. 1–15.

Hekman, Susan, *Hermeneutics and the Sociology of Knowledge* (Cambridge: Polity, 1986).

——, 'Re-Interpreting Mannheim', *Theory, Culture and Society*, Vol. 3 (1986) No. 1, pp. 137–42.

Hesse, Mary, 'Comments on the papers of David Bloor and Steven Lukes', *Studies in History and Philosophy of Science*, Vol. 13 (December 1982) No. 4, pp. 325–31.

Hibbin, Sally (ed.), *Politics, Ideology and the State* (London: Lawrence & Wishart, 1978).

Hicks, Emily, 'Cultural Marxism: Nonsynchrony and Feminist Practice' in Sargent, L. (ed.), op.cit., pp. 219–37.

Hindess, Barry, 'Power, Interests and the Outcomes of Struggles' *Sociology*, Vol. 16 (November 1982) No. 4, pp. 498–511.

——, '"Interests" in Political Analysis' in Law, J. (ed.), op.cit., pp. 120–31.

Hinshawe, Virgil G., 'Epistemological Relativism and the Sociology of Knowledge', *Philosophy of Science*, Vol. 15 (January 1948) No. 1, pp. 4–10.

Hirst, Paul Q., *On Law and Ideology* (London: Macmillan, 1979).

Hodge, H. A. 'Lukács on Irrationalism' in Parkinson, G. H. R. (ed.), op.cit., pp. 86–108.

Hollis, Martin and Lukes S., 'Introduction' to Hollis and Lukes, op.cit., pp. 1–20.

Hollis, Martin and Lukes, Steven (eds), *Rationality and Relativism* (Oxford: Blackwell, 1982).

Horowitz, Irving L., 'Science, Criticism and the Sociology of Knowledge', *Philosophy and Phenomenological Research*, Vol. 21 (December 1960) No. 2, pp. 173–86.

——, *Philosophy, Science and the Sociology of Knowledge* (Springfield, Illinois: Charles C. Thomas, 1961).

——, 'A Formalization of the Sociology of Knowledge', *Behavioural Science*, Vol. 9 (January 1964) No. 1, pp. 45–55.

Huntington, Samuel P., 'Conservatism as an ideology', *American Political Science Review*, Vol. 51 (June 1957) No. 2, pp. 454–73.

Huppert, George, 'Divinatio et Erudito: Thoughts on Foucault', *History and Theory*, Vol. 13 (1974) No. 3, pp. 191–207.

Hussain, Athar, 'Foucault's History of Sexuality', *m/f* (1981) Nos. 5 and 6, pp. 169–91.

Iggers, George G., *The German Conception of History: The National Tradition of Historical Thought from Herder to the Present* (Middletown, Connecticut: Wesleyan University Press, 1968).

Isaac, Jeffrey, 'On Benton's "Objective Interests and the Sociology of Power": A Critique', *Sociology*, Vol. 16 (August 1982) No. 3, pp. 440–4.

Jay, Martin, 'The Frankfurt School's critique of Karl Mannheim and the Sociology of Knowledge', *Telos* (1974) No. 20, pp. 72–89.

——, 'Crutches v Stilts: An Answer to James Schmidt on the Frankfurt School', *Telos* (Winter 1974/75) No. 22, pp. 106–17.

Jessop, Bob, *Traditionalism, Conservatism and British Political Culture* (London: Allen & Unwin, 1974).

Jessop, Bob *et al.*, 'Authoritarian Populism, Two Nations and Thatcherism', *New Left Review* (September/October 1984) No. 149, pp. 32–60.

——, 'Thatcherism and the Politics of Hegemony: A Reply to Stuart Hall', *New Left Review* (September/October 1985) No. 153, pp. 87–101.

Johnson, Richard, 'Thompson, Genovese and Socialist Humanist History', *History Workshop* (Autumn 1978) No. 6, pp. 79–100.

——, 'Three Problematics: elements of a theory of working-class culture' in Clarke, J., Critcher, C. and Johnson, R. (eds), op.cit., pp. 201–37.

——, 'Histories of Culture/Theories of Ideology: Notes on an Impasse' in Barrett, M. *et al.* (eds), op.cit., pp. 49–77.

——, 'Against Absolutism' in Samuel, R. (ed.), op.cit., pp. 386–96.

Journal of Contemporary History, Special Issue—'A Century of Conservatism', Vol. 13 (October 1978) No. 4.

Keohane, Nannerl O., Rosaldo, Michelle Z. and Gelpi, Barbara C. (eds), *Feminist Theory: A Critique of Ideology* (Brighton: Harvester, 1982).

Kettler, David, 'Sociology of Knowledge and Moral Philosophy: The Place of Traditional Problems in the Formation of Mannheim's Thought', *Political Science Quarterly*, Vol. LXXXII (1967) No. 3, pp. 399–426.

——, 'Culture and Revolution: Lukács in the Hungarian Revolution of 1918/19', *Telos* (Winter 1971) No. 10, pp. 35–92.

——, 'Political Theory, Ideology, Sociology: The Question of Karl Mannheim', *Cultural Hermeneutics*, Vol. 3 (May 1975) No. 1, pp. 69–80.

Kettler, David, Meja, Volker and Stehr, Nico, 'Karl Mannheim and Conservatism', *The Newsletter of the International Society for the Sociology of Knowledge*, Vol. 9 (August 1983) Nos 1 and 2, pp. 3–6.

——, 'Karl Mannheim and Conservatism: The Ancestry of Historical Thinking', *American Sociological Review*, Vol. 49 (February 1984) No. 1, pp. 71–85.

——, *Karl Mannheim* (Chichester/London: Ellis Horwood/Tavistock, 1984).

——, 'Introduction: The Design of Conservatism' to K. Mannheim, *Conservatism*, op.cit.

Kiernan, Victor G., 'Culture and Society', *New Reasoner* (Summer 1959) No. 9, pp. 74–83.

King, Roy and Morgan, Rod with Martin, J. P. and Thomas, J. E., *The Future of the Prison System* (Farnborough: Gower, 1980).

Klein, Viola, *The Feminine Character: History of an Ideology* (London: Kegan Paul, Trench, Trubner, 1946).

Knights, David and Wilmott, Hugh, 'Power, Values and Relations: A Comment on Benton', *Sociology*, Vol. 16 (November 1982) No. 4, pp. 578–85.

Knorr-Cetina, Karin and Mulkay, Michael (eds), *Science Observed: Perspectives on the Social Study of Science* (London: Sage, 1983).

Kornhauser, William, *The Politics of Mass Society* (London: Routledge & Kegan Paul, 1960).

Kruger, Marlis, 'Sociology of Knowledge and Social Theory', *Berkeley Journal of Sociology*, Vol. 14 (1969), pp. 152–63.

Kuhn, Annette and Wolpe, Ann Marie (eds), *Feminism and Materialism: Women and Modes of Production* (London: Routledge & Kegan Paul, 1978).

Laclau, Ernesto, *Politics and Ideology in Marxist Theory: Capitalism-Fascism-Populism* (London: New Left Books and Verso, 1977).

Laing, Dave, 'Interpreting Punk Rock', *Marxism Today*, Vol. 22 (March 1978) No. 4, pp. 123–8.

——, *One-Chord Wonders* (Milton Keynes: Open University Press, 1985).

Larrain, Jorge, *The Concept of Ideology* (London: Hutchinson, 1979).

——, 'On the Character of Ideology: Marx and the Present Debate in Britain', *Theory, Culture and Society*, Vol. 1 (Spring 1982) No. 1, pp. 5–22.

——, *Marxism and Ideology* (London: Macmillan, 1983).

Lash, Scott and Urry, John, *The End of Organized Capitalism* (Cambridge: Polity, 1987).

Law, John, 'Editor's Introduction: Power/Knowledge and the Dissolution of the Sociology of Knowledge' in Law, J. (ed.) op.cit., pp. 1–19.

Law, John (ed.), *Power, Action and Belief: A New Sociology of Knowledge?* (London: Routledge & Kegan Paul, 1986).

Law, John and Lodge, Peter, *Science for Social Scientists* (London: Macmillan, 1984).

Lawrence, Errol, 'In the Abundance of Water the Fool is Thirsty: Sociology and Black "Pathology"' in Centre for Contemporary Cultural Studies, *The Empire Strikes Back*, pp. 95–142.

Levin, Michael, 'Marxism and Romanticism: Marx's Debt to German Conservatism', *Political Studies*, Vol. 22 (1974) No. 4, pp. 400–13.

Levitas, Ruth (ed.), *The Ideology of the New Right* (Cambridge: Polity, 1986).

Lipset, Seymour M. and Raab, Earl, *The Politics of Unreason: Right-Wing Extremism in America, 1790–1970* (London: Heinemann, 1971).

Loader, Colin, *The Intellectual Development of Karl Mannheim: Culture, Politics and Planning* (Cambridge: Cambridge University Press, 1985).

Longhurst, Brian, *Towards the Developed Sociology of Knowledge* (Ph.D. Thesis, University of Lancaster, 1984).

——, 'The Attribution of Credit in a Scientific Community' (*Mimeo*, Department of Sociology, University of Lancaster, 1985).

——, 'On Interpretation: A Note', *Theory, Culture and Society*, Vol. 5 (1988) No. 1.

Lovell, Terry, *Pictures of Reality: Aesthetics, Politics and Pleasure* (London: British Film Institute, 1980).

——, 'Why cultural studies matter', *Capital and Class* (Spring 1982) No. 16, pp. 131–42.

Lukács, Georg, *History and Class Consciousness: Studies in Marxist Dialectics* (London: Merlin, 1971).

——, *The Destruction of Reason* (London: Merlin, 1980).

Lukes, Steven, 'Comments on David Bloor', *Studies in History and Philosophy of Science*, Vol. 13 (December 1982) No. 4, pp. 313–18.

MacCabe, Colin, 'On Discourse', *Economy and Society*, Vol. 8 (August 1979) No. 3, pp. 279–307.

——, (ed.), *High Theory/Low Culture: Analysing Popular Television and Film* (Manchester: Manchester University Press, 1986).

Mackenzie, Donald, *Statistics in Britain, 1865–1930: The Social Construction of Scientific Knowledge* (Edinburgh: Edinburgh University Press, 1981).

——, 'Notes on the Science and Social Relations Debate'. *Capital and Class* (Summer 1981) No. 14, pp. 47–60.

MacMillan, Harold, *The Middle Way: A Study of the Problem of Economic and Social Progress in a Free and Democratic Society* (London: Macmillan, 1938).

McLellan, David, *Ideology* (Milton Keynes: Open University Press, 1986).

Major-Poetzl, Pamela, *Michel Foucault's Archaeology of Western Culture: Towards a New Science of History* (Brighton: Harvester, 1983).

Mannheim, Karl, 'Structural Analysis of Epistemology', in his *Essays on Sociology and Social Psychology*, pp. 15–73.

——, 'On the Interpretation of *Weltanschauung*', in his *Essays on Sociology of Knowledge*, pp. 33–83.

——, 'The Problem of a Sociology of Knowledge', in his *Essays on the Sociology of Knowledge*, pp. 134–90.

——, 'The Ideological and the Sociological Interpretation of Intellectual Phenomena', in his *From Karl Mannheim*, pp. 116–31.

——, 'Conservative Thought', in his *Essays on Sociology and Social Psychology*, pp. 74–164.

——, 'The Problem of Generations', in his *Essays on the Sociology of Knowledge*, pp. 276–320.

——, 'Competition as a Cultural Phenomenon', in his *Essays on the Sociology of Knowledge*, pp. 191–229.

——, 'Ideology and Utopia', in his *Ideology and Utopia*, pp. 49–96.

——, 'On the Nature of Economic Ambition and its significance for the Social Education of Man', in his *Essays on the Sociology of Knowledge*, pp. 230–75.

——, 'American Sociology', in his *Essays on Sociology and Social Psychology*, pp. 185–94.

——, 'The Sociology of Knowledge', in his *Ideology and Utopia*, pp. 237–80.

——, *Ideology and Utopia: An Introduction to the Sociology of Knowledge* (London: Routledge & Kegan Paul, 1936).

——, *Man and Society in an Age of Reconstruction* (London: Kegan Paul, Trench, Trubner, 1940).

——, *Diagnosis of our Time: Wartime Essays of a Sociologist* (London: Kegan Paul, Trench, Trubner, 1943).

——, 'The Function of the Refugee: A Rejoinder' *New English Weekly*, Vol. 27 (April 1945) No. 1, pp. 5–6.

——, 'Foreword' to Klein, V., op.cit.

——, *Freedom, Power and Democratic Planning* (London: Routledge & Kegan Paul, 1951).

——, *Essays on the Sociology of Knowledge* (London: Routledge & Kegan Paul, 1952).

——, *Essays on Sociology and Social Psychology* (London: Routledge & Kegan Paul, 1953).

——, *Essays on the Sociology of Culture* (London: Routledge & Kegan Paul, 1956).

——, *Systematic Sociology* (London: Routledge & Kegan Paul, 1957).

——, *From Karl Mannheim* (New York: Oxford University Press, 1971).

——, 'Letters to Lukács, 1910–1916', *The New Hungarian Quarterly*, Vol. XVI (Spring 1975) No. 57, pp. 93–105.

——, *Structures of Thinking* (London: Routledge & Kegan Paul, 1982).

——, *Conservatism: A Contribution to the Sociology of Knowledge* (London: Routledge & Kegan Paul, 1986).

Mannheim, Karl and Stewart, W. A. C., *An Introduction to the Sociology of Education* (London: Routledge & Kegan Paul, 1962).

Maquet, Jacques, *The Sociology of Knowledge: its structure and its relation to the philosophy of knowledge: A critical analysis of the systems of Karl Mannheim and Pitirim A. Sorokin* (Westport, Connecticut: Greenwood, 1973).

Marxist-Feminist Literature Collective; 'Women's Writing: *Jane Eyre, Shirley, Villette, Aurora Leigh*', *Ideology and Consciousness* (Spring 1978) No. 3, pp. 27–48.

Matthews, Betty (ed.), *Marx: A Hundred Years On* (London: Lawrence & Wishart, 1983).

McCarney, Joe, *The Real World of Ideology* (Brighton: Harvester, 1980).

McClelland, Keith, 'Some Comments on Richard Johnson, "Edward Thompson, Eugene Genovese, and Socialist-Humanist History"', *History Workshop* (Spring 1979) No. 7, pp. 101–15.

McLennan, Gregor, 'Richard Johnson and His Critics: Towards a Constructive Debate', *History Workshop* (Autumn 1979) No. 8, pp. 157–66.

McRobbie, Angela, 'Working Class Girls and the Culture of Femininity' in Women's Studies Group, Centre for Contemporary Cultural Studies, op.cit., pp. 96–108.

——, 'Settling Accounts with Subcultures: A Feminist Critique', *Screen Education* (1980) No. 34, pp. 37–49.

McRobbie, Angela and Garber, Jenny, 'Girls and Subcultures', in Hall, S. and Jefferson, T. (eds), op.cit., pp. 209–22.

Megill, Alan, 'Foucault, Structuralism and the ends of history', *Journal of Modern History*, Vol. 51 (September 1979) No. 3, pp. 451–503.

Meja, Volker, 'The Sociology of Knowledge and the Critique of Ideology', *Cultural Hermeneutics*, Vol. 3 (May 1975) No. 1, pp. 57–68.

Merton, Robert K., 'The Sociology of Knowledge' in his *Social Theory and Social Structure*, pp. 510–42.

——, 'Karl Mannheim and the Sociology of Knowledge', in his *Social Theory and Social Structure*, pp. 542–62.

——, *Social Theory and Social Structure* (New York: Free Press, 1968).

Mepham, John, 'The Theory of Ideology in *Capital*', *Radical Philosophy* (Summer 1972) No. 2, pp. 12–19.

Meynell, Hugo, 'On the Limits of the Sociology of Knowledge', *Social Studies of Science*, Vol. 7 (November 1977) No. 4, pp. 489–500.

Mills, C. Wright, 'Review of *Man and Society* by Karl Mannheim', *American Sociological Review*, Vol. 5 (December 1940) No. 6, pp. 965–9.

——, 'Methodological Consequences of the Sociology of Knowledge in Mills, C. W., *Power, Politics and People: The Collected Essays of C. Wright Mills* (New York: Oxford University Press, 1963) pp. 453–68.

Millett, Kate, *Sexual Politics* (London: Virago, 1977).

Millstone, Erik, 'A Framework for the Sociology of Knowledge', *Social Studies of Science*, Vol. 8 (February 1978) No. 1, pp. 111–25.

Minson, Jeff, 'Strategies for Socialists? Foucault's Conception of Power', *Economy and Society*, Vol. 9 (February 1980) No. 1, pp. 1–43.

Minogue, K. and Biddis, R., *Thatcherism: Personality and Politics* (London: Macmillan, 1987).

Moi, Toril, *Sexual/textual Politics: feminist literary theory* (London: Methuen, 1985).

Morley, David, *The 'Nationwide' Audience* (London: British Film Institute, 1980).

——, 'Texts, readers, subjects' in Hall, S. *et al.* (eds), op.cit., pp. 163–77.

——, *The "Nationwide" Audience: A Critical Postscript*', *Screen Education* (Summer 1981) No. 39, pp. 3–14.

Mount, Ferdinand, *The Subversive Family: An Alternative History of Love and Marriage* (London: Cape, 1982).

Mulhern, Francis, *The Moment of 'Scrutiny'* (London: New Left Books, 1979).

Mulkay, Michael, *Science and the Sociology of Knowledge* (London: Allen & Unwin, 1979).

——, 'Sociology of Science in the West', Part One of Trend Report, The Sociology of Science in East and West, *Current Sociology*, Vol. 28 (Winter 1980) No. 3, pp. 1–184.

Mullins, Willard A., 'Truth and Ideology: Reflections on Mannheim's Paradox', *History and Theory*, Vol. XVIII (1979), p.. 141–54.

Myers, Greg, 'Texts as knowledge claims: the Social Construction of Two Biology Articles', *Social Studies of Science*, Vol. 15 (November 1985) No. 4, pp. 593–630.

Neale, R. S. *Class in English History, 1680–1850* (Oxford: Blackwell, 1981).

Neild, Keith and Seed, John, 'Theoretical Poverty or the Poverty of Theory: British Marxist Historiography and the Althusserians', *Economy and Society*, Vol. 8 (November 1979) No. 4, pp. 381–416.

Neisser, Hans, *On the Sociology of Knowledge* (New York: Heinemann, 1965).

Newton, Judith and Rosenfelt, Deborah (eds), *Feminist Criticism and Social Change: Sex, Class and Race in Literature and Culture* (New York and London: Methuen, 1985).

Nisbet, Robert, 'Conservatism' in Bottomore, Tom and Nisbet, Robert (eds), *A History of Sociological Analysis* (London: Heinemann, 1978).

——, *Conservatism: Dream and Reality* (Milton Keynes: Open University Press, 1986).

Norton, Philip and Aughey, Arthur, *Conservatives and Conservatism* (London: Temple Smith, 1981).

Nugent, Neil and King, Roger (eds), *The British Right: Conservative and Right Wing Politics in Britain* (Westmead: Saxon House, 1977).

Oakeshott, Michael, 'On Being Conservative' in his *Rationalism in Politics and other essays* (London: Methuen, 1962) pp. 168–96.

O'Brien, Martin, 'Foucism, Marxory and Histault: A Critical Appraisal of Poster's *Foucault, Marxism and History, Theory, Culture and Society*, Vol. 3 (1986) No. 2, pp. 115–23.

Offe, Claus, *Disorganised Capitalism* (Cambridge: Polity, 1985).

Orwell, George, *Nineteen Eighty-Four* (Harmondsworth: Penguin, 1954).

O'Sullivan, Noel, *Conservatism* (London: Dent, 1976).

Outhwaite, William, *Understanding Social Life: The Method Called Verstehen* (London: Allen & Unwin, 1975).

Owens, Joseph, *Dread: the Rastafarians of Jamaica* (London: Heinemann, 1979).

Parekh, Bhikhu, *Marx's Theory of Ideology* (London: Croom Helm, 1982).

Parkin, Frank, *Class Inequality and Political Order* (St. Albans: Paladin, 1972).

Parkinson, G. H. R. (ed.), *George Lukács: The Man, his work and his ideas* (London: Weidenfeld & Nicolson, 1970).

Parsons, Talcott, 'An Approach to the Sociology of Knowledge' in his *Sociological Theory and Modern Society* (New York: Free Press, 1967) pp. 139–65.

Philp, Mark, 'Foucault on Power: A Problem in Radical Translation?' *Political Theory*, Vol. 11 (Feburary 1983) No. 1, pp. 29–52.

Popper, Karl, *The Poverty of Historicism* (London: Routledge & Kegan Paul, 1961).

Poster, Mark, *Foucault, Marxism and History: Mode of Production versus Mode of Information* (Cambridge: Polity in Association with Oxford: Blackwell, 1984).

Raison, Timothy (ed.), *The Founding Fathers of Social Science* (London: Scolar, 1979) pp. 272–83.

Raulet, Gerard, 'Structuralism and Post-Structuralism: An Interview with Michel Foucault', *Telos* (Spring 1983) No. 55, pp. 195–211.

Rayner, Steven, 'The Politics of Schism: Routinisation and Social Control in the International Socialists/Socialist Workers' Party', in Law, J. (ed.), op.cit., pp. 46–67.

Remmling, Gunter W., 'Philosophical Parameters of Karl Mannheim's Sociology of Knowledge', *Sociological Quarterly*, Vol. 12 (Autumn 1971) No. 4, pp. 531–47.

——, *The Sociology of Karl Mannheim* (London: Routledge & Kegan Paul, 1975).

Remmling, Gunter W. (ed.), *Towards the Sociology of Knowledge: Origin and Development of a Sociological Thought Style* (London: Routledge & Kegan Paul, 1973).

Rempel, F. Warren, *The Role of Value in Karl Mannheim's Sociology of Knowledge* (The Hague: Mouton, 1965).

Rex, John, *Key Problems of Sociological Theory* (London: Routledge & Kegan Paul, 1961).

Ricoeur, Paul, *The Conflict of Interpretations: Essays in Hermeneutics* (Evanston: Northwestern University Press, 1974).

Ringer, Fritz, *The Decline of the German Mandarins* (Cambridge: Harvard University Press, 1969).

Roberts, David, *Paternalism in Early Victorian England* (London: Croom Helm, 1979).

Roberts, Helen (ed.), *Doing Feminist Research* (London: Routhedge & Kegan Paul, 1981).

Robinson, Daniel S., 'Karl Mannheim's Sociological Philosophy', *Personalist*, Vol. 29 (April 1948) No. 2, pp. 137–48.

Rose, Nikolas, 'Fetishism and ideology: a review of theoretical problems', *Ideology and Consciousness* (Autumn 1977) No. 2, pp. 27–54.

Roth, Michael S., 'Foucault's "History of the Present"', *History and Theory*, Vol. 20 (1981) No. 1, pp. 32–46.

Rowbotham, Sheila, 'The Trouble with "Patriarchy"', in Samuel R. (ed.), op.cit., pp. 363–9.

Russel, Trevor, *The Tory Party: its Policies, Divisions and Future* (Harmondsworth: Penguin, 1978).

Salomon, Albert, 'Karl Mannheim 1893–1947', *Social Research*, Vol. 14 (September 1947) No. 3, pp. 350–64.

Samuel, Raphael (ed.), *Peoples' History and Socialist Theory* (London: Routledge & Kegan Paul, 1981).

Saran, Awadh K., 'Sociology of Knowledge and Traditional Thought', *Sociological Bulletin*, Vol. 13 (March 1964) No. 1, pp. 33–46 and Vol. 13 (September 1964) No. 2, pp. 36–48.

Sargent, Lydia (ed.), *Women and Revolution: A Discussion of the Unhappy Marriage of Marxism and Feminism* (London: Pluto, 1981).

Saunders, Peter, 'Beyond Housing Classes: The Sociological Significance of Private Property Rights in Means of Consumption', *International Journal of Urban and Regional Research*, Vol. 8 (1984) No. 2, pp. 202–27.

Schelting, Alexander von, 'Review of *Ideologie und Utopia* by Karl Mannheim', *American Sociological Review*, Vol. 1 (August 1936) No. 4, pp. 664–74.

Schmidt, James, 'Critical Theory and the Sociology of Knowledge'. *Telos* (1974/75) No. 21, pp. 168–80.

Schmann, Hans-Gerd, 'The Problem of Conservatism—Some Notes on Methodology', *Journal of Contemporary History*, Vol. 13 (October, 1978) No. 4, pp. 803–17.

Scott, Alan, 'Politics and Method in Mannheim's *Ideology and Utopia*', *Sociology*, Vol. 21 (February 1987) No. 1, pp. 41–54.

Scruton, Roger, *The Meaning of Conservatism* (Harmondsworth: Penguin, 1980).

Segal, Lynne, 'A Question of Choice', *Marxism Today*, Vol. 26 (January 1983), No. 1, pp. 20–3.

Seliger, Martin, *The Marxist Conception of Ideology* (Cambridge: Cambridge University Press, 1977).

Shapin, Steven, 'History of Science and Sociological Reconstructions', *History of Science*, Vol. 20 (1982) pp. 157–211.

Sheridan, Alan, *Michel Foucault: The Will to Truth* (London: Tavistock, 1980).

Showalter, Elaine (ed.), *The New Feminist Criticism: Essays on Women, Literature and Theory* (London: Virago, 1986).

Simonds, A. P., 'Mannheim's Sociology of Knowledge as a Hermeneutic Method', *Cultural Hermeneutics*, Vol. 3 (1975) pp. 81–104.

——, *Karl Mannheim's Sociology of Knowledge* (Oxford: Clarendon, 1978).

Smart, Barry, *Foucault, Marxism and Critique* (London: Routledge & Kegan Paul, 1983).

Speier, Hans, 'Review of *Ideology and Utopia* by Karl Mannheim', *American Journal of Sociology*, Vol. 43 (July 1937) No. 1, pp. 155–66.

Stanworth, Michelle, 'Women and Class Analysis: A Reply to John Goldthorpe', *Sociology*, Vol. 18 (May 1984) No. 2, pp. 159–70.

Stark, Werner, *The Sociology of Knowledge: An Essay in Aid of a Deeper Understanding of the History of Ideas* (London: Routledge & Kegan Paul, 1958).

Stewart, W. A. C., *Karl Mannheim on Education and Social Thought* (London: Harrap, 1967).

Sumner, Colin, *Reading Ideologies: An Investigation into the Marxist Theory of Ideology and Law* (London: Academic Press, 1979).

Swingewood, Alan, *The Myth of Mass Culture* (London: Macmillan, 1977).

Taylor, Jenny and Laing, Dave, 'Disco-Pleasure-Discourse: On "Rock and Sexuality"', *Screen Education* (Summer 1979) No. 31, pp. 43–8.

Theory, Culture and Society, Special Issue on the Future of Modernity, Vol. 2 (1985) No. 3.

Theory, Culture and Society, Special Issue—Norbert Elias and Figurational Sociology, Vol. 4 (June 1987) Nos. 2–3.

Therborn, Goran, *The Ideology of Power and the Power of Ideology* (London: New Left Books and Verso, 1980).

——, 'Why Some Classes are more successful than others', *New Left Review* (March-April 1983) No. 138, pp. 37–55.

——, 'The New Questions of Subjectivity', *New Left Review* (January-February 1984) No. 143, pp. 97–107.

Thompson, Edward P., 'The Poverty of Theory: or an Orrery of Errors' in his *The Poverty of Theory and Other Essays* (London: Merlin, 1978) pp. 193–406.

Thompson, John B., *Critical Hermeneutics: A Study in the thought of Paul Ricoeur and Jurgen Habermas* (Cambridge: Cambridge University Press, 1981).

Thompson, Kenneth, *Beliefs and Ideology* (Chichester, Sussex and London: Ellis Horwood and Tavistock, 1986).

Tillich, Hannah, *From Time to Time* (New York: Stein & Day, 1973).

Urry, John, 'Sociology as Parasite: Some Vices and Virtues' in Abrams, Philip *et al.* (eds), *Practice and Progress: British Sociology 1950–1980* (London: Allen & Unwin, 1981) pp. 25–38.

Vallas, Steven P., 'The Lesson of Mannheim's Historicism', *Sociology*, Vol. 13 (September 1979) No. 3, pp. 459–74.

Wagner, Helmut R., 'Mannheim's Historicism', *Social Research*, Vol. 19 (1952) No. 3, pp. 300–21.

——, 'The Scope of Mannheim's Thinking', *Social Research*, Vol. 20 (Spring 1953) No. 1, pp. 100—109.

Walby, Sylvia, *Patriarchy at Work* (Cambridge: Polity, 1986).

Walkowitz, Judith R., *Prostitution and Victorian Society: Women, Class and the State* (Cambridge: Cambridge University Press, 1980).

Walter, Benjamin, 'The sociology of knowledge and the problem of objectivity', in Gross, L. (ed.), *Sociological Theory: Inquiries and Paradigms* (New York: Harper & Row, 1967) pp. 335–57.

Weber, Max, *The Methodology of the Social Sciences* (New York: Free Press, 1949).

Weinstein, Deena and Weinstein, Michael A., 'Intellectual Transcendence: Karl Mannheim's Defence of the Sociological Attitude', *History of European Ideas*, Vol. 2 (1981) No. 2, pp. 97–114.

White, Hayden V., 'Foucault Decoded: Notes from Underground', *History and Theory*, Vol. 12 (1973), pp. 23–54.

Whitson, David, 'Structure, Agency and the Sociology of Sport Debates', *Theory, Culture and Society*, Vol. 3 (1986) No. 1, pp. 99–107.

Widdowson, Peter (ed.), *Re-Reading English* (London: Methuen, 1982).

Widgery, David, *Beating Time: Riot 'n' Race 'n' Rock 'n' Roll* (London: Chatto, 1986).

Wiener, Martin J., *English Culture and the Decline of the Industrial Spirit, 1850–1980* (Harmondsworth: Penguin, 1985).

Willer, Judith, *The Social Determination of Knowledge* (Englewood Cliffs, New Jersey: Prentice-Hall, 1971).

Willett, John, *The New Sobriety 1917–1933: Art and Politics in the Weimar Period* (London: Thames and Hudson, 1978).

Williams, Gavin, 'In Defence of History', *History Workshop* (Spring 1979) No. 7, pp. 116–24.

Williams, Karel, 'Unproblematic Archaeology', *Economy and Society*, Vol. 3 (1974) No. 1, pp. 41–68.

Williams, Raymond, *Culture and Society 1780–1950* (Harmondsworth: Penguin, 1963).

——, 'A Hundred Years of Culture and Anarchy' in his *Problems in Materialism and Culture*, pp. 3–8.

——, 'Base and Superstructure in Marxist Cultural Theory', *New Left Review* (November-December 1973) No. 82, pp. 3–16. Reprinted in his *Problems in Materialism and Culture*, pp. 31–49.

——, *Politics and Letters: Interviews with New Left Review* (London: New Left Books, 1979).

——, *Problems in Materialism and Culture: Selected Essays* (London: Verso and NLB, 1980).

——, *Culture* (Glasgow: Fontana/Collins, 1981).

——, *Cobbett* (Oxford: Oxford University Press, 1983).

——, *Keywords: A Vocabulary of Culture and Society* (revised edition, London: Fontana (Flamingo), 1983).

Wirth, Louis, 'Karl Mannheim, 1893–1947', *American Sociological Review*, Vol. 12 (June 1947) No. 3, pp. 356–7.

Woldring, Henk E. S., 'Karl Mannheim's Sociology of Knowledge in Search of Truth: Sociology of Knowledge in relation to the contemporary philosophy of science' (unpublished paper).

——, *Sociology of Knowledge in Search of Truth* (Amsterdam: Free University, unpublished typescript).

——, 'Karl Mannheim's search of truth', *Sociale Wetenschappen* (1984) No. 2, pp. 137–65.

——, *Karl Mannheim: The Development of his Thought: Philosophy, Sociology and Social Ethics with a Detailed Biography* (Assen/Maastricht, The Netherlands: Van Gorcum, 1986).

Wolfe, Alan, 'Sociology, Liberalism and the Radical Right', *New Left Review* (July-August 1981) No. 128, pp. 3–27.

Wolff, Janet, *Hermeneutic Philosophy and the Sociology of Art: An approach to some of the epistemological problems of the sociology of knowledge and the sociology of art and literature* (London: Routledge & Kegan Paul, 1975).

Woff, Kurt, H., *Trying Sociology* (New York: Wiley, 1974).

——, 'Karl Mannheim: An Intellectual Itinerary', *Society*, Vol. 21 (March-April 1984) No. 3, pp. 71–4.

Wolff, Kurt H. (ed. and intro.), *Wissenssoziologie: Answahl aus dem Werk* (Berlin and Neuwied: Hermann Luchterhand Verlag, 1964).

Women's Studies Group Centre for Contemporary Cultural Studies, *Women Take Issue: Aspects of Women's Subordination* (London: Hutchinson, 1978).

Working Papers in Cultural Studies 10: On Ideology (Birmingham: Centre for Contemporary Cultural Studies, 1977).

Wynne, Brian, 'Natural Knowledge and Social Context: Cambridge Physics and the Luminiferous Ether', in Barnes, B. and Edge, D. (eds); op.cit., pp. 212–31.

Yearley, Steven, 'The Relationship between Epistemological and Sociological Cognitive Interests: Some Ambiguities Underlying the Use of Interest Theory in the Study of Scientific Knowledge', *Studies in History and Philosophy of Science*, Vol. 13 (December 1982) No. 4, pp. 353–88.

——, *Science and Sociological Practice* (Milton Keynes: Open University Press, 1984).

——, 'Interactive-Orientation and Argumentation in Scientific Texts' in Law, J. (ed.) op.cit., pp. 132–57.

Young, Robert (ed.), *Untying the text* (London: Routledge & Kegan Paul, 1981).

Zeitlin, Irving M., *Ideology and the Development of Sociological Theory* (Englewood Cliffs, New Jersey: Prentice-Hall, 1981).

Index